5000

YEARS OF SCIENCE

Shaji Sreedharan

ISBN: 978-1-0682644-0-5

First Edition

Hardback ISBN 978-1-0682644-1-2
Ebook ISBN 978-1-0682644-2-9
Audiobook ISBN 978-1-0682644-3-6

Contact: https://www.linkedin.com/in/shaji-sreedharan-croydon/

Dedication

To my Wife Aji Shaji
Daughter Sneja Shaji
Son Ajin Shaji

About the Author

Shaji Sreedharan

Shaji Sreedharan is a physicist, computer engineer, and entrepreneur. He obtained his degree in Physics (with subsidiary subjects of Mathematics and Chemistry) from University College, Kerala, India, in 1982. While pursuing an Electronics and Electrical Engineering degree at the University of Surrey in England, Shaji dropped out to launch a computing business in Croydon during the 1990s. He is currently a Senior Infrastructure Analyst and lives in Croydon, Surrey, England.

TABLE OF CONTENTS

PREFACE

I chose to write this book to understand the origins of human life on Earth. Based on the information I have gathered, I aim to pen this book on 5,000 years of scientific history. Science has been a deep passion of mine since my childhood. While pursuing my physics degree at University College, Trivandrum, Kerala, India, from 1979 to 1982, I was fortunate to attend guest lectures at the college by Dr. A.P.J. Abdul Kalam, who served as the 11th President of India and was involved with the Indian Space Research Organisation (ISRO) Thumba. His profound knowledge captivated me, and he recommended numerous physics books published by McGraw-Hill, which I obtained through the British Library in Trivandrum from England. The abundance of information in these books was crucial in helping me to understand science.

For five thousand years, humanity has looked outward and inward — to the stars above and the thoughts within — in search of understanding. From ancient temples where astronomy and ritual merged, to modern laboratories where quantum fields and neural networks are mapped, science has been our evolving language for decoding the universe.

This book is a journey through that evolution — a grand narrative of how science has transformed from counting stars to creating machines that can now count us, model us, and perhaps one day, rival our minds. But beneath every breakthrough lies something more profound—something not easily measured by equations: the *desire* to know, the *urge* to solve, the *wonder* that drives exploration.

With artificial intelligence advancing at unprecedented speed, we ask new versions of old questions: Can machines think? Can they feel? And what does it mean to be conscious? As we teach machines to learn, are we merely extending logic, or are we approaching the threshold of mind? These questions are not detours. They are the culmination of a 5,000-year journey. In telling the story of science, this book follows a thread that weaves through Mesopotamian cuneiform, the Invention of zero, Darwin's evolution, and Turing's machine, to today's neural networks and quantum mind theories.

In the chapters ahead, we move chronologically, from the birth of scientific reasoning in ancient civilisations to the speculative edge of consciousness studies and AI. At each turning point, we pause to ask how science emerged from the mind and how it might give rise to new kinds of mind. This book traces the arc of scientific discovery to honour the past and frame the future. It also offers a bold new theory—Affective Survival Theory (AST)—which redefines consciousness as an evolved tool for survival rooted in feeling. It asks not only how we know but also why we *care* to know.

5000 Years of Science is not just about progress. It's about presence—about what it means to be sentient in an age of simulation.

ACKNOWLEDGEMENTS

This book, *5000 Years of Science: From Ancient Wisdom to AI and a Bold New Theory of Consciousness*, is the product of a deeply personal journey—driven by curiosity, persistence, and a desire to understand the vast arc of human knowledge and its most profound mystery: consciousness.

I want to acknowledge that this work was conceived, researched, and written independently. Every idea, insight, and chapter in this book was formulated without outside collaboration or co-authorship. It is the result of solitary reflection, years of study, and an enduring passion for the evolution of thought, science, and the human mind.

While this has been a solitary endeavour, I stand on the shoulders of giants—scientists, philosophers, and thinkers across the millennia—whose ideas and discoveries have shaped the rich intellectual landscape from which this book draws. I am indebted to their work and to the legacy of inquiry that continues to inspire the pursuit of knowledge.

To the reader: thank you for your time, your curiosity, and your willingness to explore a new vision of science, mind, and meaning. If this book sparks a new way of seeing the world, then the effort has been more than worthwhile.

Thank you for turning these pages. The journey is yours now, too.

Shaji Sreedharan
Book cover designed by Amir N

INTRODUCTION

The Eternal Flame of Curiosity

Science is more than just a collection of facts; it represents a method through which humans think and acquire knowledge. Beyond what is known, there exists hidden knowledge that humans, as Homo sapiens, can uncover through intelligence and consciousness. This process has led to new inventions that have shaped our existence for thousands of years—something that today's artificial intelligence (AI) has yet to master fully.

AI is a vital topic, and we will explore it in depth later in this book. We will also discuss the role of consciousness in living beings. While other organisms have adapted to their environments, humans have not only adapted but have also learned to reshape their surroundings. From the discovery of fire to the harnessing of nuclear energy, our capabilities are unparalleled.

What makes science exceptional is its relentless pursuit of truth, advancement, and the exploration of the unknown, all stemming from the fundamental question: Why?

One might wonder where science originated—it's a million-dollar question. The entire journey, from the Big Bang to our current world and beyond, falls under the umbrella of science. Based on our current understanding, science began with the Big Bang. Unfortunately, humans only became aware of this phenomenon once they developed cognitive thinking abilities. You may also question what existed before the Big Bang, which presents yet another trillion-dollar question. Is there anything that existed before the Big Bang? We will explore these topics in greater depth in the coming chapters.

Long before written language, humans sought to make sense of the world. Early civilisations gazed into the sky for answers, observing the movements of stars to predict the seasons for their survival and aid their navigation. They explored the use of fire, food for their survival, accommodation, and the moon's positions, progressively developing the primitive science that paved the way for medicine, agriculture, engineering, and astronomy.

Initially, science merged with belief systems as ancient civilisations sought to explain natural events through spirits and some celestial phenomena. As they learned more about nature, they shied away from beliefs and toward the reality of nature. Ancient Egyptians utilised trial and error in medicine, Chinese scholars formulated detailed calendars based on celestial cycles, and Mesopotamians devised one of the first mathematical systems. These foundational explorations in understanding the universe initiated a continuing scientific journey, a process of discovery that would span thousands of years.

Why 5000 Years? The purpose of this book

The path of science extends well beyond any individual discovery. Over the last 5,000 years, we have witnessed a stream of knowledge that has significantly influenced our civilisation. Around 3500 BCE, early civilisations started documenting their findings, allowing knowledge to be transmitted rather than rediscovered by every generation. The advancements that ensued from the initial recorded numerals to quantum mechanics are evidence of the strength of gathered knowledge. This book takes us across those 5000 years, illustrating how human curiosity, creativity, and determination shaped today's world and the power of accumulated knowledge.

It will investigate how fire, tools, and simple observations paved the way for early scientific thought and how civilisations like Egypt, Mesopotamia, China, and Greece developed the first scientific disciplines. How the Scientific Revolution shattered old beliefs and redefined physics, chemistry, and biology. How technological advances, from the Industrial Revolution to the Digital Age, transformed society. How modern science is now tackling the frontiers of space, artificial intelligence, and the universe's mysteries. This book is more than just a history of discoveries—it celebrates the human spirit, the relentless drive to question, explore, and innovate.

I've carefully selected a range of brilliant scientists whose ingenuity has shaped our world. Their work is fundamentally important, and that's why they're in this book. I might have left out some of the contributors you are thinking of, not intentionally, and I hope you will forgive me for anyone I overlooked.

The Next 5000 Years: Science as Humanity's Greatest Adventure

If history has taught us anything, you haven't seen anything yet; science is never finished. Every breakthrough leads to new questions, and every answer opens new doors to exploration. We once believed the Earth was the centre of the universe—now we search for life on distant extrasolar planets. We once thought diseases were curses—now we edit genes with precision. The discoveries of tomorrow will be shaped by the bold questions we ask today.

The future of science may bring unimaginable possibilities—quantum computing, artificial intelligence, genetic engineering, interstellar travel—but at its core, science will always be about one thing: curiosity. The same force that drove our ancestors to light the first fires still drives us to uncover the deepest mysteries of existence.

This book is an invitation to explore the most incredible scientific journey of all time—a story that began 5000 years ago and is far from over.

Let's begin.

CHAPTER 1

Birth of Science (3000 BCE- 500 BCE)

Let's examine one of humanity's greatest intellectual leaps - the 2,500-year journey (3000-500 BCE) that transformed how we comprehend our world. Forget lab coats and peer review; ancient "science" was hands-on survival wisdom passed down through generations. What's extraordinary is how these early observers - without telescopes or microscopes - began spotting patterns that would eventually replace supernatural explanations with tangible truths. This wasn't just progress; it was the first spark of the scientific mindset that now drives our modern world.

Picture this revolution: societies that once explained eclipses as dragon attacks began meticulously tracking celestial movements instead. The game-changer? When someone (probably multiple someones across different cultures) had the brilliant idea to start writing things down. Those wedge-shaped cuneiform marks in Mesopotamia, elegant Egyptian hieroglyphs, and mysterious Indus Valley symbols - they weren't just early bureaucracy. They became humanity's first hard drives, certainly enduring far longer than contemporary hard drives, preserving astronomical observations, medical remedies, and engineering tricks that oral storytelling could never accurately maintain. This was the messy, multicultural beginning of what we now recognise as the scientific method.

Many human evolutionary theories are debated by scientists worldwide, particularly regarding the origin of humans (Homo sapiens). The oldest human remains found in Africa are still debated and may be found in other parts of the world. No matter where the oldest human remains are found in the world, they must be from when he or she survived by nature. The most probable area of survival is around the equatorial area, where humans can survive. It is not sure that he or she stayed in Arctic regions. Humans may have originated from the tropic of Cancer to the tropic of Capricorn (Latitude 0 ° to 23.5 ° North and 0 ° to 23.5 ° South), where the sunlight energy is the most, and possibly up to 45° North and South from the equator, where sunlight is enough for humans to live. It is possible to see the oldest human civilisation and remains in these areas.

Humans used stones to write on Clay tablets. This tablet records the daily beer rations for workers. An upright jar with a pointed base represents beer. The symbol for rations is a human head eating from a porridge bowl. The round and semicircular impressions represent the measurements. A cut reed produced all the signs. Papyrus is a thick paper-like material made from the pith of the papyrus plant, Cyperus papyrus, a wetland sedge that was once abundant in the Nile Delta of Egypt. Papyrus is first known to have been used in ancient Egypt and throughout the Mediterranean region. Ancient Egyptians used this plant as a writing material for boats, mattresses, mats, rope, sandals and baskets. Chemically, papyrus is composed of 60% cellulose,24% lignin, 9% minerals and 7% water. When Pangaea broke up, it caused rifts along the eastern side of Africa, and rainwater flowing through this (called the Great Rift Valley) eventually ended up in the Mediterranean Sea, and thus a river was formed. The Great Rift Valley is still the water source for the Nile.

The oldest writing example comes from Mesopotamia (the modern-day area of Iran, Syria, and Turkey) and dates to about 3300 BC. In time, different-looking writing appeared in the river valleys of Egypt, the Indus Valley, China and Central America. We cannot yet be confident whether writing spread from Mesopotamia or developed independently in these civilisations. As Mesopotamian society became more complex, writing allowed administrators to keep an account of who had been paid and what had been traded. The earliest cuneiform tablets are almost all records of accountancy. Humans have no ancient history, and the ones we believe are recorded date back as far as 2800 BC, during the first dynasty (3100 BC – 2890 BC).

I embark on my exploration from Skara Brae—it is so ancient and beautiful that one cannot forget the feeling of being there, the Orkney's windswept mainland. Walking among its stone-walled homes, you can almost hear the echoes of Neolithic life: the scrape of flint tools, the crackle of hearth fires. Every artefact dug up here—from carved stone bowls to fishbone needles—whispers secrets about how these early Britons built, worked, ate, and survived.

No wonder UNESCO slapped a World Heritage label on it, grouping it with Orkney's other Neolithic heavyweights. But Skara Brae (yes, I've been misspelling it—blame autocorrect!) isn't just pretty ruins. Dating back to 3000 BCE, this place shatters stereotypes. Forget 'cavepeople'—these folks had fitted furniture, drainage systems, and even 'storage units' for their prized tools. Fancy for a society that hadn't invented metal yet, right?

Picture this: snug, single-room houses linked by covered passageways so precisely aligned, you'd think they used protractors. Who designed these? We still don't know—but their workmanship would put some modern contractors to shame. Forget 'primitive'; this was Neolithic engineering at its sharpest.

And Skara Brae's not even Orkney's only star. Over on Papa Westray, the Knap of Howar—possibly older—boasts stone cabinets and doorways still intact after 5,000 years. Together, these sites rewrite history. Think about it: if Neolithic farmers could pull this off, is it any surprise they later orchestrated megalithic blockbusters like Stonehenge?

So, if you're itching to time-travel, Skara Brae's your ticket. No CGI (Computer-generated imagery) needed—just stand in those ancient doorways and gawk. It's proof that brilliance doesn't need microchips; sometimes, all it takes is a pile of rocks and a stubborn human mind.

Between 2000 and 3000 BC, the estimated world population was approximately 20 million, with around 5 million potentially residing in Africa. Human access to information was limited during this period, and personal discoveries were primarily dispersed among humans to acquire knowledge. Notably, individuals like Imhotep emerged as wise figures. Although there is no concrete evidence attributing the authorship of Edwin Smith's Papyrus to Imhotep, one can speculate that someone initiated more intelligent medical treatments during this time. Imhotep had no information to follow from his ancestors; instead, he created his own. This era may mark the beginning of humans acquiring crucial knowledge and passing it on to succeeding generations.

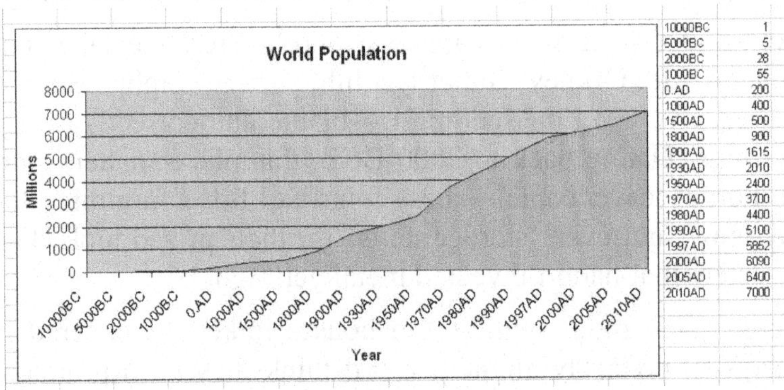

Fig 1.1 World population chart

How does one person revolutionise architecture, medicine, and philosophy? Meet Imhotep - the Leonardo da Vinci of ancient Egypt, centuries before the term "Renaissance man" existed. This commoner from Ankhtow (near modern Cairo) broke all social barriers to become Egypt's ultimate polymath. Think about it: architect, engineer, scientist, and healer - all wrapped up in one brilliant mind around 2800 BCE (give or take a few centuries). What's most remarkable? He didn't hoard his genius but used it to transform an entire civilisation.

Pinpointing Imhotep's birth year is tricky - historians place him somewhere around 2800 BCE, plus or minus 500 years (ancient record-keeping wasn't exactly precise). Tradition marks his birthday as May 31 on our calendar, but we're left connecting dots across millennia without concrete records. As High Priest of Heliopolis - Egypt's Vatican City of its day - Imhotep wasn't just another temple official. He stood at the heart of spiritual and intellectual life, bridging the sacred and the scientific in ways that would make modern minds spin.

Walking through Saqqara today, you can still feel Imhotep‘s presence... his masterpiece? The Step Pyramid at Saqqara - the world’s first pyramid and a 204-foot-tall “hello” to eternity. No foundation? No problem. Imhotep built it on solid bedrock, proving that sometimes the best innovation comes from working with what you’ve got. Those staggered levels weren’t just visually striking; they were a revolutionary leap in engineering.

But Imhotep wasn’t just about pyramids. As the founding father of medicine, he resonated through later Greek practices. Even his philosophy stuck around - that “eat, drink, and be merry” advice? The ancient equivalent of a viral quote repurposed by generations to come.

Centuries later, Hippocrates would get all the credit, but medical historian Sir William Osler set the record straight: Imhotep was the original “Father of Medicine.” Not bad for a commoner whose genius emerged from what Osler poetically called “the ancient mists of time.”

Imhotep‘s Contributions to Science: Medicine, Architecture, Engineering.

Let’s travel back to 2700 BC - when China’s first sparks of civilisation were igniting. At the centre of this cultural explosion stood Huang-di (the Yellow Emperor), born in 2704 BC and crowned in 2697 BC. Imagine living in a world where nearly everything - from writing to warfare - was being invented for the first time!

The Yellow Emperor’s era was like ancient China’s “Eureka!” moment. Need writing? Check. Transportation? He’s got ships and carts covered. Medicine, music, even kitchen utensils? All allegedly sprang from this remarkable period. And here’s something surprising - early texts credit him with developing organised warfare too. Quite the resume for a Bronze Age ruler!

Dubbed the "Originator of Chinese Culture," Huang-di's legacy is so profound that over a billion people trace their ancestry to him and Yan Di today. Think about that cultural impact! Beyond nation-building, tradition credits him with:

- Creating China's writing system
- Founding Taoist philosophy
- Inventing both the compass and pottery wheel

(Though historians debate how much one person could actually invent!)

Ancient Chinese medicine was astonishingly sophisticated. Doctors didn't just check pulses - they timed them to the hour, while factoring in seasons, gender, and age. The toolkit? Dietary plans (probably the world's first nutritionists), acupuncture needles, herbal remedies, and even what we'd now call mindfulness through Taoist practices.

Their key insight? The body follows nature's rhythms. Health wasn't just about symptoms but how ageing, seasons, and environment interacted. Master these relationships, and you could precisely tailor treatments for 2700 BC!

During Huang-di's legendary reign (where history blurs with myth), innovation flourished everywhere:

✓ Wooden houses rising from the riverbanks

✓ The first boats and bows changed transportation and hunting

✓ Even domestic life was transformed by his wife's silk-weaving workshops

(Yes, ancient China had its own power couple!)

Huang-di's contributions to Science: Medicine, Engineering.

Let's shatter some assumptions: Nearly 5,000 years ago—around 2600 BCE—a woman named Merit Ptah was practising medicine along the Nile. She wasn't just an anomaly; her story reveals how ancient Egyptian society actively fostered women in science centuries before other civilisations even considered it.

While Greek and Roman women were largely restricted to domestic roles, their Egyptian counterparts could become scribes, scholars, and even physicians. Imagine a society where a woman's education wasn't about marriage prospects, but professional mastery—that was ancient Egypt at its height.

Here's what 'breaking norms' really looked like:

- Female scribes kept court records
- Scholarly women studying astronomy
- Physicians like Merit Ptah—possibly history's first documented female doctor

Her legacy is literally set in stone, with the title 'Chief Physician' carved beside her image in Saqqara. Flourishing just generations after the legendary physician Imhotep, Merit Ptah represents a fascinating pattern: ancient Egypt's medical tradition didn't discriminate by gender. While Imhotep gets more fame, her existence proves women were equally part of medicine's early evolution. Medical training in Egypt was no casual pursuit—it required years of rigorous apprenticeship. Both women and men studied herbal remedies, surgical techniques, and even early forms of physical therapy, with knowledge accumulating across generations.

The system worked like this:

1. Apprentice to a senior physician (male or female)
2. Master diagnostic techniques through hands-on practice
3. Graduate to treating patients independently

Evidence suggests over 100 female doctors practised at medicine's peak. The most celebrated—like Peseshet, depicted teaching male students—show how deeply respected women were in this field.

Merit Ptah's contributions to Science: Medicine.

Eight centuries before the Common Era, an Indian scholar-priest named Baudhayana was quietly revolutionising mathematics. His Baudhayana Sulbasutra - essentially an ancient "construction manual" for Vedic altars - contained geometric breakthroughs that would make him famous millennia later. Think about this: while the Greeks get credit for the Pythagorean theorem, Baudhayana had already described it in his texts! He even calculated pi with remarkable accuracy for his time.

What's fascinating is how he approached problems. Using only geometric methods (algebra hadn't been invented yet), Baudhayana solved linear equations that would stump most modern high school students. His work wasn't just theoretical - these mathematical principles were literally set in stone, used to design religious altars with perfect proportions.

Let's travel back to 624 B.C. to Miletus (modern-day Balat, Turkey), where Thales - history's first Greek philosopher - was asking dangerous questions. While others explained the world through myths, this radical thinker proposed something shocking: everything originated from a single substance (he believed it was water). Aristotle would later credit Thales as the first to seek natural explanations for cosmic mysteries, effectively inventing Western philosophy during his morning walks along the Ionian coast.

This was more than mere philosophy - Thales was antiquity's ultimate polymath. As founder of the Milesian School, he wore many hats:

- Calculated pyramid heights using shadows (early geometry)
- Predicted solar eclipses (astronomy)
- Discovered static electricity (rubbing amber with fur)

Though he couldn't explain why the amber attracted feathers, this 2,600-year-old observation eventually led to our understanding of electrons. That's not bad for a guy who mentored another genius—Anaximander—while revolutionising multiple fields.

Enter Anaximander, Thales‘ star pupil and the first evolutionary thinker. Though we know little about his life (history’s cruel that way), his surviving work suggests he wrote an epic “Nature Poem” that would make Darwin nod in recognition. This was the 6th century BCE, when humanity was waking up to rational explanations of nature across civilisations from Greece to China.

Anaximander‘s bold theory? Everything began with the ‘Apeiron’ - an eternal, boundless substance. His visionary sequence:

1. Earth forms from this cosmic soup
2. Waters cover the surface
3. Life emerges in the oceans
4. Creatures adapt to land

Sound familiar? That’s because it’s evolution’s first draft - written 2,500 years before Darwin! What’s truly mind-blowing? These Ionians weren’t just explaining nature; they were inventing the very idea of scientific speculation.

Bhaskara I (c. 680-600 BCE) - a mathematical genius whose work still shapes our calculations today. This 7th-century Indian scholar made two revolutionary contributions:

1. That little circle we call ‘zero’? Bhaskara was among the first to formalise its use in the Hindu-Arabic numeral system
2. His trigonometric work produced remarkably accurate sine approximations - without calculators or computers!

What’s incredible is that these breakthroughs came while Europe was still in its so-called “Dark Ages.” While Western mathematicians struggled with Roman numerals, Bhaskara laid the foundations for modern mathematics along the banks of the Narmada River.

Let’s journey back to 6th century BCE Samos, where a young Pythagoras - yes, that Pythagoras - was soaking up wisdom from Thales and Anaximander like a sponge. This curious thinker would become more than just a mathematician-philosopher; he’d start a movement (Pythagoreanism) and discover a theorem so fundamental we still teach it today. Here's the revolutionary idea he formalised: if you square the sides of a right triangle, the biggest square (on the hypotenuse) equals the two smaller ones combined. Simple? Yes. Earth-shattering? Absolutely. Or as every math student now groans: $a^2 + b^2 = c^2$ (where 'c' is that long hypotenuse side staring back at you from geometry exams).

When Pythagoras unveiled his theorem around 530 BCE, it wasn't just another formula - it was mathematical lightning striking ancient Greece. This discovery capped centuries of Babylonian and Egyptian geometry, proving mathematics could reveal nature's hidden blueprints. Alongside medical breakthroughs and agricultural innovations, Pythagoras' work sparked something radical: the belief that humans could actually decode the universe's secrets through numbers and reason. Talk about an intellectual revolution!

In **Appendix 1**, I have explained how the Pythagorean theorem is adapted to a modified version in the space-time intervals of special relativity.

SUMMARY

By 500 BCE, humanity had already built an impressive intellectual foundation. Across the ancient world - from the banks of the Nile to Mesopotamia's fertile crescent - breakthroughs were flourishing:

- Writing Systems: Cuneiform wedges in Mesopotamia, elegant hieroglyphs along the Nile, and the revolutionary Phoenician alphabet that would shape all Western writing
- Mathematics: Sophisticated calculations that would later evolve into modern algebra
- Medicine & Philosophy: Early systematic approaches to healing and existential questions

This was not merely happenstance advancement - these were the building blocks of civilisation itself, preserved on clay tablets and papyrus scrolls that let knowledge survive across generations.

Consider Pythagoras' theorem - $a^2 + b^2 = c^2$ - discovered centuries before the Common Era. What began as a geometric curiosity in ancient Greece now underpins:

✓ Modern architecture (calculating roof angles)

✓ Space exploration (trajectory calculations)

✓ Quantum physics (wave function mathematics)

✓ Even your smartphone's GPS

This single equation demonstrates how ancient insights continue to shape our high-tech world. The Greeks couldn't have imagined that their triangle math would one day help land rovers on Mars!

Yet one critical piece was still missing - zero. This seemingly simple concept would revolutionise mathematics centuries later. But first, our ancestors would turn their attention upward, beginning around 500 BCE, to decode the mysteries of the stars. What they'd already achieved - writing systems, mathematical foundations, medical knowledge - created the launchpad for humanity's most extraordinary intellectual adventures. The stage was set for civilisation's next giant leap

CHAPTER 2

Journey through ancient science (500 BCE – 1400 CE)

Let me introduce you to the fascinating world of ancient science, spanning roughly the period mentioned above. Numerous surprises, including significant mathematical theories and scientific breakthroughs, marked this era. What's truly remarkable is that many of these discoveries, scrupulously pieced together by scholars with nothing but curiosity and crude tools, set the stage for the scientific revolution centuries later.

Take ancient Greece: Euclid's geometric proofs are still drilled into high school students (whether they like it or not!). And Aristotle? His relentless questioning of nature—why objects fall, how life functions—wasn't just philosophy but proto-science. These thinkers didn't just scribble ideas; they built frameworks we're still tweaking today.

Ready to dive in? We'll unpack game-changing inventions, meet geniuses who argued with kings (and sometimes won), and trace how shaky early theories evolved into the bedrock of modern science. Trust me, by the end, you'll see the past—and our present—differently.

Picture this: Kos, a sun-drenched Greek island in the 5th century BCE, where a young **Hippocrates** – oh, yes, that Hippocrates - was beginning his medical journey. Though history has left us few concrete details about his life, we know he came from a family of healers and honed his craft through years of travel across the ancient world. What set him apart? His revolutionary insistence on careful observation and systematic diagnosis - a radical departure from the supernatural explanations of his time. Every fever, every wound, every symptom was meticulously recorded, creating medicine's first true clinical records.

But Hippocrates' genius wasn't limited to diagnosis. Back on Kos, he established what might be history's first medical school, drilling students in both technique and ethics. That famous oath bearing his name? While scholars debate whether he actually wrote it, the principles are pure Hippocrates:

- Patient confidentiality (even in 400 BCE!)
- Respect for life above all
- Commitment to ethical practice

Remarkably, these ideals still guide doctors today - your physician's promise to "do no harm" directly echoes across 2,400 years from Hippocrates' classroom. Hippocrates' real breakthrough? Seeing patients as whole people. His treatments are considered:

✓ Nutrition ("Let food be thy medicine")

✓ Cleanliness (revolutionary for his era)

✓ Mental state (early recognition of mind-body connection)

The Hippocratic Corpus - a collection of about 60 medical works - reads like the first modern medical textbook. Its most enduring lesson? True healing addresses the person, not just the disease - a philosophy that still separates great doctors from mere technicians today.

Imagine ancient Athens, 470 BCE - a bustling city-state where a stonecutter's son named **Socrates** would become philosophy's most famous troublemaker. Unlike other thinkers of his time, this barefoot philosopher roamed the agora (marketplace) pestering politicians, poets, and craftsmen with uncomfortable questions. His mission? To expose false wisdom and show that true knowledge begins with admitting "I know nothing."

Socrates perfected what we now call the Socratic Method - a verbal jiu-jitsu that worked like this:

1. Start with a simple question ("What is justice?")
2. Follow each answer with more questions
3. Reveal contradictions in their thinking
4. Guide them to discover the truth themselves

Athenians called him their "gadfly" because he constantly stung their complacency. While others lectured, Socrates believed wisdom emerged through dialogue, making him history's first (and most annoying) life coach.

His radical ideas turned Athenian society upside down:

- "The unexamined life isn't worth living" - his famous challenge to complacency
- True virtue comes from reason, not tradition
- Real wisdom means recognising your ignorance

Unsurprisingly, this didn't win him friends in high places. When you're telling generals they don't understand courage and politicians they can't define justice, you're bound to make powerful enemies. The tension finally exploded in 399 BCE when Socrates, then 70, faced trial on trumped-up charges of corrupting youth and impiety. His defence? A typical Socratic twist:

"I'm Athens' benefactor - like a gadfly keeping a noble horse awake!"

The jury wasn't amused. Offered exile, he chose death by hemlock, proving his commitment to Athenian laws even as they condemned him. His final hours, spent philosophising with friends, became history's most famous death scene.

Ironically, Socrates' execution made him immortal. Thanks to Plato's dialogues (where Socrates always stars), his methods live on in:

✓ Modern law schools' case methods

- ✓ Scientific inquiry
- ✓ Therapy techniques
- ✓ Even Silicon Valley's "first principles" thinking

His true legacy? Teaching us that asking the right questions matters more than having all the answers - a lesson that still shapes everything from classroom discussions to AI development today. Here's the Socratic paradox: we know him only through others' accounts, yet his ideas feel intensely personal. Twenty-four centuries later, when we question our assumptions or challenge popular opinion, we're walking the path Socrates paved - one uncomfortable question at a time.

Picture Athens in 428 BCE - a city at war, where young **Plato** grew up among political turmoil and intellectual ferment. Born into Athenian aristocracy (his uncle was one of the infamous Thirty Tyrants), Plato received the equivalent of an Ivy League education: philosophy mornings, poetry afternoons, and wrestling in between. The Peloponnesian War's chaos - watching his city lose to Sparta - would later fuel his obsession with creating stable, just societies in his writings.

Then came the earthquake: meeting Socrates. The older philosopher's habit of dismantling people's certainties with simple questions ("What is courage, really?") blew Plato's mind. After Athens forced Socrates to drink hemlock in 399 BCE, a heartbroken Plato left Greece for over a decade. He studied with Egyptian priests, debated with Italian Pythagoreans, and basically became the ancient world's most dedicated grad student - all while wrestling with four big questions: What is real? What is just? How do we know? And how should we live?

Returning to Athens in 387 BCE, Plato did something revolutionary: he founded the Academy (named after the grove where it stood). This wasn't just a school - it was the world's first think tank, running continuously for 900 years! Under the olive trees, students didn't just absorb knowledge; they learned to tear ideas apart through dialogue. Plato's written works? Nearly all structured as conversations, showing philosophy in action rather than preaching conclusions.

Plato's legacy hits like a tidal wave:

- The Forms Theory: That every chair, triangle, or beautiful sunset we see is just a shadow of its perfect "Form" in a higher reality
- The Republic's Philosopher-Kings: His controversial vision of society led by truth-seeking rulers (and no poets allowed!)
- Three Big Branches of Philosophy: He essentially created the fields of ethics, aesthetics, and epistemology as we know them

Twenty-four centuries later, college freshmen still lose sleep debating his ideas - especially that alarming Allegory of the Cave, suggesting we might all be chained shadows of reality. But here's what makes Plato truly timeless - his method. The Socratic dialectic (that question-and-answer tennis match) still shapes how we:

✓ Teach law students to think

✓ Conduct scientific peer review

✓ Even design artificial intelligence

His Theory of Forms - that ultimate reality consists of abstract, perfect versions of things - solved the "problem of universals" in a way that still divides philosophers today. Like his teacher Socrates, Plato knew the real wisdom wasn't in answers, but in learning how to question everything.

"Would Plato approve of our democratic elections today?"

Next time you question assumptions at work, you're channelling Plato's Academy spirit."

Depict northern Greece in 384 BC - a boy who would become history's first true polymath was born in the small town of Stagira. **Aristotle**'s privileged upbringing (his father served as royal physician) gave him unique access to knowledge. At 17, he joined Plato's Academy in Athens, remaining a star pupil and intellectual rival for two decades. After Plato's death, this brilliant thinker would tutor a young Alexander the Great before founding his school, the Lyceum, where he literally walked while teaching (earning his followers the name "Peripatetics"). His mind ranged from biology to drama, politics to physics - making him antiquity's ultimate Renaissance man centuries before the Renaissance.

While Aristotle revolutionised biology, his physics had some...quirks. He borrowed heavily from predecessors like Empedocles, insisting the universe ran on four elements (earth, water, air, fire) - an idea that seems charmingly naive today. His cosmological works recycled pre-Socratic theories, proposing crystalline spheres carrying planets in perfect circles. Yet even these "misses" proved valuable - by being so precisely wrong, they challenged later scientists to prove otherwise.

Aristotle's real genius shone in biology. His "History of Animals" reads like an ancient field guide:

- ✓ First to systematically dissect and compare species
- ✓ Grouped animals by blood/no blood (our vertebrate/invertebrate distinction)
- ✓ Observed dolphin pregnancies to prove they're mammals
- ✓ Noted that chickens develop feathers in the egg

This was more than just making lists - he established biology as a science of careful observation and classification, creating methods still used today. Aristotle gave us the syllogism - philosophy's killer app. Here's how it works:

1. Major premise: All humans are mortal
2. Minor premise: Socrates is human
3. Conclusion: Socrates is mortal

This three-step logic machine became the foundation of Western thought, influencing everything from medieval theology to computer programming logic gates. Aristotle's influence spread like intellectual wildfire:

- Islamic scholars preserved and expanded his works during Europe's Dark Ages
- Thomas Aquinas Christianized his philosophy

- Galileo and Newton built modern science by disproving their physics
- Even today, his ethics shape virtue theory in philosophy classes worldwide

Aristotle's ideas keep evolving from Baghdad to Boston, proving his greatest lesson: knowledge grows through constant questioning.

Let's travel back to 300 BCE, Alexandria – a bustling hub of learning where **Euclid**, history's most influential geometry teacher, was quietly revolutionising mathematics. Imagine walking those sun-drenched streets where Greek, Egyptian, and Babylonian knowledge collided! While we know frustratingly little about his personal life (did he have a favourite chalkboard? Did students groan at his proofs?), his legacy is undeniable. Trained at Plato's Academy, Euclid worked under Ptolemy I's rule – that golden age when Alexandria's Library was the Google of the ancient world. Isn't it remarkable how this one man's textbook would outlast empires?

Euclid had a radical idea that still shapes how we do math today: no free passes. Every theorem had to earn its keep through ironclad proofs. Think of it as mathematical karma – no statement got accepted unless it logically followed from previous ones. His masterpiece, *Elements*, wasn't just a book; it was a 13-volume masterclass in intellectual honesty. y, I find it awe-inspiring that his "show your work" approach predates modern science by two millennia!

Elements was the ancient world's ultimate math encyclopedia:

Books 1-6: Where high school geometry still lives (yes, those triangle proofs torment students today)

Books 7-9: Number theory gems, including his famous algorithm – still used in cybersecurity!

Book 10: Mind-bending irrational numbers that challenged Greek math norms

Books 11-13: 3D geometry that would later help Newton and Einstein

Have you ever noticed how TikTok math influencers still teach these concepts? That's Euclid's 2,300-year-old curriculum at work!

Here's the twist: Euclid was more master curator than sole inventor. Like a brilliant DJ remixing the greatest hits of Greek, Egyptian, and Babylonian math, he synthesised centuries of discoveries into one coherent system. And isn't that the mark of true genius? To organise chaos into clarity? His real gift was creating the first "mathematical method" – a framework so robust that we still teach geometry his way today. I'd argue this makes him the first great math educator in history.

Euclid's fingerprints are everywhere:

- **Science**: Galileo used his deductive method
- **Philosophy**: Spinoza modelled his ethics treatise on *Elements*
- **Tech**: Your computer runs on Boolean logic descended from his proofs

Funny how an ancient geometer became the godfather of Silicon Valley, isn't it? His axiomatic approach is why we trust math to build bridges, encrypt emails, and navigate space. Not bad for a guy who probably wore a toga!

Here's the beautiful paradox: a man whose personal life vanished into history's mist, yet whose ideas illuminate every math classroom today. When students groan over geometry proofs, they're walking in Euclid's shadow. Maybe that's his greatest lesson – that truth, when logically built, outlives empires, languages, even the memory of its creators. Two millennia later, isn't that the most elegant proof of all?

A surprising fact: "The *Elements* was second only to the Bible in reprints until the 20th century!"

I shall give you some homework. Trust me, it would be fun! ☺ Try proving the Pythagorean theorem Euclid's way – no algebra is allowed!

Euclid's Elements: Book I, Proposition explained in Appendix 2.

What about **Archimedes** - the original "mad scientist" of ancient Greece! Born around 287 BCE in sunny Syracuse, Sicily, this guy wasn't just brilliant - he was the kind of genius who'd probably forget to eat while working on a math problem. (Ever been so focused you missed dinner? Archimedes would relate.)

His most famous "Eureka!" moment? Figuring out the exact relationship between a sphere's surface area, volume, and surrounding cylinder. But that's just the start - he also gave us Archimedes' Principle, that wonderful law that explains why boats float (and why your beach ball keeps popping up in the pool). Basically, if you've ever taken a bath and noticed the water rise, you've seen his principle in action!

Now, here's my personal favourite: the Archimedes Screw. This brilliant water-lifting device was so effective that farmers are still using versions of it today. Can you imagine creating something 2,300 years ago that's still practical in the 21st century? That's like inventing the wheel and having modern cars still use it!

But wait - there's more! This man revolutionised physics with his work on:

- Levers (giving us the iconic "Give me a place to stand and I shall move the Earth" quote)
- Pulleys (making heavy lifting literally easier)
- The centre of mass (crucial for everything from gymnastics to rocket science)

And let's talk about pi - that magical number we all struggled with in math class. Archimedes calculated it with remarkable accuracy, landing on 22/7 as an approximation. Not bad for someone working without calculators or computers, right? Surprisingly, it laid the groundwork for later developments in calculus.

His inventions read like an ancient tech startup's portfolio:

1. The odometer (the grandfather of your car's mileage counter)
2. War machines to defend Syracuse against the Romans
3. Mathematical proofs for spheres and exponents that still hold up today

Here's what astonishes me: all these discoveries came from one man who basically looked at everyday problems and thought, "There's got to be a better way." Whether it was moving water uphill or measuring distances, Archimedes found elegant solutions that combined math and practicality in ways we still use.

Tragically, his story ends with that heartbreaking moment in 212 BCE when a Roman soldier killed him - supposedly while he was working on a math problem. (Makes you wonder what else he might have invented given more time.) But here's the thing - even in death, Archimedes proves that human creativity is limitless. His work shows us that the most ordinary objects - a screw, a lever, even a bath tub - contain profound scientific truths waiting to be discovered.

Let's take a moment to appreciate **Eratosthenes** - the original Renaissance man who lived 2,300 years before the Renaissance! Born around 276 BC, this ancient polymath had his fingers in every intellectual pie you could imagine: mathematics, science, even music theory. But here's what really gets me - while most of us struggle to master one field, Eratosthenes excelled in multiple disciplines while working as the head librarian at Alexandria's famous library. (Makes you wonder what he could have accomplished with Wikipedia at his fingertips, doesn't it?)

Now, here's where it gets really interesting. This brilliant thinker might have actually coined the term "geography" - talk about leaving your mark on history! But his real claim to fame? He essentially invented our modern understanding of the Earth's shape and gave us the coordinate system we still use today with longitude and latitude. Not terrible for someone working without satellites or GPS!

But wait - the best is yet to come. Picture this: One summer solstice around 240 BC, Eratosthenes heard about something peculiar happening in Syene (modern-day Aswan). At noon, the sun shone directly overhead with no shadows - you could look straight down a well and see the sun reflected in the water below. Meanwhile, in Alexandria, 500 miles north, shadows were still visible. Now, most people would just say "Huh, that's neat" and move on. But not our man Eratosthenes!

Here's what he accomplished that astonishes me:

1. Measured the shadow angle in Alexandria (about 7 degrees)
2. Did some brilliant geometry (remember, no calculators!)
3. Knew the distance between the cities (~5,000 stadia)
4. Calculated Earth's circumference as 250,000 stadia (~25,000 miles)

And get this - his calculation was within about 1-15% of the actual value! How's that for accuracy without modern technology? I don't know about you, but this makes me feel pretty inadequate about my high school math grades...

But he didn't stop there. This scientific rockstar also:

- Discovered Earth's axial tilt (explaining our seasons)
- Created the first world map with parallels and meridians
- Developed an improved calendar with leap years
- Designed the ingenious "sieve" method for finding prime numbers

Here's what really gets me thinking: In an age when many believed the Earth was flat, Eratosthenes not only knew it was round, but measured it with astonishing accuracy using just sticks, shadows, and his brilliant mind. It makes you wonder - how many other groundbreaking discoveries have been lost to history?

Tragically, Eratosthenes died around 194 BC, but his legacy lives on every time we:

- Check a map (thank him for the grid system)
- Experience seasonal changes (he explained why they happen)
- Use prime numbers (his sieve method is still taught today)

In an era before modern instruments, Eratosthenes proved that careful observation and clever reasoning could unlock the universe's secrets. His story reminds us that sometimes, the most profound discoveries come from asking simple questions about everyday phenomena - like why shadows look different in two cities at the same time.

Hipparchus—the ancient Greek astronomer who basically invented celestial cartography while the rest of us would struggle to navigate without GPS! Born around 190 BCE, this visionary didn't just observe the stars; he quantified the heavens in ways that still leave modern astronomers in awe. (Ever tried stargazing without a smartphone app? Hipparchus mapped the sky with nothing but his eyes and genius.)

Stellar Detective Work

His magnum opus? Cataloguing over 1,000 stars with precise brightness and positional data—essentially creating the universe's first Google Maps. Imagine hand-drawing a cosmic atlas so accurate that astronomers referenced it for centuries! But here's what truly astonishes me: while tracking these stars, he noticed something peculiar—a gradual shift in their positions over time. This led to his groundbreaking discovery of axial precession: Earth's slow wobble (like a spinning top) that alters our view of the stars every 26,000 years. How's that for spotting a pattern no one else saw?

Moon Math & Cosmic Connections

Hipparchus made a brilliant connection during lunar eclipses: the Sun and Moon appear the same size in our sky, and Earth's circular shadow reveals their proportional distances. Using geometry (and sheer brainpower), he calculated the Moon's average distance at 63 Earth radii—only about 11% off modern measurements! Pretty good for an individual working 2,100 years before the space age.

The Importance of His Role Today

- Trigonometry's Founding Father: Those high school trig problems you hated? Thank Hipparchus—he essentially invented the field to map the stars.
- Nova Discoverer: When a "new star" (likely a supernova) appeared in 134 BCE, he recorded it—challenging the ancient belief that the heavens were unchanging.
- Precision Pioneer: His work proved that meticulous observation could reveal cosmic truths hidden for millennia.

What's most inspiring isn't just his discoveries, but his method: no telescopes, no computers—just patience, math, and an insatiable curiosity. Hipparchus dared to measure and calculate in an era when myths dominated explanations of celestial phenomena. Next time you look up at the night sky, picture him squinting at the same stars, armed only with a protractor and relentless intellect, forever changing how we understand our place in the cosmos.

Let's take a moment to appreciate **Hero of Alexandria**—the ancient world's answer to Leonardo da Vinci, working his magic nearly two millennia before the Industrial Revolution! Around 60 AD, while most of Rome was busy building aqueducts and hosting gladiator games, this Greek genius was tinkering with what might be history's first steam engine. (Makes you wonder what he could have invented if he'd had proper funding instead of relying on temple gadgetry, doesn't it?)

Steam Power Before It Was Cool

Hero's pièce de résistance? The aeolipile—a spinning, steam-powered sphere that looks like something between a rocket and a fancy kettle. While it was treated as more of a party trick than practical technology at the time, today we recognise it as the grandfather of all steam engines. Imagine showing this to James Watt 1,700 years later—he'd probably have wept at the lost potential!

More Than Just Steam

But what surprises me is that Hero wasn't just a one-trick inventor. As a scholar at Alexandria's legendary Museion (think ancient MIT), he:

- Wrote the "Metrica"—a geometry textbook so thorough it included what we now call Heron's formula for calculating triangle areas (still taught in math classes today!)
- Penned the "Mechanica," detailing machines that would make Archimedes proud
- Created what might be history's first vending machine (dispensing holy water when you inserted a coin!)

Ancient World's Gadget Guru

His "Pneumatica" reads like a 1st-century edition of Popular Mechanics, featuring over 100 devices including:

- Automatic temple doors that opened using steam power (take that, modern motion sensors!)
- A self-operating puppet theatre powered by water and gears (the ancestor of Disney animatronics)
- Musical instruments that played themselves using hydraulic pressure

Why He Remains Significant

What's most fascinating isn't just his inventions, but his mindset. While others built for utility, Hero blended science, art, and pure wonder. His steam engine might not have powered factories, but it proved the potential of steam centuries before anyone thought to harness it. And that's the real lesson—sometimes pure curiosity leads to world-changing discoveries, even if it takes 1,700 years for everyone else to catch up.

Next time you hear a steam whistle or use a vending machine, spare a thought for Hero—the original mad scientist who saw magic in boiling water and geometry in everyday shapes. His legacy reminds us that innovation often begins not with practicality, but with someone asking, "I wonder what would happen if...?"

Picture this: It's 129 CE in Pergamon (modern Turkey), and a young **Galen** is about to become medicine's most influential figure for the next 1,500 years. Isn't it astonishing that one man's ideas could dominate hospitals from London to Baghdad for fifteen centuries? This Greek physician became the medical Bible of both medieval Europe and the Islamic Golden Age – though we might cringe at some of his theories today!

Galen didn't just read medical scrolls—he got his hands bloody. As chief physician to Pergamon's gladiators (ancient Rome's NFL players), he treated gruesome sword wounds and broken bones. Can you imagine the pressure? One mistake, and an angry crowd might demand your head! These battlefield-style surgeries taught him what no classroom could: anatomy matters, and observation is everything. Personally, I think his gladiator days were the real "medical school" that made him great.

When Galen moved to Rome in 162 AD, he became the celebrity doctor of his era – the ancient equivalent of having a MD-PhD from Harvard while serving as White House physician! His patient roster read like a "Who's Who" of Roman emperors: Marcus Aurelius the philosopher-king, the volatile Commodus (yes, that gladiator-obsessed emperor from the movies), and several others. Talk about workplace stress – one bad day could mean exile or worse!

Here's where Galen gets controversial: forbidden from human dissections, he became the ancient world's top monkey anatomist. While his pig and primate studies revealed astonishing details about nerves and organs, this led to some hilarious errors. (Human livers don't actually look like monkey livers – oops!) Yet isn't it remarkable how much he got right despite these limitations? His makeshift "vivisection" experiments would give modern ethicists nightmares!

Galen's breakthroughs read like a medical thriller:

- **Nervous System:** First to recognise sensory vs motor nerves (though he thought nerves carried "animal spirits")
- **Circulation:** Proved arteries carry blood, not air – take that, ancient sceptics!
- **Pharmacology:** His plant-based "Galenicals" dominated pharmacies until the 1800s

His blood circulation theory was only half-right (missing Harvey's later discovery of full circulation), but hey – for a guy working 1,800 years before microscopes, that's still impressive!

So here's the paradox: Galen was both revolutionary and wrong, brilliant and biased. His ideas saved lives for centuries... and delayed medical progress just as long. Yet walking through any medical school today, you'll still see his shadow – in the way we classify drugs, study anatomy, and value clinical observation. Not bad for a man who never saw a human heart dissection! Makes you wonder: which of today's medical "facts" will future doctors find equally quaint?

One of the surprising facts: Some of his herbal remedies still appear in modern pharmacology textbooks!

A challenge for you! Try diagnosing disease without X-rays or blood tests – that was Galen's daily reality!

Imagine Alexandria in the 3rd century CE - while most mathematicians were obsessed with geometry, one rebel thinker was brewing a revolution. **Diophantus**, the "father of algebra," dared to ask: *What if we could solve problems using symbols instead of shapes?* His thirteen-book masterpiece, *Arithmetica*, wasn't merely academically dull - it was the ancient world's equivalent of a hacker manual, introducing radical concepts like:

- Using fractions in equations (shocking at the time!)
- Creating the first algebraic notation system
- Inventing the concept of approximate equality ("parisotes")

Isn't it remarkable how this Greek mathematician, working 1,700 years before calculus, laid the groundwork that would stump mathematicians until the 1990s?

Here's where it gets fascinating - Diophantus' "parisotes" (approximate equality) became the seed for calculus! Centuries later, Pierre de Fermat repackaged it as "adequality" to find tangent lines - essentially creating Calculus 0.5 before Newton and Leibniz. And who could forget Fermat's famous margin note about Diophantine equations? That cheeky "I have a proof too long for this margin" became mathematics' greatest cliffhanger, finally solved by Andrew Wiles in 1994 after 358 years!

But Diophantus wasn't just about serious math - he had flair! His tombstone bore this poetic riddle about his life:

"God granted one-sixth as a child,
One-twelfth as a whiskered youth,
One-seventh unwed, five years till a son -
Whose life halved mine, then four more I wept..."

Let's break this down like ancient algebra detectives:

1. Let X = Diophantus' total lifespan
2. Boyhood: X/6
3. Youth: X/12
4. Bachelorhood: X/7
5. 5 years until fatherhood
6. Son's life: X/2
7. Final mourning: 4 years

The equation? $X = (X/6 + X/12 + X/7 + 5 + X/2 + 4)$

After some fraction work (and probably a few reed-pen breakages), we find:

- Son's life (Y) = 42 years
- Diophantus' age at death = 84 years

Today, Diophantine equations (Ax + By = C, where all terms are integers) are everywhere you'd least expect:

- Cryptography: Protecting your online banking
- Coding Theory: Ensuring error-free data transmission
- Computer Science: Optimising complex algorithms

That's pretty good for a concept born when Rome still ruled Egypt! What would Diophantus think if he knew his equations now guard our digital lives? His legacy proves that pure mathematics always finds unexpected practical uses—often centuries later.

Imagine Baghdad in 965 CE - while Europe slumbered through the Dark Ages, a child named **Ibn Al-Haytham** was born who would literally change how we see the world. This polymath (who dabbled in everything from astronomy to philosophy) made his mark by asking a simple but revolutionary question: *What if our eyes don't emit light, but receive it?* In his groundbreaking *Book of Optics*, he demolished the 1,000-year-old Greek theory that vision worked like flashlights from our eyes. Can you picture the courage it took to challenge such deeply-held beliefs?

Through accurate experiments (some using camera obscura devices), Ibn Al-Haytham proved light behaves like a well-mannered guest - it enters rather than exits! His discovery that light reflects off objects into our eyes seems obvious now, but was as shocking then as quantum physics is today. This "light revolution" directly influenced:

- Kepler's planetary optics
- Descartes' light theories
- Newton's prism experiments

Funny how a medieval Iraqi scholar became the great-grandfather of modern optics, isn't it?

Ibn Al-Haytham's light investigations read like a physics treasure map:

- **Reflection Laws**: First to mathematically prove incident/reflected rays lie in one plane (still taught in high schools today)
- **Refraction Mysteries**: Discovered light takes the fastest path through different media - a principle later named after Fermat
- **Rainbow Physics**: Explained atmospheric refraction centuries before European scientists.

I'm amazed how he nailed these concepts without lasers or precision instruments - just brilliant experimental design and geometric reasoning!

Visualise this: It's 980 CE in Persia, and an infant named Ibn Sina (we'd later call him Avicenna) is born who will become the medical rockstar of the Islamic Golden Age. Imagine being so brilliant that 1,000 years later, medical students still study your work! This polymath didn't just practice medicine - he revolutionised it while simultaneously mastering philosophy, astronomy, and mathematics. His two masterpieces, *The Book of Healing* and *The Canon of Medicine*, became the medical bibles of both East and West for centuries. Isn't it astonishing that one man could influence medicine longer than any textbook in history?

The Canon of Medicine wasn't just a book - it was a five-volume medical revolution that:

- Synthesised Greek knowledge (Hippocrates, Galen) with Persian and Arabic innovations
- Introduced quarantine for epidemics (centuries before Europe caught on)
- Described 760 drugs and their effects

- Included the first clinical descriptions of meningitis

What's most impressive? He compiled this while working as a full-time physician and vizier! Makes our modern work-life balance struggles seem trivial, doesn't it?

Here's the mind-blowing part: by day, Avicenna served as royal physician and political advisor (no pressure - just keeping kings alive and empires running!). But nights? That's when the real magic happened. By candlelight, he'd:

Write groundbreaking medical texts

Debate philosophy with students

Conduct scientific experiments

Personally, I can't decide what's more impressive - his intellect or his ability to function on what must have been severe sleep deprivation!

When *The Book of Healing* reached Europe in the 12th century, it hit medieval universities like an intellectual tsunami. Translated into Latin, this philosophical masterpiece covered:

- **Psychology**: Early theories of consciousness
- **Cosmology**: The nature of the universe
- **Mathematics**: Advanced geometry proofs
- **Logic**: Systems of reasoning

Funny how this "book of healing" healed minds rather than bodies - though medieval scholars probably needed aspirin after wrestling with its complex ideas!

Today, Avicenna stands shoulder-to-shoulder with Hippocrates and Galen in medicine's hall of fame. But here's what's truly remarkable: while Western medicine eventually moved beyond Galen's errors, Avicenna's *Canon* remained standard in Islamic hospitals until the 19th century! His legacy lives on every time an Iranian medical student quotes his texts or a philosopher cites his ideas. Makes you wonder - how many other geniuses from the Islamic Golden Age deserve similar recognition?

Nishapur in 1048 CE - while Europe was still deep in the Middle Ages, **Omar Khayyam** was born, who would become Persia's ultimate Renaissance man centuries before the Renaissance! This wasn't just another mathematician - imagine being so brilliant that you could:

- Solve cubic equations geometrically (basically doing calculus before calculus existed)
- Revolutionise calendar systems
- Write poetry that would be quoted for a millennium
- All while working as an astronomer for the Sultan!

Isn't it remarkable how one 11th-century polymath could excel in such diverse fields? Khayyam's astronomical work was nothing short of revolutionary. Leading a team of scientists, he: developed the Jalali calendar (still used in Iran today!) - so accurate it only drifts one day every 5,000 years

1. Calculated the solar year to within 5 decimal places of modern measurements
2. Created astronomical tables that would guide navigators for centuries

What's more impressive - that he achieved this without telescopes or computers, or that we still use his calendar nearly a millennium later? But here's the real surprise - this hardcore scientist was also history's most quotable poet! His Rubaiyat (quatrains) explore life's big questions with a wine glass in hand:

"The moving finger writes, and having writ, moves on..."

"A book of verses underneath the bough... jug of wine, loaf of bread - and thou"

"Be happy for this moment - this moment is your life"

Isn't it fascinating that the same mind calculating celestial mechanics could pen such timeless verses about life's fleeting beauty? Personally, I find this duality - rigorous scientist and free-spirited poet - absolutely captivating. Khayyam's legacy teaches us that genius isn't one-dimensional. Who says a mathematician can't be a poet? That an astronomer can't ponder life's meaning? His work shines through the centuries as proof that:

- Science and art aren't opposites - they're partners
- Precision and passion can coexist
- True understanding requires both calculation and contemplation

As we use his calendar, solve his equations, and quote his poetry today, we're keeping alive the spirit of a man who saw no boundaries between numbers and nature, between stars and stanzas.

12th-century Persia – a golden age of science where scholars like **Al-Khazini** (c. 1115–1130 CE) pushed the boundaries of knowledge. This Iranian polymath wasn't just a scientist; he was a *medieval science detective*, cracking the secrets of physics with experiments that still impress today. His magnum opus, *The Book of the Balance of Wisdom*, reads like a proto-lab manual, tackling questions like:

- Why do objects float or sink?
- How does density affect buoyancy?
- Can we measure liquid properties systematically?

In one iconic experiment, Al-Khazini dunked metals into water, proving denser objects displace more liquid – a hands-on validation of Archimedes' principle centuries before modern hydrodynamics. (Who knew medieval labs could be so thrilling?)

But here's what's wild: this hydrostatics genius *also* moonlighted as an astronomer and mathematician! His work on:

- Astrolabes (the GPS of the medieval world)
- Celestial motion models
- Trigonometry breakthroughs

…laid the groundwork for future astronomers. How one person mastered so many fields remains a mystery – maybe Persian coffee was stronger back then?

Yet despite his contributions, Al-Khazini's name often gets lost in the history of science. Isn't it time we gave this polymath his due? After all, where would modern physics be without minds like his, blending meticulous experimentation with cross-disciplinary curiosity?

Córdoba in 1126 CE - a vibrant crossroads of Islamic, Jewish, and Christian thought where a sibling named **Ibn Rushd** (we'd later call him **Averroes**) was born. Isn't it remarkable that his warning - "Ignorance leads to fear, fear leads to hatred, and hatred leads to violence" - feels chillingly relevant today? This polymath didn't just study philosophy; he became its bridge between civilizations, mastering:

- Aristotle's complex works
- Groundbreaking medicine
- Precise astronomy

...all while navigating the political minefields of medieval Spain. Averroes' true genius lay in making Aristotle *speak Arabic* - not just translating the Greek master's works like *Metaphysics* and *De Anima*, but breathing new life into them. In smoky candlelit scriptoriums, he crafted commentaries so insightful that:

- Jewish scholars called him "The Commentator"
- Christian theologians debated his ideas for centuries
- Islamic philosophers found new ways to reconcile reason with revelation

His radical idea? That faith and science aren't enemies but partners in truth. How tragic that some contemporaries burned his books while European universities later made them required reading!

But wait - this philosopher had a day job as a physician! His medical encyclopedia Colliget (Arabic: al-Kulliyat) was the Gray's Anatomy of its time:

- Systematised Galen's work with new observations
- Catalogued drugs and their effects
- Included early neuroscience insights

...becoming standard reading at Montpellier and other early medical schools. Who knew that a man debating metaphysics by night could revolutionise hospitals by day?

Here's the beautiful irony: though condemned in his lifetime, Averroes became the intellectual godfather of Europe's Renaissance. His books - rescued by Jewish translators and carried across borders - fueled:

- Thomas Aquinas' theology
- The scientific method's development
- Medieval Europe's rediscovery of reason

Today, as we grapple with science-religion debates, perhaps we should revisit this 12th-century sage who insisted the mind and soul could harmonise. After eight centuries, isn't that a vision still worth pursuing?

It's time to gaze through medieval Italy, the place I visit most often- while most European merchants struggled with clunky Roman numerals, a young **Leonardo Fibonacci** (c.1170-1240) returned from North Africa with a mathematical bombshell: Hindu-Arabic numerals. His 1202 masterpiece *Liber Abaci* ("Book of Calculation") didn't just introduce 0-9 to Europe; it sparked a numerical revolution that would make everything from banking to astronomy possible. Can you picture merchants' shock when they realised "XLVII x IX" could now be solved as 47×9 with this new system?

But here's where it gets magical - while solving a rabbit breeding puzzle, Fibonacci stumbled upon nature's secret code:

- Sunflower seeds spiralling in 55/89 patterns (both Fibonacci numbers)
- Nautilus shells grow in perfect logarithmic spirals
- Tree branches dividing at Fibonacci angles

This "golden ratio" sequence (0,1,1,2,3,5,8...) now predicts stock markets, designs apps, and even tunes violins! Who knew medieval math could become Silicon Valley's favourite pattern?

Yet the sequence was just Fibonacci's side gig! This math superhero also:

- Wrote Europe's first algebra manual for businessmen
- Developed currency exchange formulas (medieval Forex trading!)
- Calculated compound interest tables
- Solved cubic equations geometrically

We should call him the "Steve Jobs of medieval math" - he didn't just calculate, he built tools that transformed everyday commerce!

Here's the bittersweet truth: Fibonacci died before seeing his work's true impact. But like a mathematical time capsule, his ideas blossomed during the Renaissance and still shape:

- Modern financial systems
- Computer science algorithms
- Architectural design principles

Eight centuries later, isn't it poetic that the man who brought us zero (0) ultimately became... well, a hero (1) of mathematics?

13th-century England - while most monasteries focused solely on scripture, a young friar in Somerset was about to shake up medieval science. **Roger Bacon** (c.1219-1292) wasn't your typical Franciscan brother; imagine a man who could:

- Debate theology at Oxford
- Experiment with lenses like a medieval "MacGyver"

- Predict flying machines and submarines centuries before their invention
- All while wearing his friar's robes!

Isn't it astonishing how this polymath thrived in an age when science was often viewed with suspicion? Bacon's Opus Majus (1267) was nothing less than a medieval manifesto for the scientific method. At a time when scholars debated ancient texts, Bacon insisted:

- "Don't take Aristotle's word for it - go test nature yourself!"
- "Mathematics is the key to unlocking nature's secrets"
- "Record everything - even failed experiments teach us"

Personally, I'm thrilled by how this 13th-century friar grasped principles that wouldn't become mainstream for another 400 years. How many modern scientists wish they'd had his insight?

Here's why Bacon deserves the title "Father of Experimental Science":

- He turned alchemy labs into proper research spaces
- Demanded repeatable results - no mystical handwaving allowed
- Saw mathematics as nature's native language
- Predicted microscopes, telescopes, and even steam engines!

While his peers debated how many angels could dance on a pinhead, Bacon laid the groundwork for everything from chemistry labs to NASA missions. Talk about visionary!

Bacon's optical breakthroughs read like a science fiction novel:

- Ground glass into lenses despite primitive tools
- Understood light refraction before Snell's Law
- Predicted corrective lenses centuries before spectacles
- Described telescope principles 300 years before Galileo

Imagine being the first person to see a magnified leaf's veins or a distant tower brought near - no wonder his contemporaries called it magic! Today, we celebrate Bacon not just as a scientist, but as science's first revolutionary. His legacy lives on every time a researcher:

1. Designs a controlled experiment
2. Reaches for a microscope
3. Insists on mathematical proof
4. Dares to imagine the impossible

Is it not bad for a friar who worked by candlelight eight centuries ago? Perhaps his most significant lesson was this: accurate understanding comes not from ancient texts but nature's book - if we dare to read it carefully.

Southeast of England, Surrey in 1285, is where I live today - while most medieval villagers focused on harvests and hymns, a boy named William was born who would change how humanity thinks. We know frustratingly little about young William of Ockham's life (did he question his village priest as a child? Argue with sheep about logic?), but by the time he reached Oxford, this Franciscan friar had honed a mind so razor-sharp we still measure intellectual elegance by it today. Isn't it remarkable how someone from such humble beginnings could reshape entire disciplines?

Occam's gift to the world? His legendary "razor" - not a physical blade, but a mental scalpel that slices through intellectual clutter. The principle is deliciously simple: when faced with competing explanations, the one making the fewest assumptions is probably right. Modern scientists use it daily to:

- Choose between quantum theories
- Design cleaner experiments
- Debunk conspiracy claims ("Aliens built the pyramids? Really?")

Personally, I wish more people would apply this principle to social media debates! Can you imagine how much simpler online arguments would be if we all wielded Occam's Razor?

- But Occam was no one-trick philosopher. This medieval rebel also:
- Redefined faith as reasonable, not blind obedience
- Defended the separation of church and state (dangerous in the 1300s!)
- Argued for moral philosophy grounded in reality

His boldness came at a cost - ever been called into your boss's office? Try being summoned by the Pope himself to defend "heretical" ideas! Yet he stood firm, proving intellectual courage isn't a modern invention.

Here's the bitter irony: the very church that excommunicated Occam later adopted his methods. His "heresies" became foundations for:

- The scientific revolution (thank him next time you use a smartphone)
- Modern legal systems
- Even the U.S. Constitution's church-state separation

Reasonable for a medieval friar branded a troublemaker, eh? Makes you wonder: which of today's "radical" ideas will be tomorrow's common sense?

Today, Occam stands as the patron saint of clear thinking in our age of information overload. His legacy challenges us to:

1. Question even "sacred" assumptions
2. Value simplicity over showy complexity
3. Defend ideas with logic, not volume

In an era of fake news and conspiracy theories, perhaps we need Occam's Razor more than ever. After seven centuries, isn't it time we all became a little more "Occam-ish" in our daily lives?

Let's time-travel to 14th-century Kerala, where a mathematical revolution was brewing beneath palm trees, rather than in European universities. While Newton and Leibniz get all the credit, **Madhava of Sangamagrama** (1340-1425) was solving calculus-level problems 300 years earlier! Isn't it shocking how Western narratives nearly erased this genius from history? His story isn't just about math—it's about correcting the historical record.

Though history left few records of Madhava's youth (did he count coconut rows as a child? Debate geometry with temple priests?), his leadership of the Kerala School reveals extraordinary insights:

- Developed infinite series for π with mind-boggling precision (3.14159265359!)
- Created trigonometric tables more accurate than European versions
- Pioneered early "calculus" concepts using Sanskrit verses as equations

Imagine deriving these breakthroughs without modern notation—just palm leaves and relentless intellect!

- Madhava's calculus revelations read like magic:
- Infinite Series: Solved what we now call Taylor series expansions
- Trigonometry: Expressed sine functions as infinite sums
- Early Integration: Calculated areas under curves
- Derivatives: Analysed instantaneous rates of change

All this in the 1300s—centuries before European "discoveries"! The Kerala School deserves its own Hollywood biopic. Who wouldn't watch "The Man Who Knew Infinity: Part 1"?

But wait—this math wizard also tracked the stars! His astronomical feats included:

- Eclipse predictions are accurate to minutes

- Planetary models rivalling Copernicus' later work
- A revolutionary calendar system

Kerala fishermen still use their lunar calculations! How many 14th-century theories remain practical today?

Madhava's legacy demands more than remembrance—it requires celebration. Next time you:

1. Use GPS (thanks to his trigonometry)
2. See a physics equation (applaud his calculus)
3. Hear "Eastern vs Western science" (cite Kerala's proofs)

...remember the palm-leaf manuscripts that held these secrets first. After 600 years, isn't it time we gave Sangamagrama's son his rightful place in the math hall of fame?

Let's play a thought experiment: if Gutenberg walked into a modern coffee shop and saw people scrolling smartphones, he might nod and say "Ah, you've got your own printing presses!" Because his 15th-century invention—the movable-type printing press—was nothing less than the medieval internet. Both technologies:

- Democratized information
- Broke knowledge monopolies
- Sparked cultural revolutions
- And terrified authorities

Isn't it fascinating that history's biggest leaps always involve setting information free?

Here's why historians call it the "Gutenberg Galaxy": within 50 years of his press:

- Book production exploded from thousands to millions
- Literacy rates tripled across Europe
- Heretical ideas spread faster than the Church could burn them

The Renaissance without Gutenberg would be like the internet without WiFi—all the content, no delivery system!

Gutenberg‘s genius wasn't inventing printing—it was industrialising it. This Mainz goldsmith (yes, he trained as a jeweller!) solved three key problems:

1. Metal movable type that didn't wear out
2. Oil-based ink that adhered cleanly
3. A modified wine press for perfect pressure

The result? Books became 300 times cheaper practically overnight. Imagine the 15th-century equivalent of Amazon book prices crashing from 300 to 1!

Gutenberg‘s path was messier than a printer's ink-stained apron:

- Went bankrupt funding his experiments
- Lost his workshop to a lawsuit (medieval patent battles!)
- Saw fires destroy precious type sets

Yet he kept pressing on—literally. The man even printed indulgences to pay his debts, proving that innovators have always needed to hustle.

The aftershocks changed everything:

- Martin Luther's 95 Theses went viral (16th-century style)
- Scientists could replicate experiments using identical texts
- Recipes, maps, and news spread like never before

Within decades, Europe went from scriptoriums to street-corner bookstalls. How different might history be if Gutenberg had given up after the first lawsuit?

Gutenberg‘s true legacy? Turning "knowledge is power" into "knowledge is participation." Every time we:

1. Share an article online
2. Download an ebook
3. Debate ideas on social media

...we're using spiritual descendants of his press. Six centuries later, his revolution still isn't finished—it's just changed fonts from Gothic to Times New Roman, as it is in this book!

SUMMARY

Let's pause and appreciate humanity's greatest glow-up! Between 500 BCE and 1400 CE, our ancestors didn't just evolve—they revolutionised thought itself. While Europe slept through its so-called Dark Ages, the Mediterranean and Asia hosted history's first intellectual supernovas. Was this the original "Renaissance" we rarely discuss?

This era birthed the tools that still shape modern minds: Hippocrates' oath became medicine's moral compass. Socrates' questioning method—ancient Athens' version of critical thinking 101, Plato's Academy (the world's first think tank), where "What if?" became a lifestyle.

These Greek innovations travelled further than Alexander's armies ever did! Meanwhile, the math revolution was heating up: Euclid's "Elements" – the original math bible (still assigned in grad schools!), Archimedes shouting "Eureka!" in his bathtub (history's most famous bath time), Both laid the groundwork for Newton and Einstein centuries later. These ancients did more with parchment and sticks than some do with supercomputers!

Not to be outdone, the scientists were: Galen dissecting (mostly animal) bodies to map human systems. Eratosthenes measured the Earth with sticks and shadows (off by just 1%!). Hipparchus catalogued stars without telescopes. Calculating our planet's size using just well shadows and geometry makes GPS look easy.

But the real game-changer? Gutenberg's printing press—the medieval information superhighway. Within decades, Book prices crashed 300-fold, Ideas spread faster than the Black Death, and Power structures trembled as knowledge escaped its chains.

Does this sound familiar? It should—we're living through Gutenberg 2.0 with the digital revolution! These weren't just incremental advances—they were intellectual earthquakes whose aftershocks shaped the Scientific Revolution, the Age of Exploration, and our modern technological era.

As we turn to Chapter 3's next wave of discoveries, remember: today's "cutting-edge" often stands on parchment-and-quill foundations. Who knows—maybe future historians will call our era "Digital Antiquity"!

CHAPTER 3

The Scientific Revolution (14th - 17th centuries)

Imagine living in a world where questioning church doctrine could get you burned at the stake—until suddenly, it made you famous. Europe underwent a radical transformation between the 14th and 17th centuries, where "because God wills it" gave way to "let me prove it." The Renaissance wasn't just about pretty paintings; it was humanity's first science fair on a continental scale. What began in Florence's workshops soon spread like intellectual wildfire, replacing medieval guesswork with measurable evidence. This was history's greatest upgrade from faith-based to fact-based thinking.

While Italy often steals the spotlight, similar revolutions were brewing worldwide—from Timbuktu's astronomers to Constantinople's manuscript preservers. The Renaissance's true spark? When Copernicus dared to suggest Earth wasn't the universe's VIP section. Picture the audacity: a Polish mathematician upending 1,500 years of Ptolemaic astronomy without even a telescope! His heliocentric theory, later proven by Galileo's stargazing and Kepler's calculations, became the ultimate mic-drop moment. And thanks to Gutenberg's printing press (the 15th-century internet), these ideas spread faster than the Black Death ever did.

Static electricity wasn't new—ancient Greeks knew rubbing amber created sparks. But William Gilbert's 1600 *De Magnete* transformed parlour tricks into real science. This Renaissance rockstar coined the term "electricity" from "elektron" (Greek for amber), built the first electroscope to detect charges, and proved Earth itself was a giant magnet.

Not too shabby for a guy who moonlighted as Queen Elizabeth I's physician! His work inspired Otto von Guericke's sulfur globe generator—essentially the first battery, though it could barely power a modern doorbell.

The 17th century saw electricity move from curiosity to quantifiable science. When Robert Boyle discovered conductivity in 1675, it was like finding the universe's hidden wiring diagram. Metals became highways for electrons, while glass and rubber were roadblocks—knowledge that would later enable everything from lightbulbs to laptops. Meanwhile, in medicine, Andreas Vesalius risked execution to steal corpses for dissection, creating eerily beautiful anatomy sketches that corrected 1,300 years of medical errors. Talk about dedication to your craft!

By the 1700s, the Leyden jar could store enough juice to knock out a grown man (volunteers lined up for this shocking "entertainment"). This glass-bottle capacitor paved the way for Franklin's kite experiment and Volta's battery. What started as rubbing amber in curiosity became the foundation of our electrified world—proving once again that Renaissance minds didn't just paint ceilings... they raised them for all of humanity.

Envision an 11-year-old boy starting university today— **Johannes Müller** (1436 – 1476 CE), also better known as Regiomontanus, in 1447. Born in humble Königsberg, this prodigy would become the "human calculator" of his era. Isn't it remarkable how a miller's son could rise to advise popes and reshape astronomy? His journey from rural Germany to Vienna's intellectual circles proves that genius can blossom anywhere.

At Vienna University, young Johann found his mentor in Georg Peuerbach - think of him as the 15th century's equivalent of a superstar professor. Together, they decoded Ptolemy's ancient star maps in the *Almagest,* invented new trigonometric methods (our modern sine/tangent calculations owe him!), and Wrote *De*

Triangulis Omnimodis, essentially the first trigonometry textbook. His work was so advanced that 16th-century navigators still used his tables to cross oceans!

Regiomontanus didn't just study the stars - he reinvented how we track them: built astronomical instruments precise enough to shame modern protractors, created eclipse predictions used for decades, partnered with Gutenberg to print scientific texts (the original "academic publishing")

His 1474 *Ephemerides* became the GPS of the Age of Exploration - Columbus allegedly carried a copy to the New World! How's that for lasting impact? This Renaissance polymath wore more hats than a Venetian noble: Professor at 21, bestselling author, Scientific instrument designer, and Vatican consultant

His greatest legacy? Bridging medieval and modern science. When Copernicus cited his work decades later, it proved that good ideas outlive their creators. Tragically dead at 40 (possibly poisoned by political rivals), Regiomontanus left us wondering - what more could he have achieved? Yet in his brief life, he:

1. Gave trigonometry its modern form
2. Made astronomy accessible through printing
3. Inspired generations of scientists

In our age of AI and quantum computing, we'd remember Regiomontanus - proof that human curiosity, not just technology, drives real progress.

A Star Is Born. Visualise young **Nicolaus Copernicus** (1473-1543 CE) in 1483 Toruń - a grieving 10-year-old whose merchant father had just died, leaving him to an uncle who happened to be an influential bishop. Talk about an unlikely start for a man who would challenge the Church's cosmic worldview! At Kraków University (1491-1495), this Renaissance polymath-in-training Studied math by day under Albert Brudzewski (who secretly taught cutting-edge astronomy), collected astronomy texts like Sacrobosco's *Tractatus de Sphaera* (1220) like cosmic treasure, and painted celestial maps that perhaps first hinted at his revolutionary ideas.

Isn't it poetic that the man who moved Earth literally started as an art student? Those painting skills later helped him illustrate celestial motions!

The Book Collector Who Changed History. By 29, Copernicus had assembled the 15th century's ultimate astronomy library: Euclid's *Elements* (1482 Venice edition) - his geometry bible, Alfonsine Tables for calculating planetary positions, Regiomontanus's *Tables of Directions*(1490) - the GPS of its day. Yet something troubled him. His wooden yardstick measurements (no telescopes yet!) showed discrepancies that Ptolemy's Earth-centred model couldn't explain. Imagine his "Eureka!" moment realizing: *What if we're the ones moving?*

At Olsztyn Castle, Copernicus didn't just *study* the heavens—he *rewrote* them. Armed with nothing but wooden yardsticks, a metal viewing tube, and sheer brilliance, he turned a castle wall into his laboratory, painting. His meticulously drawn sundial wasn't just a timekeeper but a silent protest against centuries of flawed cosmology. Every shadow it cast whispered: *"The Sun doesn't revolve around us."* While Europe clung to the idea of Earth as God's chosen centre, Copernicus sketched the unthinkable: our planet as a mere traveller, circling the Sun like Jupiter or Saturn. Imagine the audacity—declaring humanity *not* the centre of creation with nothing but math and observation! His orbital sequence—Mercury, Venus, Earth, Mars, Jupiter, Saturn—was flawless (Uranus and Neptune remained unseen)—no guesswork, no divine intervention—just cold, complex calculations.

The Seven Bombshells That Shattered Medieval Thought

Copernicus didn't just tweak the model—he torched it. His propositions were cosmic heresy wrapped in logic:

1. "The Universe Has No VIP Section"

   Translation: Earth isn't special. Stars don't dance around us.

2. "We're Not the Main Character"

The ultimate plot twist: Earth is just another actor in the solar system's play.

3. "The Sun is the Local Landmark"

   Not the universe's centre, but the anchor of our celestial neighbourhood.

4. "Stars Are *Really* Far Away"

   His realization that stellar distances dwarfed Earth-Sun space foreshadowed modern astronomy.

5. "We're Spinning, Not the Sky"

   Those "moving" stars? Just an illusion from Earth's 24-hour pirouette.

6. "Seasons Aren't Magic—They're Orbital"

   Summer and winter are explained by tilt *and* motion, not celestial whims.

7. "Planetary Backtracking? Just Perspective"

   Mars' retrograde motion finally made sense—a cosmic "passing lane" illusion.

The Tools of Rebellion

No telescopes. No computers. Just:

- A wooden triquetrum (think medieval protractor) to measure star angles
- A metal sighting tube—Galileo's telescope, decades before Galileo
- Naked-eye observations so precise they embarrassed professional astronomers

Why It Terrified the World

This was more than mere science—it was a philosophical earthquake. If Earth weren't central, what else might the Church be wrong about? No wonder he waited until death to publish.

Legacy in Stone and Starlight

That wall calendar at Olsztyn? Still there. Those seven propositions? Still taught. The revolution? Still unfolding—every time a child learns planets orbit the Sun, not the other way around.

In an age of AI and space telescopes, we forget how radical it was to trust *math* over doctrine. Copernicus didn't just move Earth—he moved humanity toward the light of reason.

A Quiet Departure (1543 CE)

Copernicus held back *De Revolutionibus* until his deathbed (May 24, 1543), fearing backlash. The first printed copy reached him hours before dying—legend says he awoke from a coma to touch it, then expired. His epitaph? A silent model of a solar system that outshone any words.

That simple metal tube he peered through? It shattered humanity's cosmic ego forever.

Andreas Vesalius (1514-1564 CE): The Rebel Anatomist Who Redrew the Human Body. A 16th-century teenager crouched in a Brussels alley, dissecting stray mice with kitchen knives. This wasn't macabre curiosity—it was the childhood of the man who would dismantle 1,300 years of medical dogma. How did this privileged physician's son become history's most determined grave robber?

Born into a dynasty of court physicians, young Andreas didn't settle for reading Galen's texts—he *tested* them. While his Paris professors lectured from yellowed scrolls (never touching a scalpel themselves), Vesalius bribed gravediggers and dodged the law to secure cadavers. Imagine the scandal when this 23-year-old upstart took over dissections from the barber-surgeons—considered "butchers" by the academic elite!

The Padua Revolution

At Europe's finest medical school, Vesalius broke every rule:

- Hands-On Heresy: Insisted on performing dissections himself (unheard of for professors)
- Art Meets Science: Commissioned lavish illustrations from Titian's workshop
- "Fabrica" – The First Medical Blockbuster: His 1543 masterpiece *De Humani Corporis Fabrica* wasn't just a book—it was a 700-page mic drop proving Galen's "facts" (based on animal anatomy) were often wrong

Those intricate woodcuts of flayed "muscle men" posing in landscapes didn't just educate—they turned medicine into art.

The Cost of Truth

Vesalius paid dearly for his breakthroughs:

- Grave-Robbing Charges: Rumoured to have taken a noblewoman's body mid-autopsy
- Inquisition Woes: Accused of heresy when beating hearts were found in "corpses"
- Exile & Mystery: Died at 49 en route to Jerusalem—possibly shipwrecked, possibly poisoned.

A Legacy Carved in Flesh

Today, every medical student traces their knowledge to Vesalius' radical principles:

1. See for Yourself: Autopsy over Authority
2. Mistakes Are Progress: Correcting Galen saved lives

3. Beauty in Truth: His anatomical art still takes your breath away

In our age of AI diagnostics, Vesalius reminds us that medicine begins with human hands—and the courage to question.

The Logarithmic Revolution: How **John Napier***(1550-1617),* Made Math Multiply. It's 1590s Scotland, and an eccentric landowner named John Napier obsessively scribbles numbers in his castle tower. While his neighbours worry about crops and clan wars, Napier battles a bigger problem—how to save astronomers from drowning in endless calculations. Could there be a shortcut through the numerical wilderness?

Napier's Bones: The Original Calculator. Before silicon chips, there were ivory rods. Napier's ingenious "bones" weren't medical tools but the 16th century's answer to a pocket calculator, 10-numbered rods with multiplication tables with Slide-and-read functionality that could handle 5-digit numbers, and no batteries required—just Scottish ingenuity.

Watching students today groan over calculators, I wonder if they'd prefer Napier's tactile math sticks!

His *Mirifici Logarithmorum Canonis Descriptio* wasn't solely a textbook—it was a mathematical superweapon: **First 57 pages with** A bombshell explanation of logarithms. A **90-page book of tables,** the "Google Sheets" of its day, cutting calculation times from months to minutes. And another Napier's Rules, a Spherical trigonometry shortcut for navigators.

Imagine charting a ship's course without logarithms, calculating compound interest by hand, or predicting planetary motions with raw multiplication?

Napier's logs became the invisible engine behind:

✧ Kepler's planetary laws

✧ Newton's physics

✧ Even modern algorithms

A Legacy Carved in Numbers

When Napier died at Merchiston Castle in 1617, he left behind:

1. A calculation revolution is still used in everything from pH scales to decibels
2. The concept of the decimal point (yes, we owe our 3.14 to him too!)
3. A challenge: How many modern "innovations" will still be relevant in 400 years?

In our age of quantum computing, it's humbling that Napier's logs still run silently beneath every digital calculation—proof that brilliant simplicity never goes obsolete.

Put yourself as **Galileo Galilei** (1564 – 1642 CE) in 1610, peering through his handmade telescope at Jupiter's moons, only to realise you're seeing proof that could get you burned at the stake. That was the dangerous truth behind his confirmation of Copernicus' heliocentric model. While 16th-century Europe clung to Earth-as-centre dogma, this stubborn Italian physicist gathered evidence that would rewrite cosmic history. Isn't it ironic that the same Church that condemned him later used his pendulum clocks?

The most significant moment: The Rolling Ball Experiments That Changed Physics Forever. Galileo didn't just challenge Aristotle—he demolished him with simple wooden ramps and bronze balls:

- Mass Myth Busted: Showed a 10-pound and 1-pound ball hit the ground simultaneously (take that, ancient Greeks!)
- Parabolic Revelations: Traced the elegant arcs of projectiles—foundations for modern ballistics
- Pendulum Precision: Discovered timekeeping doesn't care about swing width, birthing the first accurate clocks

His inclined planes were the 17th-century equivalent of a viral physics TikTok—simple, brilliant, and impossible to ignore.

A Toolkit of Cosmic Rebellion, 20x Telescopes, Hand-ground lenses revealing lunar craters and Jupiter's moons. Pulse-Powered

Pendulums, using his heartbeat to time swings. Sneaky Manuscripts, publishing heretical findings as “hypotheses” to avoid Inquisition wrath.

The Legacy That Wouldn’t Be Silenced, Even under house arrest, his ideas kept orbiting:

1. Newton‘s Launchpad: Those falling bodies became F=ma
2. Space Age Navigation: Jupiter’s moons now help spacecraft orient
3. Modern Scientific Method: Showed math + experiment > ancient authority

When today’s scientists face “alternative facts,” they walk the path Galileo paved—one stubborn observation at a time.

A young German mathematician in 1600, nervously joining the court of the eccentric Tycho Brahe in Prague. Little did **Johannes Kepler** (1571-1630 CE) know that this partnership would become one of history’s most fruitful scientific collaborations—even if it began with Brahe withholding his precious Mars data like a dragon guarding treasure! How did this former theology student become the man who would forever shatter Aristotle‘s crystalline spheres?

Kepler’s career took a celestial turn when Emperor Rudolph II—a rare ruler who valued stargazers over soldiers—paired him with Brahe. The contrast couldn’t have been sharper: Brahe, the flamboyant observational genius with his golden nose and island observatory. Kepler, the quiet theorist with crippled hands but a mind that could bend mathematics to the heavens

When Brahe died mysteriously in 1601 (possibly from a burst bladder at a banquet), Kepler inherited decades of precise planetary observations, including Mars’s that would become the Rosetta Stone of orbital mechanics.

The Laws That Rewrote the Cosmos

Armed with Brahe's data, Kepler made discoveries that still form the bedrock of astronomy:

1. **First Law (1609): Planets Move in Ellipses**
2. That eureka moment when Kepler realised Mars' orbit wasn't a perfect circle but a "squashed" ellipse shattered 2,000 years of Aristotelian dogma. His *Astronomia Nova* didn't just tweak cosmology—it launched a revolution.
3. **Second Law: The Cosmic Speedometer**
4. Planets don't glide at constant speeds but *accelerate* as they near the Sun. His equal-area law explained why Mercury zips around while Pluto crawls—all with elegant geometry that would make Euclid weep.

It's humbling to think that today's Mars rovers navigate using math Kepler derived with just quill pens and Brahe's naked-eye observations!

Against All Odds, Kepler's life reads like a tragic opera with a triumphant finale:

- Exiled from Graz for his Lutheran faith
- Lost his wife and son to the plague
- Constantly bankrupt (even Emperor Rudolph paid him in wine!)
- His mother was nearly burned as a witch

Yet through it all, he kept calculating—proving that scientific progress often depends as much on stubbornness as genius.

The Ripple Effect

Kepler's legacy orbits far beyond astronomy:

- Newton's Gravity: Without elliptical orbits, there's no Principia

- Space Exploration: NASA's Voyager trajectories use his math
- Exoplanet Hunting: Modern telescopes apply these laws to alien worlds

In our age of supercomputers, Kepler reminds us that universe-changing insights can come from a single human mind—armed only with data, determination, and the courage to question everything.

An example calculation of Mercury's average distance from the sun is shown in Appendix 3

William Harvey (1578-1657): The Man Who Made Blood Move: A young Englishman in 1600, fresh from Cambridge, trekking across Europe to study at Padua's famed medical school—the same institution where Vesalius had revolutionised anatomy decades earlier. Little did William Harvey know he was about to solve one of medicine's oldest mysteries: how blood actually moves through the body. How many centuries had doctors clung to Galen's mistaken belief that blood sloshed back and forth like ocean tides?

The Circulatory Revelation (1628), Harvey's De Motu Cordis wasn't just a medical text but a detective story written in blood. Through meticulous dissections and calculations, he proved:

- The Heart as a Pump: Not some mystical furnace, but a muscular machine pushing 1.3 gallons of blood daily
- Closed-Loop System: Blood travels in continuous circuits, not consumed by organs as previously thought
- Valve Logic: Those tiny flaps in veins meant blood could only flow toward the heart

Harvey essentially discovered plumbing 200 years before modern pipes—imagine diagnosing circulation without even knowing about capillaries!

Beyond the Veins: A Renaissance Medical Mind

Harvey's curiosity pulsed through every branch of medicine:

- Embryology: Challenged "spontaneous generation" by studying chick development day-by-day
- Royal Physician: Served Charles I during the English Civil War—perhaps the only man who could calm the king's temper as well as his palpitations
- Evidence-Based Practice: Insisted on repeatable experiments over ancient texts

The Reluctant Revolutionary

Despite his courtly position, Harvey faced fierce opposition:

- Traditionalists mocked his "impossible" circulation theory
- Colleagues clung to Galen's 1,400-year-old teachings
- Even poets like John Donne referenced the controversy in their works

Yet by his death in 1657, Harvey had outlasted his critics—his ideas flowing as steadily as the blood he championed.

A Legacy That Still Circulates

Today, every:

- Heart surgery
- Blood pressure measurement
- CPR technique

...traces back to Harvey's stubborn insistence on seeing rather than assuming. In an age of AI diagnostics, his hands-on approach remains medicine's lifeblood.

When you feel your pulse today, remember that Harvey first understood what that rhythmic thump truly meant: not magic but magnificent machinery.

René Descartes (1596-1650): The Philosopher Who Put the 'I' in Idea

Picture a young Frenchman in 1618, lying awake in a Bavarian winter garrison (where he'd enlisted as a mercenary!), staring at the ceiling as geometry problems danced in his mind. This was Descartes' "stove-heated room" moment—the literal warmth that sparked modern philosophy. How many of history's greatest breakthroughs began with such ordinary moments of quiet reflection?

Descartes didn't just philosophise—he engineered thought itself. His *Discourse on the Method* (1637) was the ultimate intellectual toolkit:

- Radical Doubt: Wiping the mental slate clean ("What if all my teachers were wrong?")
- Mathematical Certainty: If $a^2 + b^2 = c^2$ is irrefutable, why not build philosophy with similar rigour?
- The Ultimate Soundbite: *"Cogito, ergo sum"*—four Latin words that made the thinking self the bedrock of existence

In our age of AI and deepfakes, Descartes' insistence on the primacy of conscious experience feels more relevant than ever.

The Graph Paper Revolution, Before Descartes, algebra and geometry lived in separate worlds. His coordinate system changed everything:

- X Marks the Spot: That simple horizontal line (now called the x-axis) became reality's grid
- Y Not?: Adding the vertical y-axis lets mathematicians "map" equations visually

Origin Story: The (0,0) intersection point became the Big Bang of analytic geometry

Every GPS coordinate, video game sprite, and MRI scan today owes him royalties!

The Mind-Body Split That Still Divides Us

Descartes‘ most controversial idea—that mind and body are separate substances—sparked debates that rage in neuroscience labs today:

- Body as Machine: His description of animal (and human) bodies as clockwork automata
- The Ghost in the Machine: The non-physical "thinking thing" (res cogitans) that somehow pilots the physical body
- Quantum Echoes: Modern physicists still grapple with how consciousness interacts with matter

His well-known phrase "I think. Therefore, I exist,"

In his Dutch exile, Descartes became tutor to the brilliant Princess Elisabeth of Bohemia (their letters revolutionised the philosophy of emotions). He fell victim to Queen Christina of Sweden's brutal 5 AM philosophy lessons in freezing Stockholm and dried his lungs in the Scandinavian cold—an ironic fate for the man who reduced bodies to machinery.

As we debate AI consciousness and upload brains to clouds, we're still living in Descartes' world—still asking "What can I truly know?" just as he taught us.

Pierre de Fermat (1607-1665): The Lawyer Who Outsmarted Mathematicians for Centuries

Envision this: A 17th-century French lawyer, quill in hand, scribbling mathematical theorems in the margins of legal documents by candlelight. By day, Pierre de Fermat argued cases in Toulouse's courts; by night, he conducted a secret love affair with numbers that would change mathematics forever. How many of his colleagues suspected that the quiet man reviewing contracts was simultaneously inventing modern number theory?

The Theorem That Launched a 358-Year Chase.

Fermat's most famous taunt – written casually in 1637 – became mathematics's ultimate mic drop:

"I have discovered a truly marvellous proof that this margin is too narrow to contain."

This throwaway comment about equations like $x^n + y^n = z^n$ (where $n > 2$) tormented mathematicians until:

- 1994: Andrew Wiles cracked it using elliptic curves and modular forms
- The Twist: Fermat likely didn't have the proof he claimed (the required math didn't exist yet!)
- The Legacy: A 358-year treasure hunt that advanced entire fields of mathematics

Fermat's Last Theorem became the mathematical equivalent of a viral cliffhanger—the "Who shot J.R.?" of number theory.

The "Amateur" Who Outplayed the Professionals. Don't let his "Prince of Amateurs" title fool you—Fermat was a heavyweight who:

- Pioneered Calculus Early: His method for finding curve maxima/minima predated Newton and Leibniz
- Invented Probability Theory: Through lively correspondence with Pascal about gambling odds
- Laid Foundations for Optics: With his principle of least time (light takes the fastest path)

Fermat's brilliance came with quirks:

- The Correspondent: Preferred sharing discoveries in letters rather than publishing
- The Lost Works: Many breakthroughs known only through others' references

- The Collaborator: Despite his secrecy, he mentored younger mathematicians

Imagine what we might know today if his papers hadn't been used to wrap fish or line birdcages!

Fermat proved that Genius Needs No Title. You can revolutionise fields outside your "day job." One Good Tease Can Inspire Generations; his last theorem fueled centuries of research. Mathematics is a Conversation: His collaborative spirit lives on in modern arXiv preprints.

In our age of academic specialisation, Fermat reminds us that sometimes the most revolutionary ideas come from outsiders—those daring enough to scribble in margins rather than follow established paths.

The Gambling Problem That Changed Mathematics Forever

It's 1654 France, and a gentleman gambler named Chevalier de Méré poses a dice problem that would spark one of history's most brilliant intellectual partnerships. Who stepped up to the challenge? None other than Pierre de Fermat and **Blaise Pascal** (1623 - 1662) - two mathematical giants who essentially invented probability theory over their correspondence. (Who knew that gambling disputes could lead to scientific revolutions?)

While working on probability, Pascal also engineered the Pascaline - the 17th century version of a calculator. But here's what really blows my mind: this brass gear contraption could only add and subtract, yet it paved the way for every computing device we use today.

It makes you appreciate your smartphone's calculator a bit more, doesn't it?

Pascal's most elegant contribution? That beautiful numerical pyramid we now call Pascal's Triangle. By decoding its hidden patterns, he gave us:

- Formulas to calculate probabilities in repeated events
- The foundation for binomial distributions
- Tools to understand combinations (perfect for modern statistics)

What many don't realise is that Pascal was also a physics pioneer. His work on fluids led to Pascal's Law - the principle that makes hydraulic lifts possible. Next time you see construction equipment or car brakes working, remember: that's Pascal's 350-year-old discovery in action!

Today, we measure pressure in Pascals (Pa), and programmers still use the Pascal language. Not bad at all for a man who did his most famous work through letters about dice games!

Robert Boyle (1627 - 1691): The Aristocrat Who Reinvented Chemistry

It's 1627 in an Irish castle, and a boy named Robert Boyle is born into wealth and privilege. But unlike most aristocrats of his time, young Boyle would trade courtly pleasures for laboratory experiments, ultimately earning the title "father of modern chemistry". (Who knew chemistry could have aristocratic roots?)

Educated at home and at Eton before touring Europe's intellectual hotspots, Boyle developed what I like to call a "Renaissance man" approach to science. In 1660, he published *Touching the Spring of the Air* - a work that contained his famous gas law. The equation $PV=k$ might look simple today, but imagine being the first person to realise that:

- Pressure (P) and volume (V) of gases are inversely related
- This relationship holds true as long as the temperature stays constant
- The product always equals some constant (k)

But Boyle's real masterpiece came in 1661 with *The Sceptical Chemist*. This groundbreaking book:

- Challenged alchemical traditions
- Proposed that matter consists of tiny "corpuscles" (what we'd now call atoms)
- Established chemistry as its own scientific discipline (not just a branch of physics or medicine)

It is fascinating to mention Boyle's "mechanical philosophy" - his view of the universe as an enormous, precise clock. While this might sound quaint today, it was revolutionary thinking in an age when most scientists still believed in mystical explanations for natural phenomena.

As a founding member of the Royal Society (1663), Boyle mentored brilliant minds like Robert Hooke. His insistence on rigorous experimentation over philosophical speculation set the standard for modern scientific practice. *Astonishing, for an aristocrat who could have spent his life sipping tea in castles!*

It's 1629 in The Hague, and a boy is born into a family where science isn't just a hobby—it's a way of life. **Christiaan Huygens** (1629 – 1695) grew up in what we might call the "Dutch Scientific Royalty" of his time. But here's what's fascinating—while most kids played with toys, young Huygens was busy dreaming about the stars. (Ever met a teenager who grinds his telescope lenses because the store-bought ones aren't good enough? That was Huygens!)

So fed up with existing telescopes, Huygens did what any obsessive 17th-century scientist would do—he became his own lens manufacturer. Through painstaking polishing (can you imagine doing this without modern machinery? I wonder how long it took!), he created lenses with such precision that in 1665 he spotted something nobody had seen before: Saturn's largest moon, Titan. And let's not forget his brilliant insight about Saturn's rings—he correctly guessed they were composed of countless small particles orbiting the planet.

This theory wouldn't be confirmed until spacecraft visited Saturn centuries later!

While Isaac Newton insists that light travels as particles (the "corpuscular theory"), Huygens has a different idea. In his 1690 masterpiece Traité de la Lumière, he proposed light travelled as waves through an invisible "ether." His wave theory is beautifully explained:

- Why light bends when entering water (refraction)
- How mirrors work (reflection)
- Those strange patterns when light passes through small openings (diffraction)

The irony? Both Newton and Huygens were partially correct! It took until the 20th century and quantum mechanics to show light behaves as a particle and a wave. I am amazed by the revelations of these intelligent individuals!

Huygens' recognition came early, though—he was elected to the Royal Society in 1663 as one of its first foreign members, proving that good science transcends borders.

It's the 17th century in Delft, Netherlands, and a textile merchant with no formal scientific training is peering through a tiny, handcrafted lens at a drop of water. What he sees will change science forever. **Antonie van Leeuwenhoek** (1632–1723) was the first to lay eyes on the hidden universe of bacteria and sperm cells, earning him the title **"Father of Microbiology."** (Who would've thought fabric inspection could lead to such groundbreaking discoveries?)

Leeuwenhoek was a Self-Taught Lens Grinder; his obsession began with magnifying glasses, which he used to inspect cloth threads. But soon, his curiosity outgrew textiles. He perfected lens-grinding techniques with relentless patience, crafting microscopes so powerful for a whopping three hundred times magnification! that they surpassed anything else in his era. Imagine doing this without modern tools—just raw skill and determination. He became the first person to observe bacteria and protozoa, calling them little animals.

In 1677, Leeuwenhoek turned his lens toward human semen—and became the first to describe living sperm cells, marvelling at their wriggling motion. (Talk about an awkward dinner conversation!) His detailed sketches and letters to the Royal Society of London left scientists both amazed and sceptical. Could this Dutch shopkeeper really be seeing microscopic life? Yet, his observations were so meticulous that he was eventually elected as a Fellow of the Royal Society—an extraordinary honour for a man with no university degree.

A Legacy Written in Letters

Leeuwenhoek's discoveries weren't published in fancy journals but in over 190 handwritten letters to the Royal Society, filled with vivid descriptions and sketches. These letters, preserved in the Royal Society Library, reveal a man driven by pure curiosity, reshaping our understanding of life.

The Significance of His Position Today?

- Founded bacteriology & protozoology (without him, no Pasteur or germ theory!)
- Proved the existence of microscopic life, challenging old beliefs about spontaneous generation.
- Pioneered single-lens microscopy, inspiring modern lab equipment.

So next time you wash your hands to kill germs, remember—it all started with a Dutch draper and his tiny glass lenses!

Robert Hooke: The Poor Orphan Who Redefined Science

A penniless orphan waits tables to scrape together tuition money, only to become one of the most brilliant scientific minds of the 17th century. That was **Robert Hooke** (1635–1703), the Isle of Wight, one of my favourite places I visit, a native who literally worked his way from servant to scholar at Christ Church, Oxford. (Who says you need family connections to make history?)

From Lab Assistant to Legend:

Hooke's big break came when he caught the attention of Robert Boyle - yes, THAT Boyle of gas law fame. As Boyle's assistant, the young Hooke didn't just fetch coffee - he helped design vacuum pumps and conducted groundbreaking experiments. Talk about an internship that paid off!

The Spring That Changed Physics:

Ever wonder why your mattress bounces back after you get up? Thank Hooke's Law ($F = kx$), which he formulated in 1660. In plain terms:

- F = The force you apply (like sitting on a spring)
- x = How much the spring compresses
- k = The spring's stiffness constant

This deceptively simple equation became the foundation of elasticity theory - crucial for everything from earthquake engineering to memory foam mattresses!

The Michelangelo of Microscopes:

Hooke's masterpiece, *Micrographia*, was the first scientific best-seller. With stunning hand-drawn illustrations, he revealed a hidden universe:

- Fleas with intricate armour-like exoskeletons
- Cork structures he called "cells" (because they reminded him of monastery rooms)
- Crystalline patterns in snowflakes

The Forgotten Genius

Here's what breaks my scientific heart - while everyone remembers Newton, Hooke's contributions often get overlooked. He:

- Built some of the first Gregorian telescopes
- Designed London buildings after the Great Fire
- Proposed the wave theory of light before Huygens

Yet history nearly forgot him - perhaps because of his famous feud with Newton. Next time you use a spring or look through a microscope—*remember the orphan-turned-genius who made it possible!*

The Farmer's Son Who Moved the Universe

A lonely boy, born prematurely on Christmas Day 1643 in a simple Lincolnshire farmhouse, who would grow up to explain the very workings of the cosmos. **Isaac Newton's** story begins at Woolsthorpe Manor, where sheep outnumbered books and his widowed mother nearly condemned him to farm life. (Can you imagine science without calculus or gravity?) Thankfully, his uncle and schoolmaster saw his genius, pushing him toward Cambridge instead of ploughshares.

From Poverty to Cambridge

As a "sizar" (essentially a scholarship student who waited tables), Newton devoured knowledge like a man starved. While Aristotle dominated the curriculum, Newton's notebooks reveal his secret obsession with Descartes, Galileo, and Kepler. His mathematics professor, Isaac Barrow, initially dismissed him as "unpromising" in Euclid - an ironic assessment of history's greatest mathematical mind!

The Plague Years That Changed Science

When Cambridge closed during the Great Plague of 1666, Newton returned to Woolsthorpe with the collective wisdom of:

- Copernicus' heliocentrism
- Galileo's falling bodies
- Kepler's planetary laws
- Hooke's elasticity theories

...all missing crucial explanations. Armed with nothing but quills and genius, he would spend "the miracle year" solving them all.

The Birth of Modern Science

Under that legendary apple tree (*yes, it really existed! When I visited his birthplace, the tour guide mentioned that another branch had grown from its root since the storm blew down the original apple tree. I can see the old root on the ground, convincing me that the new tree grew from it. The taste of the soup they supplied; it is the best I have ever had, claiming Newton always loved that recipe!)* Newton connected cosmic and earthly motion through:

Calculus

Invented because existing math couldn't describe changing quantities. Your physics homework? Thank Newton.

Optics Revolution

Proving white light contains all colours using prisms (take that, Aristotle!)

Laws of Motion

1. Objects keep doing what they're doing (inertia)
2. $F=ma$ (force equals mass times acceleration)
3. Every action has an equal reaction

Universal Gravitation

That famous equation ($F=G(m_1m_2)/r^2$) explained everything from falling apples to orbiting moons.

Principia Mathematica

His 1687 masterpiece described nature and showed that the universe runs by mathematical laws, sparking the Enlightenment.

The Bitter Ironies

Newton feuded with Hooke over credit for gravity, refused to acknowledge Leibniz's parallel calculus work, and spent the later years as Master of the Mint. He died in 1727, leaving over 10 million words of unpublished notes - some on alchemy and biblical prophecy.

The Importance of His Role Today

Newton's fingerprints are everywhere, from your smartphone's GPS (which relies on his gravitational equations) to modern engineering. Not too shabby for a farmer's son who almost didn't go to school!

Edmund Halley: The Wealthy Soap Heir Who Mapped the Stars

One thousand six hundred fifty-six in London, and a baby boy is born to a wealthy soap manufacturer - hardly the typical start for an astronomy legend. Yet young **Edmund Halley** (1656-1742) would grow up to become the man who gave us both celestial maps and the most famous comet in history. (Who knew soap money could buy telescopes that would change science forever?)

From Schoolboy to Stargazer: Halley's privileged upbringing had its perks - private tutors, the best education at St. Paul's School, and most importantly, an indulgent father who bought him expensive astronomical instruments. By the time he entered Queen's College, Oxford in 1673, he was already rubbing shoulders with John Flamsteed, the Astronomer Royal. But here's where Halley's story takes an adventurous turn...

The Ultimate Study Abroad Trip: In 1676, at just 20 years old, Halley made a radical decision - he dropped out of Oxford to embark on a celestial treasure hunt to St. Helena (yes, the same island where Napoleon would later be exiled!). Funded by both his soap-baron father and King Charles II himself, Halley packed:

- A 24-foot telescope (imagine transporting that by ship!)
- Precise sextants and quadrants
- A pendulum clock to track time

For months, he braved the island's unpredictable weather to catalogue 341 southern stars - a feat no European had accomplished before. His persistence paid off when he became the first to observe Mercury's transit across the sun in 1677.

The Matchmaker of Physics: Halley's greatest contribution might have been playing cosmic matchmaker between ideas. When he, Christopher Wren, and Robert Hooke were puzzling over planetary motion in 1684, they suspected an inverse-square law governed orbits but couldn't prove it. Enter Halley's brilliant move - he travelled to Cambridge to consult a reclusive math professor named Isaac Newton. Their historic conversation went something like this:

Halley: "What shape would planets' orbits take under an inverse-square law?"

Newton (casually): "Ellipses. I proved it years ago but lost the notes."

Halley (probably screaming internally): "Please recalculate it!"

This fateful meeting led to Newton's *Principia Mathematica* , which Halley not only edited but personally funded in 1687. Talk about recognising genius when you see it!

The Comet That Bears His Name: While Halley didn't discover his famous comet (it had been observed for centuries), he made the groundbreaking realisation that comets could be periodic visitors. By calculating its 75-76 year orbit, he predicted its return in 1758 - long after his death. When the comet appeared right on schedule, it cemented his legacy and Newtonian physics's power.

A Life of Celestial Firsts

Halley's other pioneering work included:

- Proposing the Venus transit method to measure Earth-Sun distance
- Suggesting the universe was infinite (to prevent gravitational collapse)
- Serving as Astronomer Royal for over 20 years
- Creating the first magnetic charts of the Atlantic
- Welcomed a soap magnate's son who dropped out of college to stargaze from a remote island!

Thomas Savery: The Forgotten Father of Steam Power

It's 1698 in England, and a self-taught engineer named **Thomas Savery** (1650 – 1715**)** is about to patent a machine that will change the world—though he doesn't know it yet. His "Miner's Friend" steam engine, clunky and dangerous by today's standards, would become the spark that ignited the Industrial Revolution. (Who knew solving a mining problem would eventually lead to locomotives and factories?)

The Mine Drainage Maverick

Savery's world-changing invention addressed a deadly problem:

- Mines flooded constantly, risking lives and livelihoods
- Traditional methods (bucket chains, horse-powered pumps) were slow and ineffective
- His 1698 patent described a steam-powered vacuum pump that could:
    - Create suction through condensing steam
    - Lift water 50 feet using atmospheric pressure

It's ironic that an engine designed to remove water was powered by boiling it!

How the "Miner's Friend" Worked

The genius—and limitations—of Savery's design:

The Good ☑

- First practical steam-powered water pump
- Used a clever vacuum-and-pressure cycle (steam in → cool → vacuum → repeat)
- Proved steam could replace muscle power

The Bad ✕

- Fuel-guzzling: Required constant coal to maintain steam
- Dangerous: Prone to boiler explosions (early OSHA nightmare!)
- Limited lift: Couldn't pump beyond ~50 feet vertically

Savery's original patent lasted 14 years—an early example of intellectual property protection!

The Ripple Effects of Rough Genius

Though flawed, Savery's engine:

- Inspired Thomas Newcomen's improved atmospheric engine (1712)
- Indirectly led to James Watt's revolutionary separate condenser (1765)
- Proved steam could transform industries beyond mining

More Than Just Steam

Savery was a Renaissance troubleshooter who also invented:

- Marine engines (attempting steam-powered boats)

- Firefighting pumps (early “fire engines”)
- Agricultural devices (helping farmers before tractors existed)

Legacy: The First Domino

While we remember Watt and Newcomen more, Savery:

- Broke psychological barriers about machine power
- Connected theory to industry (a model for future engineers)
- Proven patents could drive innovation

Visit His Memory: The Science Museum in London displays models of his engine—humble beginnings of the steam age!

Thomas Newcomen: The Blacksmith Who Kickstarted the Industrial Revolution

It’s 1712 in a coal mine in England, and a blacksmith-turned-inventor watches as his massive steam engine—standing three stories tall—sputters to life. **Thomas Newcomen** (1664-1729), built the *first practical steam engine* that would power the world into a new age. (Who knew solving a mining problem would change civilisation?)

From Dartmouth Blacksmith to Steam Pioneer

Newcomen’s journey was anything but conventional:

- No formal education, just hands-on experience in ironworking
- Teamed up with plumber John Calley to solve mine flooding
- Spent 10 years tinkering before perfecting his atmospheric engine

His story proves innovation isn’t about diplomas—it’s about solving real problems.

How the Atmospheric Engine Worked

Newcomen's genius was in simplicity:

1. Steam fills a cylinder, lifting a piston
2. Cold water injected → steam condenses → vacuum created
3. Atmospheric pressure slams piston down (with a satisfying *whoosh!*)
4. Pump attached to piston rod removes water from mines

Each engine cycle took ***5 minutes****—slower than a snail, but stronger than 50 horses!*

The Good, The Bad, and The Steam-Powered

Revolutionary Advantages ☑

- Could pump water from 150+ feet deep (unlike Savery's 50-foot limit)
- First commercially successful steam engine (installed in 300+ mines by 1800)
- Reliable in harsh mining conditions

Quirky Limitations ✖

- Fuel-hungry: Burned coal like a dragon (only 1% efficiency!)
- Slow as molasses: 12 strokes per hour (Watt later boosted this to 30+ per *minute*)
- Giant footprint: Required a dedicated engine house

The Ripple Effect of Rough Genius

Though clunky, Newcomen's engine:

- Inspired James Watt's separate condenser (1769)
- Proved that steam could replace animal/water power

- Funded deeper coal mining → cheaper fuel → more steam engines (a virtuous cycle!)

More Than Just Mines

Newcomen also pioneered:

- Water pumps for towns (early municipal utilities)
- Engine adaptations for factories (pre-Watt industrial use)
- Safety mechanisms (learning from explosive failures)

Legacy: The First Spark of Industry

While Watt gets more fame, Newcomen:

- Proved steam's practical potential
- Created a template for engineering innovation (trial + error + persistence)
- Enabled the coal boom that fueled the Industrial Revolution

Visit His Legacy: The Dartmouth Engine (the oldest surviving Newcomen engine) still stands in England—a monument to gritty ingenuity.

SUMMARY

From 1400 CE to 1700 CE, science underwent a dramatic transformation, evolving from the rediscovery of ancient knowledge to the development of the modern scientific method. From the 14th century, scientists like Regiomontanus hazed into the skies to get an accurate picture of our universe. Sky exploration was a major scientific endeavour during this time. He published an astronomical calendar for predicting planetary movements and solar eclipses. This paved the way for some insights into Copernicus' ideas and predicted the heliocentric model of the universe. From here onwards, the pursuit of understanding the universe has expanded immensely to what we know today.

Andreas Vesalius's contribution to medical science on the human body was a step towards a deeper understanding of it. John Napier introduced logarithms to mathematics, making large-scale calculations easy. Galileo Galilei accepted Copernicus's heliocentric model, and free-falling objects accelerate towards the Earth at the same speed, regardless of mass, which gave insights into gravitation, a precursor to Newton's gravitational force. Kepler's planetary laws contributed to the elliptical path of planets' orbits. Rene Descartes intertwined algebra and geometry. Pierre de Fermat developed theorems and a step towards developing calculus. Blaise Pascal developed the Pascaline mechanical calculator, a foremost step towards computation. Robert Boyle developed Boyle's Law, a contribution to the advancement of chemistry. Christiaan Huygens introduced the ether medium in the universe. During this time, magnifying lenses were created by Antonie van Leeuwenhoek, a step towards magnification.

One of the most significant contributors to science during this period was Newton, who made substantial scientific advancements, introducing the laws of motion and gravity, and developing calculus, which were essential for the mathematical calculations of these phenomena. One could say Newton's contribution paved the way for the Industrial Revolution in Britain, a prominent scientific achievement.

As we can see, many humans gathered a lot of information during this period; we are evolving! And now, in the subsequent chapter, it's time for the next scientific revolution.

CHAPTER 4

The Age of Scientific Enlightenment (17th - 19th centuries)

One would be surprised to see the incredible amount of advancements in science that began in the seventeenth century. Science moved away from reliance on religious beliefs toward rigorous fact-checking and experimental observations to understand the physical world.

It is evident that Franklin's demonstration of lightning as electricity sparked the origin of electricity and how lightning can produce electricity. This was food for thought for many scientists on their quest to learn more about electric energy.

Later, Volta made a significant contribution to the invention of the battery. Surprisingly, today's technology used in electric vehicles is only a modified version of the fundamental technology that Volta invented.

Faraday's discoveries of electricity generation and motors shaped electrical engineering today. Then came Maxwell's equations, which brought together electricity and magnetism, a phenomenon of electromagnetism. This ushered in a new era of scientific inquiry that no one had even thought of proving by mathematical equations, inspiring countless scientists with limitless opportunities to learn the intricacies of electricity and magnetism.

Most of our school science studies have taught us that energy cannot be created or destroyed, only converted. Joules's experiments proved this and led to the first law of thermodynamics. Remember, before Joule's time, the heat and the work were separate entities.

Lavoisier's discovery of oxygen in combustion altered chemistry, replacing old theories with quantitative science and transforming understanding of reactions and respiration. Though refined, Dalton's atomic theory also changed chemistry, and its essential ideas still underpin atomic science today. Mendeleev's periodic table developed chemistry by establishing a logical framework for element properties and interactions, and the modern periodic table development.

James Watt's steam engine advanced modernised industry and transportation, establishing modern mechanical engineering and earning him recognition as a pioneering inventor.

Jenner's smallpox vaccine reformed medicine, demonstrating safe immunity induction. His work saved millions and established vaccination, leading to smallpox's unique eradication.

Morse's telegraph modernised communication, using electrical pulses for instant global connections, fundamentally transforming how society shares information. Bell's telephone transformed communication, enabling instant long-distance talk and shaping the modern telecommunications networks we depend on today.

Louis Pasteur revolutionised medicine and microbiology, demonstrating that microbes cause disease. His contributions laid the groundwork for vaccines and sterilisation, making him historically significant. Charles Darwin's evolutionary theory explains life's changes and significantly influences modern biology, medicine, and genetics. Mendel's findings transformed biology, establishing genes as hereditary units and influencing modern genetics and biotechnology.

This chapter examines some renowned scientists whose contributions to science changed our understanding.

The Bernoulli Principle: Why Planes Stay Up and Perfume Bottles Spray

Have you ever wondered how a massive aeroplane stays airborne or why spraying perfume feels like a mini science experiment? The answer lies in the work of **Daniel Bernoulli** (1700-1782)—an 18th-century genius who cracked the code on fluid dynamics. (Who knew the same principle explains both flight and fragrance?)

From Medicine to Mathematics: A Rebel Scientist: Born in 1700 in the Netherlands, Daniel Bernoulli was supposed to follow his father's wishes—study business, then medicine. And he did… at first. By 21, he'd earned a medical degree with a thesis on respiration, inspired by William Harvey's blood circulation discoveries. But his real passion? Math and physics.

Defying his father (a famous mathematician himself), Daniel dove into Galileo's mechanics, Newton's laws, and Boyle's gas theories—laying the groundwork for his groundbreaking fluid research. (Imagine telling your dad, a math legend, that you're ditching medicine for equations!)

The "Eureka" Moment: Water, Pressure, and Energy: As a professor at the University of Basel, Daniel conducted a deceptively simple experiment:

- He filled a tank with water and measured how fast it flowed out at different heights.
- The higher the water level, the faster the flow.
- Key insight: The water's potential energy (from height) converted into kinetic energy (speed)—proving energy is conserved in fluids.

This led to Bernoulli's Principle (1738), which states:

As a fluid moves faster, its pressure drops, and vice versa.

Mathematically, it's captured in his famous equation:

$P + \frac{1}{2}\rho v^2 + \rho g h = \text{constant}$

- P = Pressure

- ρ (rho) = Density
- v = Velocity
- g = Gravity
- h = Height

Why This Matters Today

1. Aviation: Airplane wings are shaped so air moves faster over the top, creating lower pressure above and lift below—keeping planes aloft.
2. Carburetors & Perfume Sprayers: Fast-moving air in the carburetor lowers pressure, sucking in fuel vapor—just like spraying perfume creates a mist by accelerating air.
3. Weather & Pipelines: The principle explains wind patterns, blood flow, and even why your shower curtain clings to you!

Beyond Fluids: A Pioneer in Probability & Public Health

Bernoulli didn't stop there. He also:

- Pioneered probability theory, using math to model real-world risks.
- Advocated for smallpox inoculation, using stats to prove vaccines saved lives—an early example of epidemiology.

Legacy of a Reluctant Physicist: Bernoulli passed away in 1782, but his equation remains a cornerstone of aerospace engineering, medicine, and meteorology. Next time you board a flight or spritz cologne, remember: an 18th-century doctor-turned-mathematician made it all possible.

Benjamin Franklin: The Original American Renaissance Man

It's 1706 in Boston, and a bright child would become America's ultimate multitasker—scientist, inventor, diplomat, and even party favourite (more later). Benjamin Franklin was more than merely a founding father; he was the *cool uncle* of American innovation. *(Who else could flirt with French aristocrats and tame lightning?)*

The Kite That Shocked the World: In 1752, Franklin didn't just fly a kite—he *harnessed the sky itself.* His famous (and dangerous) experiment proved lightning was electrical, leading to the lightning rod. This invention saved countless buildings from becoming kindling and set the foundation for improvements in electrical theory.

French scientists replicated his experiment but used a metal rod instead of a kite—smart move, given Franklin probably singed his eyebrows a few times!

More Than Just Electricity

Franklin's genius buzzed through multiple fields:

- Meteorology: Mapped the Gulf Stream, cutting weeks off transatlantic voyages. (Take that, Columbus!)
- Thermodynamics: Studied heat conduction, paving the way for modern insulation.
- Oceanography: Charted currents so accurately that his maps were used for over a century.

Inventions That Stuck: From cosy homes to clearer vision, Franklin's creations included:

- The Franklin Stove: A heater so efficient, it made colonial winters bearable.
- Bifocals: Because even geniuses get tired of switching glasses.

- Glass Armonica: A musical instrument played by *rubbing wet fingers on glass bowls* (Mozart even composed for it!).

Politics & Lightning Rods: An Unlikely Pair

While inventing, Franklin also:

- Helped draft the Declaration of Independence (casually, between kite flights).
- Served as a diplomat in France, charming everyone with his wit and *lack* of powdered wigs.

Franklin proved you could be a world-class scientist *and* a revolutionary politician—all while writing snappy one-liners like "An ounce of prevention is worth a pound of cure." (Try dropping *that* at your next Zoom meeting.)

Leonhard Euler: The Mathematician Who Gave Us the "Most Beautiful Equation"

It's 1707 in Basel, Switzerland, and a prodigy named **Leonhard Euler** is dutifully studying theology to please his pastor father. But fate—and a brilliant mentor named Johann Bernoulli—had other plans. *(Can you imagine how different math would be if Euler had stuck to sermons instead of sums?)*

From Theology to Theorems: Euler's pivot from divinity to mathematics was a career change—a *revolution*. Under Bernoulli's guidance, his genius exploded like a supernova. By his 20s, he dazzled the Russian and Prussian academies, churning out proofs like a human supercomputer.

The Man Who Gave Math Its Language: Euler didn't just *do* math—he *reinvented its vocabulary*. His contributions read like a "Greatest Hits" of modern mathematics:

- Calculus & Analysis: Turned differential equations into an art form.

- Graph Theory: Solved the "Seven Bridges of Königsberg" puzzle, birthing network theory (ever used GPS? Thank Euler).
- Mechanics & Fluids: Derived laws still used in aerospace engineering today.
- Notation: We owe π, *e*, *i*, and *f(x)* to his obsession with clarity.

But his crowning jewel? Euler's Identity (*e^iπ + 1 = 0*), dubbed "the most beautiful equation" for linking five fundamental constants. Even Feynman gushed over it—and that guy *invented* cool!

Blindness? Just a Speed Bump: Here's the kicker: Euler lost his eyesight *twice* (first in one eye, then both). Did he slow down? Nope—he *dictated* proofs from memory, producing *half his life's work* while blind. *(Makes your "I'm too tired to do homework" excuses sound weak, huh?)*

Legacy: The Invisible Architect: From Google's algorithms to NASA's rockets, Euler's fingerprints are everywhere. His relentless curiosity—over 800 papers published!—proves math isn't just about numbers; it's the *hidden scaffolding of reality*.

Next time you see π or use a map app, whisper a thanks to the Swiss genius who saw the universe in equations.

Henry Cavendish: The Millionaire Scientist Who Weighed the Earth

It's the late 1700s, and while most scientists beg for funding, a shy British aristocrat is quietly revolutionising physics in his private lab. Meet **Henry Cavendish** (1731–1810)—the reclusive genius who *literally weighed the planet* and discovered hydrogen, all while dodging small talk like it was the plague. *(Who knew introverts could reshape science?)*

The Experiment That Defied Gravity: After Newton proposed gravity, everyone nodded sagely... then avoided testing it (those lead spheres weren't cheap!). But Cavendish—armed with inherited wealth and obsessive precision—built the first lab to measure gravitational attraction in 1798. His setup?

- **A torsion balance** with two lead balls (158 kg each!)
- **A wire so sensitive** it twisted when the balls attracted smaller weights
- **Painstaking measurements** taken in a dark room to avoid air currents

The result? He calculated Earth's density (5.45 g/cm^3 vs today's 5.51 g/cm^3) and indirectly found the gravitational constant (**G**). His value for *G* was off by just **1.2%**—basically a bullseye with 18th-century tools.

Hydrogen, the "Inflammable Air" Breakthrough: 1766 Cavendish isolated a gas that made metals fizz in acid. Naming it "inflammable air" (later **hydrogen**), he:

- Proved it was **lighter than air** (hello, future balloons!)
- Showed it burned to form water—hinting at H_2O's composition
- Essentially **founded pneumatic chemistry** while peers were still debating phlogiston

The Electricity Research Everyone Missed. Cavendish's notebooks reveal he:

- Anticipated Ohm's Law (V=IR) 60 years early
- Conceptualised electric potential and capacitance
- Used fish as conductors (yes, really)

Tragically, he never published these findings. When James Clerk Maxwell rediscovered them in 1879, science had to play catch-up.

Science's Quiet Titan, Cavendish, proved two things:

1. Money helps (his lab was the 1700s version of a SpaceX budget)

2. Genius thrives in silence (he spoke so rarely, servants communicated via notes)

Next time you see a hydrogen balloon or use a capacitor, tip your hat to the hermit who weighed the world—then went back to his lab without a word.

Joseph Priestley: The Accidental Chemist Who Gave Us Oxygen

In 1774, in a small English lab, a clergyman-turned-scientist named Joseph Priestley stared at a flickering candle inside a jar of mysterious gas. To his shock, the flame burns *brighter* than ever. Little does he know, he's just discovered oxygen—and is about to kickstart a chemical revolution! (Who knew a curious preacher would change how we breathe?)

The "Dephlogisticated Air" Discovery, Priestley's eureka moment came when he:

- Heated red mercuric oxide (HgO) and collected the gas that bubbled off
- Noticed candles burned fiercely in it
- Watched mice thrive in sealed jars of the gas (18th-century ethics, anyone?)

Dubbing it "dephlogisticated air" (blame the then-popular phlogiston theory), he'd found oxygen—though he didn't fully grasp its significance.

The Game-Changing Coffee Chat: During a 1774 trip to Paris, Priestley casually mentioned his discovery to Antoine Lavoisier over (presumably) coffee. Lavoisier, the "father of modern chemistry," ran with it:

- Repeated the experiments
- Proved oxygen's role in combustion and respiration
- Coined the name "oxygen" (Greek for "acid-former")

Talk about the most productive scientific gossip session ever!

Gas Guru: More Than Just Oxygen

Priestley's lab was a gas factory—he also isolated:

- Nitrous oxide (N_2O): Later used as laughing gas in dentistry
- Carbon monoxide (CO): The silent killer (and future car exhaust villain)
- Ammonia (NH_3): Today's cleaning agent and fertilizer staple

His work laid the groundwork for pneumatic chemistry—proving air wasn't just "nothingness" but a cocktail of reactive gases.

Franklin's Electric Influence, Priestley's brilliance wasn't confined to chemistry. After befriending Benjamin Franklin in 1767, he:

- Wrote a groundbreaking book on electricity
- Proposed the inverse-square law for electrical attraction (before Coulomb!)
- Showed charcoal could conduct electricity (a precursor to batteries)

This earned him a Royal Society fellowship—rare for a self-taught scientist.

Priestley's story teaches us:

1. Curiosity thrives anywhere—even in a clergyman's spare time.
2. Collaboration sparks revolutions (that Parisian chat changed chemistry forever).
3. Science and faith can coexist—he saw gas experiments as "revealing God's natural laws."

Next time you take a deep breath or flip a light switch, remember the minister who lit the fuse of modern chemistry—between sermons.

Sir William Herschel: The Musician Who Redefined the Cosmos

A young German musician, moonlighting as an amateur astronomer, grinds his own telescope mirrors in his spare time—only to discover a new planet and rewrite our understanding of the galaxy. Meet **William Herschel** (1738–1822), the ultimate Renaissance man who proved that curiosity knows no bounds. (Who knew stargazing could be this revolutionary?)

From Music to Mirrors, A Self-Taught Stargazer: Herschel's journey began with a borrowed book—*Smith's "A Compleat System of Opticks"*—that taught him to craft telescopes from scratch. Obsessed with perfection, he:

- Hand-ground mirrors using custom blends of copper, tin, and antimony
- Built telescopes so powerful that they outperformed Greenwich Observatory's tools
- Spent countless nights testing lenses (likely muttering, *"Just one more polish..."*)

By the 1770s, his DIY spirit paid off: he'd constructed the largest reflector telescope of its time, unlocking unprecedented views of the cosmos.

The Night He Discovered Uranus: On March 13, 1781, Herschel spotted a faint object moving strangely across the sky. At first, he thought it was a comet—but his detailed notes revealed the truth:

- It was a new planet: Uranus, the first discovered since antiquity
- The finding doubled the size of the known solar system overnight
- It shattered the ancient belief that only five planets existed

Herschel initially named it Georgium Sidus (George's Star) to flatter King George III. (Scientists: sometimes just as political as the rest of us!)

The Dynamic Duo, William and Caroline Herschel: Behind every great astronomer was his brilliant sister, Caroline Herschel:

- Trained by William, she became the first woman to discover a comet (and found eight more!)
- Her precise calculations and observations were critical to their joint success
- Proved that science thrives on collaboration—not just lone genius

Mapping the Milky Way, Using his 40-foot telescope (the "Google Earth" of the 18th century), Herschel:

- Conducted the first systematic star survey
- Deduced the Milky Way's disk-like structure (with the Sun near the centre)
- Paved the way for modern astrophysics

From Amateur to Royal Astronomer

Herschel's accolades were as bright as the stars he studied:

- Copley Medal for discovering Uranus
- Fellowship in the Royal Society (thanks to Dr. William Watson's recommendation)
- Personal astronomer to King George III (with a salary to match)
- A monument in Slough, UK, honouring his legacy

Herschel taught us that:

1. Passion trumps pedigree (no formal training? No problem!)
2. Great discoveries demand great tools (sometimes homemade)
3. Science is a team sport (shoutout to Caroline!)

Next time you gaze at the night sky, remember the musician-turned-astronomer who expanded our cosmic horizons—one hand-polished mirror at a time.

Antoine Lavoisier: The Architect of Modern Chemistry

In late 18th-century Paris, a young tax collector passionate about precision is about to turn chemistry on its head. Antoine Lavoisier (1743–1794) didn't just study chemicals—he gave them a *language* and proved matter can't simply vanish into thin air. (Who knew weighing stuff carefully would revolutionise science?)

The Scale That Changed Everything:

While others saw mysterious transformations, Lavoisier saw math. His experiments proved:

- Mass isn't magic: In sealed containers, the weight before/after reactions stayed the same → Law of Conservation of Mass
- Phlogiston was nonsense: Combustion wasn't some mystical "fire element" escaping—it was oxygen reacting (take that, alchemists!)
- Water = H_2O: He literally assembled water from hydrogen and oxygen like a molecular Lego master

The Nomenclature Revolution:

Chaos reigned in chemical naming (e.g., "oil of vitriol" for sulfuric acid). Teaming up with Berthollet and others, Lavoisier:

- Ditched poetic names for systematic ones (goodbye, "inflammable air" — hello, *hydrogen*!)
- Classified elements by properties, creating the first modern chemical dictionary
- Made formulas intuitive: *Oxygen* + *Hydrogen* → *Water* instead of *"Dephlogisticated air* + *Phlogiston* → *River juice"*

The Textbook That Built a Science:

His 1789 *Traité Élémentaire de Chimie* —it was a manifesto for:

✓ Quantitative experiments (measure everything!)

✓ Oxygen's starring role in fire and life

✓ Clear definitions (no more alchemical mumbo-jumbo)

His wife, Marie-Anne, illustrated the book and translated papers—science's first power couple!

Lavoisier's work is why today we can:

- Balance chemical equations (thank that conservation law!)
- Name compounds without a medieval poetry degree
- Understand respiration as slow combustion

The man who proved *matter is eternal* met his end in the guillotine during the French Revolution. His colleague Lagrange lamented: *"It took only a moment to cut that head, but a century may not produce another like it."*

Alessandro Volta: The Spark That Lit Up the Modern World

In 1800, in Como, Italy, a curious physicist stacked coins, soaked cardboard, and metal plates—creating the world's first battery. Little did **Alessandro Volta (1745–1827)** know that his "voltaic pile" would power everything from smartphones to electric cars. *(Who knew a stack of wet metal could change civilization?)*

When fellow scientist Luigi Galvani claimed electricity came from *animal tissue* (thanks to twitching frog legs), Volta was sceptical. His brilliant counter-experiment proved the real power was in the metals, not the legs (sorry, frogs!). The brine-soaked paper worked as well (creating the first chemical battery). This revealed that the electrochemical series ranks metals by their electric potential.

The Voltaic Pile: A Tower of Power

Volta's 1800 invention of the battery for humankind—it was a *revelation*:

- Design: Zinc + Copper + Saltwater Cardboard (like a savoury science sandwich)
- Impact: Enabled the first steady electric currents, demolishing the idea that electricity was just fleeting sparks
- Legacy: Paved the way for lead-acid car batteries, alkaline AA cells, and even lithium-ion tech

The basic theory behind his invention of battery technology remained the same, but it significantly improved its life expectancy later. Will we soon invent alternative battery technology for storing energy? This remains to be seen.

Napoleon was so impressed that he made Volta a count and awarded him gold medals. Move over, Nobel Prize!

From Frog Legs to Future Tech

Volta's work answered two big questions:

1. How to store electricity? (Hello, batteries!)
2. How to generate it reliably? (Goodbye, static shocks as the only option)

His discoveries laid the groundwork for:

- Ohm's Law (voltage = current × resistance)
- Faraday's electrolysis
- Modern electrochemistry

A Legacy Measured in Volts

Honours poured in during his lifetime:

- Royal Society Fellowship (1791)

- Copley Medal (1794)
- Immortalised by the "volt" (V), the unit of electric potential

Next time you charge your phone, remember the Italian maestro who proved electricity wasn't magic—just brilliantly harnessed chemistry.

In 1796, in rural England, a country doctor was about to make a bold gamble that would save millions of lives. **Edward Jenner** (1749–1823), a man who split his time between treating patients, studying cuckoo birds, and playing the violin, noticed something peculiar about milkmaids—their cowpox scars seemed to shield them from deadly smallpox. *(Who knew a dairy observation would lead to the world's first vaccine?)*

The Scourge of Smallpox

In the 18th century, smallpox was a ruthless killer:

- No social immunity: Kings and peasants died alike
- Survivors bore scars—if they survived at all
- Variolation, the risky practice of infecting people with mild smallpox, sometimes backfired tragically

Jenner's "Eureka" Moment

While others saw just milkmaids, Jenner saw nature's vaccine:

- Cowpox (a mild cattle disease) left similar but harmless pustules
- Milkmaids who caught it never got smallpox
- His hypothesis: *Cowpox could train the body to fight smallpox*

The Experiment That Changed Medicine

In May 1796, Jenner made history:

1. Collected pus from milkmaid Sarah Nelmes' cowpox blisters
2. Injected it into 8-year-old James Phipps (brave kid!)
3. Later exposed Phipps to smallpox—no infection!

By 1798, after more trials, Jenner published *"An Inquiry into the Causes and Effects of the Variolae Vaccinae"*—coining the term "vaccination" (from *vacca*, Latin for cow).

From Scepticism to Salvation

Despite initial ridicule ("*You're turning people into cows?*"), Jenner's vaccine:

- Spread globally (Napoleon vaccinated his army!)
- Inspired modern immunology
- Eradicated smallpox by 1980 (WHO declared it gone!)

The Renaissance Man Behind the Vaccine

- A bird behaviourist (published on cuckoos)
- A musician (regular violin performer)
- A poet (though his rhymes didn't save lives)

Today, if you would like to explore the history of medicine, a must-visit place is Jenner's home, Dr Jenner House, which serves as a museum in Gloucestershire GL13 9BN—where you can stand where the first vaccine was born!

John Dalton: The Quaker Schoolteacher Who Saw the Atomic World

It's the late 1700s in rural England, and a self-taught Quaker scientist is peering at the sky, taking notes on the weather. Little did **John Dalton** (1766–1844) know that his humble meteorological observations would lead him to crack one of chemistry's greatest mysteries—the atomic nature of matter. *(Who knew studying clouds could reveal the building blocks of reality?)*

From Humble Beginnings to Manchester's Intellectual Hub

Dalton's journey began in a small Quaker school in Eaglesfield, where:

- Limited formal education didn't stop his curiosity
- Meteorology became his gateway to science (he kept weather records for 57 years!)
- A move to Manchester in 1793 connected him with thinkers who fuelled his atomic theories

The Gas Law That Changed Everything

While studying gases, Dalton noticed something peculiar:

- In mixtures, gases behaved independently—like strangers ignoring each other at a party
- This led to Dalton's Law of Partial Pressures (1801): *Total pressure = Pressure of Gas A + Pressure of Gas B + …*
- Hinted that gases were made of discrete particles—a clue to his atomic theory

The Atomic Theory: A Revolution in a List

In 1803, Dalton proposed ideas so radical that they reshaped chemistry:

1. Atoms exist (and they're indivisible—take that, nuclear physicists!)
2. Each element has unique atoms (oxygen ≠ carbon)
3. Compounds form in fixed ratios (H_2O is always 2:1, no exceptions)
4. Atoms just rearrange in reactions (RIP alchemical transformations)

His handwritten atomic symbols (○ for oxygen, ● for carbon) were the first chemical "emojis".

The Scientist Who Colored His World

Dalton had colour blindness, which he studied scientifically, giving us:

- "Daltonism" (the old term for colour vision deficiency)
- The realisation that perception is personal (his red looked like your green)

The Unseen Architect of Chemistry

Though his atomic weights were later refined, Dalton:

- Gave chemistry its atomic foundation
- Inspired the periodic table (Mendeleev stood on his shoulders)
- Proved humble origins don't limit genius

Visit the Lit & Phil Society in Manchester, where he worked, and you'll still find his original atomic models on display.

Joseph Fourier: The Orphan Who Unlocked Nature's Hidden Rhythms

What does heat flow have in common with your Spotify playlist? More than you'd think - and we owe this surprising connection to Joseph Fourier (1768–1830), the brilliant but often overlooked French mathematician whose work touches nearly every aspect of modern science. His life story reads like a historical novel, complete with revolution, war, and groundbreaking discoveries.

From Orphan to Scientific Revolutionary

Imagine being orphaned at 8 years old in 18th century France. Fourier beat the odds, rising from humble beginnings to:

- Teach at Paris's prestigious École Polytechnique
- Serve as Napoleon's scientific advisor during the Egyptian campaign (1798-1801)
- Govern the Isère region while still pursuing cutting-edge research (Grattan-Guinness, 1972)

"How did he manage it all?" Through sheer brilliance and relentless curiosity - traits that would lead him to discoveries still vital today.

The Heat Equation That Changed Everything

While serving as a provincial administrator (of all things!), Fourier made his greatest breakthrough. His 1822 masterpiece *Théorie analytique de la chaleur* revealed that:

- ✓ Heat flows like a mathematical melody, predictable through trigonometric series
- ✓ Even jagged temperature patterns could be expressed as smooth wave combinations
- ✓ This "Fourier series" applied far beyond heat - to sound, light, and vibration (Fourier, 1822)

Your WiFi router uses Fourier's math to untangle overlapping signals right now!

The Accidental Climate Scientist

Decades before global warming was understood, Fourier noticed something peculiar:

- Earth should be colder given its distance from the sun
- The atmosphere acts like "an invisible blanket" (his words!), trapping heat
- His 1827 paper essentially described the greenhouse effect (Fourier, 1827)

"Why don't more people know about this?" Perhaps because his mathematical legacy overshadowed his insights into climate change.

A Legacy That Echoes Through Time

Fourier's fingerprints are everywhere in modern tech:

- **Medical imaging**: MRI scans rely on Fourier transforms
- **Audio engineering**: Spotify uses his math to compress your music
- **Quantum physics**: Schrödinger's equation builds on his work

As he wisely noted: *"Nature is the most fertile source of mathematical discoveries."* How right he was - his methods now help us decode everything from DNA to distant galaxies.

Alexander von Humboldt: The Last Man Who Knew Everything

Around 1799, a Prussian explorer wades through the Orinoco River, taking measurements of electric eels while scribbling notes about howler monkeys. Meet **Alexander von Humboldt** (1769–1859)—the original interdisciplinary genius who connected nature's dots decades before specialisation narrowed our vision. *(Who else could make a rainforest sound like a symphony of data?)*

The Father of Biogeography, while others collected specimens, Humboldt observed patterns in climate-vegetation links, proving that similar latitudes support similar plant species (think of palm trees aligning along the equator). Isothermal lines depict his global temperature maps, predicted climate zones—the birth of modern climatology. Vertical zonation showed that mountain ecosystems change with altitude, like layers of a cake.

His work was the 19th-century version of Google Earth—revealing nature's hidden algorithms.

The Magnetic Maverick

During his epic American expedition (1799–1804), Humboldt:

- Mapped Earth's magnetic fields using handmade instruments
- Discovered magnetic storms (now called geomagnetic storms)
- Inspired the first international scientific conference (the "Magnetic Crusade")

His magnetic data was so precise, NASA still references it!

Kosmos: The Original Theory of Everything

His magnum opus, *Kosmos* (1845–1862)—it was a manifesto for interconnected science:

- Merged astronomy, geology, and biology
- Inspired Charles Darwin ("My whole career traces back to Humboldt")
- Predicted human-caused climate change (in 1800!)

Nature's Networker

Today, Humboldt's fingerprints are everywhere:

- 4 countries, 300+ plants/animals, and even an ocean current bear his name
- The national parks movement stems from his conservation ethos
- Systems thinking in ecology owes him everything

Visit His Berlin: The Humboldt University displays his original butterfly collections!

Carl Friedrich Gauss: The Mathematician Who Bent Reality With Numbers

A 7-year-old boy in 1784 Germany stares at his arithmetic slate, then shocks his teacher by instantly solving a problem that had been meant to occupy the class for hours. Little did anyone know, young **Carl Friedrich Gauss** (1777–1855) would grow up to become the "Prince of Mathematicians" – a man whose work would shape everything from your smartphone's GPS to MRI scans. *(Who knew adding numbers could lead to such power?)*

The Child Prodigy Who Outsmarted His Teacher

That legendary classroom moment revealed Gauss's genius:

- The problem: Sum the first 100 numbers
- His insight: 1+100=101, 2+99=101... creating 50 pairs of 101
- The formula born: $S = n/2[2a + (n-1)\times d]$ (still taught today!)
- The outcome: A scholarship to university at age 11

Most kids count sheep—Gauss counted mathematical revolutions.

Number Theory's Architect, his 1801 *Disquisitiones Arithmeticae*—it was a blueprint for modern math. It cracked quadratic forms like a safe. Laid foundations for cryptography (yes, your online banking security traces back to him). Introduced modular arithmetic (the math behind 24-hour clocks)

From Stars to Statistics: A Polymath's Playground

Gauss's mind refused boundaries:

Astronomy

- Predicted Ceres' orbit using just 3 observations (saving the "lost" dwarf planet)
- Developed celestial mechanics methods still used by NASA

Electromagnetism

- Formulated Gauss's Law (cornerstone of electromagnetism)
- Helped build the first telegraph in 1833

Statistics

- Invented the least squares method (vital for data science today)
- Defined the normal distribution (the famous "bell curve")

The Magnetic Earth Explorer

With physicist Wilhelm Weber, Gauss:

- Mapped Earth's magnetic field (foundation for modern geophysics)
- Established global magnetic observatories
- Created absolute units for magnetism (the "gauss" unit honours him)

The Hidden Mathematician

Gauss hated publishing (much was discovered posthumously), yet his work powers:

- Every regression analysis in machine learning
- GPS satellite calculations
- MRI imaging technology

Next time your phone finds your location instantly, thank the boy who saw numbers as living things.

Joseph Louis Gay-Lussac: The High-Flying Chemist Who Tamed Gases

It's 1804, and a daring French scientist is ascending in a hydrogen balloon to 24,000 feet—higher than any human had gone before—with nothing but a thermometer and barometer to study the atmosphere. Meet **Joseph Louis Gay-Lussac** (1778–1850), the chemist who quite literally *rose to new heights* in science. (Who knew studying gases could be such an adrenaline sport?)

The Gas Law Maverick

While others tinkered in labs, Gay-Lussac *lived* his experiments:

- **Gay-Lussac's Law**: Showed gas pressure rises with temperature ($P \propto T$) – crucial for everything from pressure cookers to car engines
- **Law of Combining Volumes**: Proved gases react in simple whole-number ratios ($2H_2 + O_2 \rightarrow 2H_2O$), giving Avogadro the clues he needed for his famous hypothesis

His work was the 19th-century version of a chemistry "rulebook" – suddenly, gases made sense.

The Ballooning Scientist

In that record-breaking balloon flight, he:

- Collected air samples at extreme altitudes
- Proved atmospheric composition stays constant (no "breathable air layer" myth!)
- Measured Earth's magnetism aloft – making him the first *aerial geophysicist*

His balloon was filled with hydrogen – the same gas he helped characterise!

Halogen Hero & Atomic Architect

Gay-Lussac didn't stop at gases:

- Iodine: Discovered its disinfectant power (paving the way for antiseptic surgery)
- Chlorine: Unlocked its bleaching properties (revolutionising textiles)
- Atomic theory: His volume ratios secretly supported Dalton's atomic ideas

The Invisible Hand in Modern Chemistry

Next time you:

- Use a pressure cooker (thanks to his gas law)
- Sterilise a wound (iodine's gift)
- See a weather balloon (he pioneered atmospheric science)

...remember the Frenchman who made chemistry *predictable.*

The Accidental Discovery That Electrified Physics: Biot & Savart's Magnetic Moment

Paris, 1820. Two scientists stare in wonder as a compass needle twitches near a wire carrying an electric current. **Jean-Baptiste Biot** and **Félix Savart** had just stumbled upon a fundamental truth of nature—that electricity and magnetism were secret dance partners. (Who knew a wiggling needle would reveal the invisible forces powering our world?)

The Experiment That Changed Everything

Their deceptively simple setup—a vertical wire and magnetic needle—produced revolutionary insights:

- The Biot-Savart Law: A precise mathematical description of how electric currents create magnetic fields
- The equation: *dB = $(\mu_0/4\pi)$ * $(I\, dl \times \hat{r})/r^2$* (don't worry—we'll unpack this!)
- Practical magic: This law became the blueprint for electric motors, MRI machines, and even particle accelerators

Their work was so foundational that James Clerk Maxwell later built his electromagnetic theory upon it.

Breaking Down the Biot-Savart Law

Let's make sense of that intimidating equation:

1. **dB** = Tiny magnetic field created
2. **I** = Current flowing through the wire
3. **dl** = Tiny segment of the wire
4. **r** = Distance from wire to measurement point

In plain terms? *The stronger and closer the current, the stronger the magnetic field.* This is why wrapping wire into coils supercharges electromagnets!

Biot's Bonus: The Light Polariser

While Savart focused on acoustics, Biot made another breakthrough:

- Discovered circular polarization in quartz crystals
- Invented polarimetry—now used to:
    - Test sugar purity in food science
    - Analyse protein structures in biochemistry
    - Detect atmospheric pollutants

It's remarkable how studying light through crystals led to quality control in candy factories!

Hidden Forces, Visible Impact

Next time you:

- Use a **blender** (thank their law for the motor)
- Get an **MRI scan** (their discovery powers the magnets)
- Eat **store-bought honey** (polarimetry checks its purity)

The Electromagnetic Trinity: How Three Scientists Lit Up the World

It's 1820, and across Europe, three brilliant minds are simultaneously realising that electricity and magnetism are two sides of the same coin. **Hans Christian Ørsted** (1777- 1851 CE) in Denmark and Jean-Baptiste Biot with Félix Savart in France were all racing to unravel nature's best-kept secret. (Who knew that compass needles and wires would spark a technological revolution?)

Ørsted's Eureka Moment: When Electricity Met Magnetism

Ørsted's groundbreaking observation was beautifully simple:

- A current-carrying wire made a nearby compass needle twitch
- Proved that electricity could produce magnetic fields
- His law showed the circular nature of these fields around wires

It's poetic that the first electromagnetic effect was seen in a compass - nature's magnetic detector!

Biot-Savart: The Mathematicians of Magnetism

While Ørsted showed the "what," the French duo revealed the "how much":

- Their law **quantified** the magnetic field strength
- Introduced the **inverse square relationship** (like gravity's reach weakening with distance)
- Gave engineers the **precise calculations** needed to build motors

Their equation is still used today to design everything from MRI machines to maglev trains!

Two Perspectives, One Revolution

The subtle but crucial differences:

Ørsted's Law	Biot-Savart Law
Qualitative (shows a relationship exists)	Quantitative (calculates exact strength)
Directional (circular fields)	Precise (accounts for wire shape/distance)
Inspired Faraday	Enabled Maxwell

The Legacy That Powered the Modern World

This trio's work became the foundation for:

- **Electric motors** (thank them for your blender)
- **Generators** (the backbone of power plants)
- **Maxwell's equations** (the full theory of electromagnetism)

James Watt: The Sickly Scotsman Who Supercharged the Industrial Revolution

It's 1765 in Glasgow, and a 29-year-old instrument maker is walking through a park when he suddenly stops dead in his tracks. James Watt (1736–1819) had just had a flash of inspiration about steam condensation that would change the world. (Who knew a Sunday stroll could spark an industrial revolution?)

The Boy Who Tinkered With Steam

Watt's journey began unconventionally:

- Home-schooled due to chronic illness (asthma and migraines)

- Obsessed with mechanics – took apart his aunt's teakettle to study steam at age 15
- University instrument maker, where he first repaired a Newcomen engine – and was shocked by its inefficiency

It's poetic that the man who improved steam power was literally breathless himself.

The Eureka Moment That Changed Everything

That fateful 1765 walk led to Watt's breakthrough:

- Separate condenser: Kept the cylinder hot while condensing steam elsewhere
- 75% less coal needed than Newcomen engines
- Double-acting piston: Power on both up *and* down strokes (doubling output)

Watt's first full-scale engine took 6 years to build – proving even genius requires grit!

More Than Just Engines

Watt was a Renaissance inventor who also gave us:

- The copying press (early photocopier)
- The horsepower unit (to market his engines)
- Rotary motion (transforming factories from water wheels to steam)

The Industrial Revolution's Architect

Watt's engines powered:

- Textile mills (1 engine could replace 50 horses)
- Iron forges (enabling railroads)
- Global trade (steamships and locomotives)

By 1800, over 500 Watt engines were humming across Britain.

The Man Behind the Machine

Despite fame, Watt remained:

- Humble: Declined a baronetcy from the King
- Collaborative: Partnered with Matthew Boulton for manufacturing
- Philanthropic: Supported technical education

Visit His Legacy: The Science Museum London displays his original workshop – complete with tea-stained blueprints!

Sir Humphry Davy: The Rockstar Chemist Who Lit Up Mines and Labs

It's 1815 in England, and miners are dying in horrific coal mine explosions caused by their lanterns igniting flammable "fire damp" gas. Enter **Humphry Davy** (1778–1829)—a brilliant, self-taught chemist who would trade his laughing gas experiments for a life-saving mission. (Who knew the man who discovered recreational nitrous oxide would also prevent mining catastrophes?)

The Miner's Guardian Angel

Davy's safety lamp breakthrough was born from tragedy:

- 1812 Felling Colliery disaster: 92 miners killed by methane explosions
- Existing lamps were flame traps waiting to happen
- His 1815 solution: A wire-gauze enclosure that:
    - Allowed light out
    - Cooled flames below ignition temperature
    - Became known as the Davy Lamp

It's ironic that the man who made miners safer also discovered the gas that would later fuel their pain relief in surgeries!

How the Davy Lamp Worked

The genius was in its simplicity:

1. Fine metal mesh surrounds the flame
2. Heat dissipates through the mesh
3. Flame can't escape to ignite methane outside
4. Bonus feature: Flame changes colour in dangerous gas (an early warning system!)

Miners loved it so much they reportedly carried it like a protective talisman—even after electric lamps arrived!

From Laughing Gas to Lightning in a Bottle

Before saving miners, Davy was the 19th century's "mad scientist":

- 1799: Discovered nitrous oxide's euphoric effects (hosting legendary "laughing gas parties")
- 1807: Used Volta's battery to isolate potassium (it burst into purple flames!)
- 1808: Isolated sodium, calcium, and magnesium through electrolysis

The Accidental Anaesthetist

His nitrous oxide research had unexpected medical benefits:

- First documented surgical anaesthesia in 1844 (though he never pursued it)
- Paved the way for modern anesthesiology

Science's First Celebrity

Davy's fame was unprecedented for a scientist:

- Knighted by George IV
- Two-time Copley Medal winner
- Royal Society president at just 41
- Mentored Michael Faraday (though their relationship later soured)

Visit His Legacy: The original Davy Lamp is displayed at the Royal Institution—next to Faraday's induction ring!

Jacob Berzelius: The Swedish Architect of Modern Chemistry

In 1810, in Stockholm, a meticulous Swedish chemist is weighing silver compounds with such precision that he's about to redefine our understanding of the atomic world. **Jacob Berzelius** (1779–1848) wasn't just a chemist—he was chemistry's *first systematiser*, turning alchemical chaos into an orderly science. (Who knew a doctor-turned-chemist would give us the language of elements we still use today?)

The Atomic Weight Maestro, Berzelius's obsession with precision led to the creation of atomic weight tables for 45 elements (1818) – some values were accurate to within 1% of today's measurements. Modern chemical symbols (H for hydrogen, O for oxygen) replace alchemical squiggles. Confirmation of Dalton's theory through painstaking experiments.

His lab must have looked like a mad scientist's workshop—with less lightning and more meticulous note-taking.

Building on Volta and Davy's work, Berzelius proposed:

- Electrochemical dualism: Atoms are either + or –, bonding like magnets

- First theory of chemical bonding (predating electrons by 80 years!)
- Discovered elements through electrolysis:
    - Cerium (1803) – named after the asteroid Ceres
    - Selenium (1817) – named for the moon (Selene)
    - Silicon (1824) – the bedrock of computer chips today

His silicon discovery literally changed the Earth—it's 28% of our planet's crust!

Beyond the lab, Berzelius was a *science communicator*:

- Textbook of Chemistry (1808–1830): The "bible" for 19th-century chemists
- Annual Reviews: Early version of *Nature* or *Science* journals
- Mentored future giants like Friedrich Wöhler (who later shattered vitalism)

The scientific community recognised him with numerous honours: ennobled by Sweden's king in 1818, foreign member of the Royal Society since 1813, and recipient of the Copley Medal in 1836 – science's first "Nobel Prize."

Visit His Legacy: The original atomic weight tables are preserved at the Swedish Academy of Sciences—written in his elegant hand.

Michael Faraday: The Bookbinder Who Electrified the World

London, 1812. A 20-year-old bookbinder scribbles furiously in the margins of a chemistry text, dreaming of a life beyond leather and glue. Little did **Michael Faraday** (1791–1867) know that his notes would become the blueprint for the electrical age—all thanks to a free ticket to a lecture and an insatiable curiosity. (Who knew binding books could lead to unlocking the secrets of electromagnetism?)

From Apprentice to Scientific Prodigy, Faraday's remarkable journey began in poverty. He was self-educated through books such as *Conversations on Chemistry*—imagine learning science from a book intended for stitching! He attended lectures at the City Philosophical Society alongside other working-class enthusiasts of science. A life-changing moment came when he received tickets to Humphry Davy's lectures in 1812. Faraday took such meticulous notes that Davy eventually hired him as an assistant.

It's poetic that a man who bound books would later "bind" electricity and magnetism together.

The Grand Tour That Sparked a Revolution: As Davy's assistant (and sometimes valet), Faraday met Volta in Milan and received a handmade voltaic pile, which is still on display at the Royal Institution. He learned from Ampère in Paris, witnessing firsthand how electric currents generate magnetic fields. This knowledge was crucial for fuelling his own experiments.

That voltaic pile was like giving a future race car driver their first bicycle!

The Birth of Electromagnetism

In his cluttered lab at the Royal Institution, Faraday made history:

1821: The First Electric Motor

- Noticed a current-carrying wire rotated around a magnet (not just attracted/repelled)
- Built a mercury-filled device proving electricity → motion
- Essentially invented the principle behind every electric motor today

1831: Electromagnetic Induction

- His famous iron ring experiment (still on display!) showed:
    - Moving magnets create electricity
    - The foundation of generators and transformers

- Formulated Faraday's Law (later part of Maxwell's equations)

The Faraday Effect & More

His genius didn't stop there:

- Diamagnetism (1845): Some materials repel magnetic fields
- Faraday rotation: Magnetic fields twist light (now used in fiber optics)
- Faraday cage: Blocks electromagnetic fields (protects your phone from lightning!)

The Humble Genius

Despite revolutionising science, Faraday refused knighthood, preferring to be known as "plain Mr. Faraday." He rejected patents, believing that knowledge should be freely accessible. Additionally, he gave Christmas lectures to inspire working-class youth.

Legacy in Every Outlet: Next time you turn on a light, thank his dynamo. When using a credit card, remember the magnetic strip on the chip. And if you ride a train, know that electromagnetic induction powers the tracks.

...remember the bookbinder who taught us how to harness invisible forces.

Charles Babbage: The Genius Who Dreamed of Computers 100 Years Early

It's 1820s London, and a grumpy mathematician is scribbling designs for a machine that could "think"—while his contemporaries are still using quill pens and abacuses. **Charles Babbage** (1791–1871) wasn't just ahead of his time; he *invented* computer science a century before the first computer was built. (Who knew steam-powered calculators could foreshadow your laptop?)

The Difference Engine: A Calculator Before Its Time

Babbage's first marvel was born from frustration:

- Tired of error-filled astronomical tables (human "computers" made 1 error per 60 pages!)
- Designed a mechanical calculator that could:
    - Solve polynomial equations using the method of differences
    - Print results automatically (the first "printer"!)
- 1822 prototype worked perfectly—but his full-scale version was never completed

Ironically, the man who hated inaccuracy died before seeing his precision machine built.

The Analytical Engine: A Victorian Computer

When government funding dried up for the Difference Engine, Babbage dreamed bigger:

The World's First General-Purpose Computer (1837)

- Processor ("The Mill"): Performed calculations
- Memory ("The Store"): Held 1,000 numbers (50-digit precision!)
- Punched cards: Adapted from Jacquard's looms (the first "programming language")
- Conditional branching: Could make "if-then" decisions

Ada Lovelace wrote the first "computer program" for this unrealised machine!

Why Babbage Matters Today

His concepts became computer science fundamentals:

Babbage's Terms	Modern Equivalent
The Mill	CPU
The Store	RAM
Punch Cards	Software
Conditional Branching	If/Else Statements

Visit His Legacy: The Science Museum London has working replicas of his engines—proof that his ideas *did* work!

Joseph Henry: The Forgotten Father of Electromagnetism

During 1831, two scientists on opposite sides of the Atlantic—Michael Faraday in London and **Joseph Henry** (1797-1878) in Albany—were simultaneously unravelling the secrets of electromagnetic induction. Yet while Faraday became a household name, Henry's breakthroughs quietly powered the modern world. (Why do some geniuses fade into history's shadows?)

The American inventor you might not know is Henry. His overlooked contributions include: electromagnetic induction (independently discovered in 1831), self-inductance (that buzzing sound in your speakers? Thank Henry!), and the electric relay (1835), which served as the "neuron" of early telegraph networks.

Ironically, the man who enabled long-distance communication couldn't make his voice heard across the Atlantic.

Every day, he created magic. Henry's workshop gave birth to inventions we still use. First electric doorbell (1831) - The great-grandfather of your Ring doorbell. Practical electromagnets - Lifting 2,300 lbs with just a battery (a party trick that wowed 19th-century crowds). Relay systems - Making Samuel Morse's cross-country telegraph possible.

Henry refused to patent his relay, calling it a "gift to mankind"—while Morse got rich from the telegraph!

The SI Unit That Keeps His Name Alive

Though overshadowed, Henry earned immortality:

- The Henry (H): Unit measuring how coils resist current changes
- Found in every:
    - Power grid transformer
    - Car ignition system
    - Wireless charger

Visit His Legacy: The original electromagnet that lifted a ton is displayed at the Smithsonian—where Henry became the first Secretary.

SUMMARY

The Spark That Lit the Modern World: How the 17th-19th Centuries Rewrote Reality

A single 300-year period where humanity went from fearing lightning to harnessing it, from guessing star patterns to mapping galaxies, and from manual calculations to dreaming of artificial intelligence. (When was the last time your century revolutionised *everything*?)

Electricity: From Parlour Tricks to Power Grids

The charge began with Benjamin Franklin's kite-flying adventure (1752) - proving lightning was electricity and leading to lightning rods. Alessandro Volta's "pile" battery (1800) - the great-grandfather of your smartphone batteryØrsted, Biot & Savart's electromagnetic discoveries - revealing the invisible threads connecting electricity and magnetism. Michael Faraday's dynamo (1831) - turning motion into electricity and powering the modern world

It's shocking (pun intended) how many "eureka moments" came from playing with sparks and magnets!

Medicine & Chemistry: From Alchemy to Science

While some tinkered with electricity, others revolutionised health:Edward Jenner's smallpox vaccine (1796) - saving more lives than any other medical discovery. Antoine Lavoisier's conservation of mass - proving matter can't magically disappear (take that, alchemists!)

The Cosmic & Computational Revolutions

The same era saw eyes turn both outward and inward: William Herschel's Uranus discovery (1781) - doubling the size of the known solar system overnight, Gauss & Euler's mathematical wizardry - creating the language of modern physics and engineering Charles Babbage's analytical engine - a Victorian computer complete with:

- Store (RAM)
- Mill (CPU)
- Punch cards (software)
- Input/output - just like your laptop!

The Industrial Engine That Changed Everything

At the heart of it all: James Watt's steam engine (1776) - turning heat into motion and powering:

- Factories that birthed cities
- Traits that shrank continents
- Ships that connected empires

Legacy: The Foundations of Our World

This era gave us:

- Electricity we can harness
- Vaccines that prevent plagues
- Telescopes that map the cosmos
- Computers... before computers

At this point, humanity had a comprehensive understanding of mathematics, science, medicine, electricity and magnetism, steam engine-driven machinery, and electrical devices, paving the way for enhanced data collection and technological advancements. In the following chapters, we will explore these technologies in depth.

CHAPTER 5

The Industrial and Technological Revolutions (19th -20th Century)

The Industrial Revolution, one could ask, where it all began! Where on earth could it be possible? It is none other than Great Britain which spread to the rest of the world from the late eighteenth to the nineteenth centuries and beyond. I must admit that the people who lived in this era likely enjoyed their lives with the technological advancements that enhanced their day-to-day experiences. From a smoke-puffing steam locomotive with a roaring whistle sound, one cannot forget that experience. Then, the modern silicon chips, the heart of processing power, and the Industrial and Technological revolutions have enhanced human life for the better.

Steam power, mechanised textile production, and the iron manufacturing industry boosted efficiency and productivity with inventions like the steam engine and the power loom. People migrated to industrial areas for more job opportunities, and cities became centres of commerce, culture, and innovation, driving economic growth and societal change.

The introduction of modern transportation, including steam power in railways, boats, and even roads, enabled the efficient movement of goods and people, connecting industrial centres to sources and markets while increasing distribution to rural regions. Of course, any revolution can also cause significant drawbacks.

Major changes occurred in the social and labour sectors. There was a shift towards capitalism and a low-wage scenario, resulting in the working class facing challenging conditions with long work hours. Consequently, trade unions and the right to fight for workers' rights and better wages emerged.

Undoubtedly, innovations in Physics, chemistry, biology, and medical science further fuelled economic growth. This period also drove the expansion of European colonial empires, as nations sought access to raw materials such as cotton and minerals, thereby driving industrial production and enhancing economic growth through extensive trade networks.

On the other hand, I am pretty sure that no one considered the consequences of such advancements during the Industrial Revolution; they primarily focused on technological advancements, wealth, and prosperity. Today, whole generations are suffering from climate change, the aftermath of pollution, habitat destruction due to fossil fuel use, and deforestation. Ultimately, the Industrial Revolution has altered how we perceive the world today, transforming cultures, societies, technology, and economies worldwide.

I will focus on the remarkable individuals whose ingenuity shaped the Industrial Revolution.

Matthew Fontaine Maury: The Lame Sailor Who Charted the Invisible Highways of the Sea

Around 1842, a limping naval officer in Washington, D.C, is poring over stacks of dusty ship logs—not for military strategy, but to decode the ocean's hidden pathways. **Matthew Fontaine Maury** (1806–1873), grounded by injury, would become the father of oceanography by turning sailors' scribbled notes into a roadmap of the seas. (Who knew being benched could lead to such profound discoveries?)

From Cabin Boy to Chartmaster, Maury's journey was far from straightforward. In 1839, a stagecoach accident left him with a lame leg, effectively ending his sea duty. He was "promoted" to a desk job, where he was put in charge of the Navy's chart depot—a position often viewed as a dead end. However, there was a silver lining: he gained access to thousands of ship logs containing valuable observations about winds and currents.

Sometimes life's storms blow us toward unexpected harbours—Maury's injury gave the world oceanography!

Mapping the ocean's currents, Maury noticed what others overlooked. The Gulf Stream was not just a body of water; it functioned as a liquid highway, significantly reducing transatlantic travel times. The trade winds followed predictable patterns, but only if you knew where to look. He created the first wind and current charts in 1847, enabling ships to ride the currents like escalators, avoid the doldrums where winds died down, and cut the journey from New York to California from 200 days to just 135.

His charts were so accurate, clipper ship captains called them "Maury's Bible."

The Confederate controversy regarding Maury's legacy is complex. He resigned from the U.S. Navy to join the Confederacy in 1861 and spent the war years in England and Mexico promoting the use of electric mines. Later, he reconciled with science rather than politics by founding Virginia Tech's meteorology program.

Legacy: The GPS of the Age of Sail

Every time today's ships:

- Use ocean current data to save fuel
- Rely on global wind models
- Access satellite navigation (the spiritual heir to his charts)

...they're following trails Maury first mapped with quill and ledger.

Visit His Legacy: The U.S. Naval Observatory in D.C. still displays his original charts—with coffee stains and all!

Louis Agassiz: The Man Who Saw Ice Ages in Fish Scales

(Or: How a Swiss Perfectionist Changed Science While Hating Darwin)

Who would guess that a boy from Moutier, Switzerland (population: tiny) would become America's most famous ice-and-fish-obsessed scientist? **Jean Louis Rodolphe Agassiz** (1807–1873) was a biologist/geologist/palaeontologist—he was a human hurricane of curiosity who made glaciers exciting and fish fossils revolutionary.

School Days, Where Passion Met Pedantry: Agassiz's education at Zürich, Heidelberg, and Munich reads like a 19th-century academic thriller. Imagine: young Louis hunched over microscopes, arguing with professors twice his age, and developing theories that would later embarrass Darwin. His 1829 Munich doctorate wasn't just a degree—it was a declaration of war on scientific complacency.

Modern grad students complain about lab hours—Agassiz probably dissected fish by candlelight and thanked them for the privilege.

The Ice Age Revelation (Cue Dramatic Music): Here's where it gets wild: Agassiz's glaciology work began when he noticed strange scratches on Alpine rocks. "These weren't made by tools," he realised, "but by mile-thick ice sheets!" (Hall, 2009, p. 112). His 1840 ice age theory was initially mocked—until geologists found matching evidence worldwide.

*How many scientists get to say **"I told you so"** to an entire continent?*

Fish Fossils, Where Obsession Meets Art:Agassiz's *Recherches sur les poissons fossils* (1833–1843) wasn't just science—it was Renaissance-level artistry. His illustrations captured fish scales so precisely that modern biologists still use them as references.

Contradiction alert: This man who documented evolution in fish ironically became Darwin's most vocal critic. The irony? His work proved Darwin right (Gould, 2002, p. 154).

Legacy: Museums, Mentorship, and Modern Irony

Before "science communication" was trendy, Agassiz built two landmark museums (Neuchâtel and Harvard's MCZ) and mentored future Nobel winners. His opposition to evolution? A footnote compared to his teaching genius.

Charles Darwin: The Accidental Revolutionary Who Redefined Life

(And Why We're Still Arguing About Him Today)

One of the most influential figures of this period was born on February 12, 1809, in Shrewsbury. Evolutionary theory was a significant discovery in the 19th century. I will explore Darwin's theory, which received so much attention in that era. Charles Robert Darwin (1809–1882), born in England, was a British naturalist and biologist whose revolutionary research laid the groundwork for the **theory of evolution by natural selection**.

Darwin's passion for natural history grew at Cambridge, deepening his knowledge of botany and geology, and improving his fieldwork and sample collection skills. To their surprise, Darwin was offered a voyage aboard the HMS Beagle as the ship's naturalist under the command of Captain Robert FitzRoy. This voyage was a life-changing experience for him, as it deepened his passion for understanding nature profoundly. The voyage took him to South America, Australia, the Galápagos Islands, and Cape Verde. He documented all the natural observations and collected specimens that his hand could reach. Darwin recorded all the available data, which was crucial to developing his theory upon his return home.

During his travels, Darwin was struck by the distinct adaptations among species to their respective environments on different islands, particularly the variations in the shapes and sizes of finches' beaks. Darwin wondered about the causation of the differences in the species, which led him to develop the theory of evolution. He published his theory and findings in his book "On the Origin of Species "In 1859, which gathered much attention from the broader public.

In his book, he has highlighted four distinct features.

A. Battle of survival: Organisms generate a greater number of offspring than can be sustained, resulting in a struggle for scarce resources like food, shelter, and partners.

B. Variation: Within a species, individuals display differences in traits like size, strength, and behaviour. These differences are typically inherited from one generation to the next.

C. Decent with alteration: Over time, small changes accumulate, leading to the evolution of new species. All species share a common ancestry.

D. The most vital individuals will survive: Individuals with characteristics more compatible with their surroundings have a higher chance of survival and procreation, allowing them to pass these favourable traits to their offspring.

Darwin laid down the basic principles of evolution. There are debates in the 21st century; while I write this book, the theory does not convince the public, as we still do not know how exactly life is formed on Earth. I have researched this field, including the origin of life on Earth and the evolutionary process that led to the current state of the species. Any human today with existing knowledge will struggle to grasp how life forms on earth, as we know very little about the subject, perhaps at the low end of the numerical digit percentage. One of the reasons is that the subjects are so advanced on their own that one cannot study all of them, mainly chemistry, biology, physics, geology, or, to be more specific, all the science subjects, as well as environmental science, in a lifetime. We need to rely on AI technology for assistance; however, AI is programmed by humans, which has its limitations. It could take many years for humans to acquire the knowledge to understand how life began on Earth.

I have been intrigued by Erwin Schrödinger's book "What is Life? " It depicts, "How can the events in space and time which take place within the spatial boundary of living organisms be accounted for by physics and chemistry?" Schrodinger explained life as "the essential part of a living cell—the chromosome fibre—may suitably be called an aperiodic crystal." It is the material carrier of life.

Periodic crystals have a uniform atomic arrangement, while aperiodic crystals have an intricate and non-repetitive structure.

Critical characteristics of aperiodic crystals are: 1. non-periodic structure: a pattern never repeats exactly. 2. Fractals: where smaller portions of the crystal resemble the larger structure. 3. Physical properties: aperiodic crystals can show distinct physical characteristics like electrical conductivity, optical properties, and mechanical strength that differ from those of periodic crystals. Here, **electrical properties** play a crucial role in transferring energy and information.

Life on Earth began approximately 3.7 to 4.5 billion years ago, and human ancestors emerged around 7 million years ago. Lucy, a female Australopithecus afarensis specimen, the oldest so far found in Ethiopia, was discovered in 1974 and is believed to be approximately 3.2 million years old. Since we rely on fossils, anything much older than Lucy would be disintegrated by nature, and if we find any, we would be fortunate to see it as evidence. Lucy was described as a hominin who walked on two legs like modern humans, known as bipedal. Her brain was smaller than that of modern humans, yet it exhibited characteristics resembling those of apes, as indicated by her skull and teeth. Based on her skeletal structure, it appears she was skilled at climbing, implying she likely moved in both trees and on land. Lucy seems to be transforming from a common ancestor to a human-like species, perhaps home sapiens.

We can examine the cell structure within a membrane and the DNA structure to gain a deeper understanding of the evolution of life. One of the detailed studies by James Watson and Francis Crick involved building a model of DNA's double helix structure, which opened up many possibilities for understanding cell structure. Genetic fingerprinting and DNA profiling, pioneered by British scientist Sir Alec John Jeffreys, have also significantly advanced the field of DNA research. The study of **DNA switches** (cis-regulatory elements) involves DNA regions that control gene expression. These switches are typically located near the genes they regulate and consist of brief DNA sequences that interact with specific proteins known as transcription factors. When a transcription factor connects to a DNA switch, it can turn the gene's expression on or off. They determine when, where, and to what extent a gene is turned on or off, which plays a crucial role in natural selection, leading to the emergence of new species.

Research indicates that specific DNA sequences govern embryo formation, yet the mechanism by which DNA selects information to facilitate adaptation remains unclear. It is conceivable that dietary intake and survival instincts may influence the alteration of gene sequences, both of which stem from evolutionary pressures such as fear or necessity. DNA can preserve vital information for subsequent generations, ensuring survival or driving speciation. Additionally, particle physicists aim to delve deeper into understanding the transmission of information at subatomic levels, shedding light on processes Darwin recognised but could not elucidate regarding the conveyance of data to future generations.

We will delve into how consciousness plays a crucial role in survival according to Darwin's theory of evolution in the last chapter, a new frontier.

To explore Charles Darwin's legacy today, a must-visit place is his home, Down House, located in Orpington, BR6 7JT, England. I have visited a couple of times, and it is not too far from where I live.

Ada Lovelace: The Poetess of Programming

(Or: How a 19th-Century Countess Invented Software Before Hardware Even Worked)

Let's be real: When you picture a computer pioneer, you probably don't imagine a Victorian countess who wrote algebra equations alongside love poems. But Augusta Ada King, Countess of **Lovelace** (1815-1852)—Lord Byron's only legitimate daughter—was precisely that glorious contradiction. Her 1843 notes contained what we now call the first computer program—a full century before ENIAC!

Babbage & Lovelace

Picture London, 1833: 17-year-old Ada, already a math prodigy thanks to her tutor Mary Somerville, gets introduced to eccentric inventor Charles Babbage. When he shows her his **Difference Engine**—a clunking brass calculator the size of a piano—most Victorian ladies would've swooned. Not Ada. She took one look at those gears and said, *"This could do so much more"*.

Forget "tech bros"—the first programmer wore corsets and wrote sonnets. Take that, Silicon Valley.

Note G: The Algorithm That Changed Everything

In 1843, Ada dropped what we'd now call a microwave manual for the future. Her famous *Note G* contained:

- Step-by-step instructions for calculating Bernoulli numbers (the world's first published algorithm)
- Mind-blowing predictions: *"This engine might compose music... or draw fractals!"* (Lovelace, 1843)
- The killer insight: Machines could manipulate symbols, not just numbers

How many 27-year-olds today could explain algorithmic logic without Googling?

The Tragic Irony

Here's the twist: Babbage's Analytical Engine never got built. Ada's program remained untested—like a recipe for moon cheese written before rockets existed. Yet her vision was so precise that modern coders still debug her work using emulators.

If she'd lived past 36, we might've had TikTok in 1860.

James Joule: The Beer-Brewing Physicist Who Changed Thermodynamics

(And Got No Respect While Doing It)

A 19th-century English brewery owner, elbow-deep in ale vats by day, conducts world-changing physics experiments by night. Meet **James Prescott Joule** (1818-1889)—the ultimate "amateur" scientist whose work *powered* the modern world, yet spent years being ignored by London's elite Royal Society.

From Electric Hobbyist to Energy Revolutionary

As a kid, Joule and his brother zapped each other with homemade batteries (parenting was... different in 1820s Lancashire). His mentors—chemistry heavyweight John Dalton and engineer Eaton Hodgkinson—nurtured this curiosity. But here's the twist: Joule never stopped tinkering, even while running the family brewery.

Imagine your local microbrew owner casually inventing thermodynamics between IPA batches.

The Eureka Moment (Involving Paddles & Beer)

In 1843, Joule rigged up a paddle-wheel contraption in his brewery's basement. His goal? Prove that steam engines could be replaced with electric motors. The result? Something far bigger:

- 772 ft-lbs of work = 1°F water temp rise (Joule, 1845)
- The mechanical equivalent of heat—a foundational concept
- The kicker: London's scientific elite dismissed it as "brewery nonsense" for *years*

How many rejected papers does it take to change physics? (Answer: At least 7, in Joule's case.)

Joule-Thomson & The Ultimate "I Told You So"

Teaming up with Lord Kelvin (then just "William Thomson"), Joule proved gases cool when expanding—the Joule-Thomson effect. This paved the way for:

1. First Law of Thermodynamics (Energy can't be created/destroyed—just converted)
2. Modern refrigeration (Cheers for your AC, courtesy of 1840s beer science)
3. The joule (J)—now the SI energy unit, because naming stuff after yourself is the ultimate flex

Joule's gravestone should read: "Told you energy was conserved."

Foucault: The Parisian Showman Who Made Physics Appealing

During 1851 in Paris, Crowds gasp as a 28kg brass ball swings ominously from the Pantheon's dome, its path mysteriously shifting over hours. No magic trick - this was **Jean-Bernard-Léon Foucault**'s pendulum delivering the first visceral proof that Earth rotates beneath our feet. The audacity! A self-taught physicist upstaged academia with what amounted to a fancy chandelier.

Foucault's 67-meter pendulum wasn't just science - it was theatre. As Parisians watched, the bob's plane appeared to rotate clockwise (11°/hour in Paris). No invisible hand touched it - just Earth's sly rotation doing the work. Today, these pendulums swing in museums worldwide like taunting metronomes to flat-Earthers.

How many "geniuses" can claim that their experiment became a tourist attraction?

Never one to rest, Foucault then invented:

1. The gyroscope (1852): A spinning top that laughs at gravity, now guiding everything from smartphones to Mars rovers

2. Light speed tests (1850): Proving light slows in water like "a carriage hitting mud" (Foucault's actual analogy)
3. Telescope mirror tests: His knife-edge technique remains the gold standard for astronomy mirrors today

Foucault was the Elon Musk of 1850s Paris - minus the tweets, plus actual breakthroughs.

Why This Still Matters

That pendulum is not just about Earth's spin - it revealed how simple experiments can overturn centuries of dogma. As Foucault quipped: *"I don't need theories when I can show the truth dancing on a string."*

Gregor Mendel: The Monk Who Cracked Life's Code (And Nobody Listened)

(Or: How a Pea-Obsessed Priest Became the Unwitting Father of Genetics)

A 19th-century Austrian monk, knee-deep in pea plants, discovers the rules governing all life... only to be ignored for 35 years. **Gregor Mendel**'s (1822-1884) story is the ultimate case of scientific irony - a man who solved nature's puzzle but couldn't make his contemporaries care.

God, Peas, and Rockstar Science

At Brno's St. Thomas Monastery, Mendel had the perfect setup:

- Day job: Augustinian friar duties
- Side hustle: Breeding 28,000 pea plants (!) in the monastery garden
- Secret weapon: His physics training helped him quantify biological traits

In today's terms, Mendel was running a medieval biotech startup in his backyard.

The Two Laws That Changed Everything

Through meticulous cross-breeding, Mendel uncovered:

1. The Law of Segregation:
    - Parents' traits don't blend - they're discrete "packages" (alleles)
    - Like getting half your mom's playlist and half your dad's on your phone
2. The Law of Independent Assortment:
    - Traits shuffle independently (brown eyes don't dictate your height)
    - Nature's version of a poker dealer mixing decks

How could anyone ignore rules this elegant?

Science's Most Painful Snub

When Mendel presented his findings in 1866:

- The Brno Natural History Society politely applauded... then forgot him
- His papers gathered dust until 1900 (16 years after his death)
- Even Darwin had a copy - but never read it!

The ultimate vindication? In 2022, scientists sequenced Mendel's DNA to commemorate his 200th birthday, confirming through his genes what he'd discovered through his experiments with peas (Masaryk University, 2022).

Louis Pasteur: The Microbe Whisperer Who Changed Medicine Forever

(How a Wine-Tinkering Chemist Became the Godfather of Vaccines)

Let's be real: Most 19th-century scientists worked in labs. Pasteur? He hung out with frustrated French brewers and rabid dogs—and somehow revolutionised modern medicine. This is the story of how a crystal-obsessed chemist (yes, really) defeated spontaneous generation, saved the wine industry, and invented vaccines as we know them.

From Crystal Geek to Germ Theory Guru

Young Pasteur at École Normale Supérieure was that kid who:

- Got way too excited about tartaric acid crystals (weird flex, but okay)
- Noticed some crystals bent light left, others right—discovering molecular chirality
- *Basically invented 3D chemistry before 3D glasses existed*

Who knew wine gunk would reveal that molecules have "handedness"? (Take that, flat-Earthers.)

"Wait, Germs Cause Disease?!" – Pasteur to 1860s Europe

After saving France's wine industry with pasteurization (heat-killing microbes without ruining the bouquet), Pasteur made his big leap:

1. Debunked spontaneous generation with swan-neck flasks (no, maggots don't spawn from old meat)
2. Connected microbes to disease (revolutionary for an era that blamed "bad air")
3. Anthrax vaccine (saved cows → saved beef → saved steak dinners)

The Rabies Vaccine: Science's Greatest Hail Mary

The rabies vaccine story reads like a thriller:

- Grew virus in rabbit spines (dark, but effective)
- Dried infected tissue to weaken it (medieval-sounding, yet brilliant)
- First human test on 9-year-old Joseph Meister (1885)

Spoiler: The kid lived, Pasteur became a legend, and the Pasteur Institute was born.

Lord Kelvin: The Child Prodigy Who Redefined Temperature

Picture this: A 10-year-old boy walks into Glasgow University in 1834 - not as a visitor, but as a full-fledged student. This was **William Thomson** (1824-1907), the Scottish wunderkind who would later become Lord Kelvin and fundamentally change our understanding of heat, energy, and communication.

Kelvin's career reads like a superhero origin story: He entered university before most kids finish elementary school. Graduated from Cambridge as Second Wrangler (translation: math genius). Got hooked on thermodynamics after reading Fourier's work like it was beach reading

Meanwhile, most of us at 22 were still figuring out how to do laundry...

Thermodynamics: Kelvin's Greatest Hit

His groundbreaking work included:

1. The Second Law of Thermodynamics (1840s):
    - Proved heat flows one way only (like your ex's texts)
    - Introduced the concept of entropy - nature's "you can't win" rule

2. Absolute Zero & the Kelvin Scale (1848):
    - -273.15°C isn't just "cold" - it's where molecules stop dancing
    - Gave scientists the ultimate yardstick for temperature

From Theory to Transatlantic Texts

Never one for ivory towers, Kelvin:

- Teamed up with Maxwell on electromagnetism
- Saved the transatlantic cable project with his mirror galvanometer
- Got knighted by Queen Victoria (the 19th-century version of a Nobel Prize)

George Stoney: The Irish Visionary Who Named the Electron

(Before Anyone Even Found It!)

Let's settle this: Who really deserves credit for the electron? Was it J.J. Thomson who "discovered" it in 1897? Or the brilliant Irish physicist George Johnstone Stoney (1826-1911), who predicted its existence decades earlier? (And let's be honest - gave it a much cooler name than "corpuscle," Thomson's original term.)

Ahead of His Time (Literally)

In the 1870s, while studying electrolysis, Stoney had a revolutionary thought:

- Electricity isn't a continuous fluid (as everyone believed)
- It comes in discrete packets of charge ("electrons," from Greek *ēlektron* for amber)
- These were fundamental units of nature

Imagine naming a particle 20 years before its discovery - that's like calling your unborn child "Doctor"!

Natural Units: Stoney's Forgotten Masterpiece

Long before Planck invented quantum units, Stoney proposed:

1. Elementary charge (e) - the "atom" of electricity
2. Combined with:
    - Speed of light (c)
    - Gravitational constant (G)
      To create nature's own measurement system

The Ultimate Scientific Prophet

Stoney's genius wasn't just in being right - it was in setting the table for:

- Thomson's cathode ray experiments
- Quantum theory's birth
- Modern electronics

Every time you charge your phone, thank Stoney - the man who saw electrons everywhere before anyone could prove they existed.

Joseph Lister: The Surgeon Who Made Hospitals Less Deadly

(And Gave Us That Minty Mouthwash Taste)

Let's face it: Going under the knife in the 1860s was basically a death lottery. That is, until a British surgeon named Joseph Lister (1827-1912) had a radical idea - what if we *didn't* perform surgeries with blood-crusted tools? Inspired by Pasteur's germ theory, this medical maverick launched the antiseptic revolution.

From Carbolic Acid to Common Sense

Lister's game-changing innovations read like a hygiene wake-up call:Phenol power: Discovered carbolic acid could nuke microbes (though it smelled like a tar factory). Spray-then-slice: Invented the first antiseptic spray for surgical tools. Infection rates plummeted from 45% to just 15% in his wards

The Royal Treatment (Literally)

Lister's success brought him:

- Every major science medal (Royal, Copley, Albert)
- Queen Victoria's favor (she made him Baron Lister)
- An emergency royal consult when King Edward VII needed an appendix removed

The Listerine Twist

In a quirky turn:

- 1879: American chemist Joseph Lawrence names his surgical antiseptic *Listerine*
- Today: That same formula burns your mouth at 7 AM
- Full circle moment: What saved lives in ORs now saves dates after garlic bread

Kekulé's Dream: How a Dozing Chemist Solved Organic Chemistry's Biggest Puzzle

It's 1865, and a sleep-deprived German chemist named **August Kekulé** (1829-1896) is staring at his fifth cup of coffee when—*bam!*—the solution to organic chemistry's biggest mystery comes to him... in a dream about snakes eating their tails. This wasn't just any midnight brainwave—it was the benzene ring structure, the discovery that would revolutionise how we see molecules.

Breaking Chemistry's Straight-Chain Addiction: Before Kekulé, chemists were stuck in a linear mindset. All molecules were thought to be straight chains (boring!). Benzene's weird behaviour made no sense (C_6H_6 but acted like it had fewer hydrogens?). Then came Kekulé's "Eureka!" moment: *"What if the chain bites its tail?"*

The Snake Dream That Changed Everything

That fateful vision gave us:

1. The benzene ring: 6 carbons in an alternating double-bond dance
2. Aromatic compounds: Not just smelly—now a whole chemical class
3. Structural theory: Atoms aren't just glued together—they have relationship rules (valence)

Why Your Shampoo Bottle Owes Kekulé

That simple ring structure unlocked:

- Drug development (aspirin, anyone?)
- Plastics revolution
- Modern organic synthesis

James Clerk Maxwell: The Forgotten Titan of Physics

(How a Victorian Scotsman Out-Einsteined Einstein Before Einstein Existed)

Let's settle this now: If physics had an "Avengers" team, **James Clerk Maxwell** (1831-1879) would be its Tony Stark—the brilliant, underrated genius who built the theoretical framework for our modern world. Yet ask anyone on the street about him, and you'll likely get blank stares. Why does the man who predicted radio waves, explained light, and laid the groundwork for Einstein's relativity remain so obscure? Maybe because his equations made Victorian heads explode.

Child Prodigy Turned Cosmic Detective

Young Maxwell wasn't just brilliant—he was **"read-Cauchy-and-Fourier-for-fun"** smart. By 14, he was devouring advanced math texts like kids today binge-watch Netflix. But his first big breakthrough came from an unlikely source: Saturn's jewellery.

- The Ring Mystery: How could Saturn's rings stay intact for centuries?
- Maxwell's Eureka: After 2 years of calculations (winning Cambridge's Adams Prize), he proved there must be millions of orbiting particles—correct nearly 120 years before Voyager confirmed it
- "Brick-bats": His adorable term for what we now call moonlets

Imagine being so ahead of your time that NASA eventually texts you "u were right lol" from space.

The Equations That Built Your WiFi

At King's College London, Maxwell had his actual legacy moment—unifying electricity and magnetism into four elegant equations (later simplified by Heaviside):

1. Gauss's Law: How electric charges create fields
2. Gauss's Law: Why there are no magnetic "charges"
3. Faraday's Law: Changing magnetic fields create electricity
4. Ampère-Maxwell Law: How electric currents create magnetism

Colour Photos, Gas Theory, and a Lab That Changed Everything

Maxwell wasn't a one-trick pony:

- First colour photograph (1861) using red, green, and blue filters
- Kinetic theory of gases linking heat to molecular motion
- Designed Cambridge's Cavendish Lab—future birthplace of DNA and neutron discoveries

The tragic twist: Dying at 48, just as quantum mechanics was emerging. Had he lived longer, might he have beaten Planck to quantum theory? We'll never know.

Mendeleev: The Card Shark of Chemistry Who Played Elemental Poker

Let's be honest: Most of us struggled to memorise the periodic table in school. But imagine being the mad genius who *invented* it—not by chance, but by recognising nature's hidden card game. **Dmitri Mendeleev** (1834-1907), the Russian chemist with a prophet's beard and a gambler's intuition, didn't just list elements—he predicted the future of chemistry.

The Eureka Moment, In 1869, while writing a chemistry textbook (as one does), Mendeleev noticed something revolutionary: Elements weren't just random—they formed patterns when ordered by atomic weight. Like a deck of cards, they grouped into "suits" with similar properties. But here's the kicker—he left blank spaces for undiscovered elements and *dared* to describe them.

This would be like publishing a crossword puzzle with half the clues missing—and still winning the tournament.

Mendeleev's 6 Rules of Elemental Poker

His bold predictions read like a cheat code for chemistry:

1. Weight = Destiny: Atomic mass determines properties (your "hand" in the game)
2. Family Resemblance: Similar elements cluster together (alkali metals = the wild cousins)
3. Gaps Are Opportunities: Left spaces for "eka-aluminium" (gallium), "eka-silicon" (germanium)
4. Future-Proofing: Knew atomic weights might need tweaks (like updating player stats)
5. Chemical Crystal Ball: Predicted densities, melting points—and was *right*
6. The Royal Flush: Valency matters as much as weight (the "trump card" of bonding)

Mendeleev wasn't just a one-table wonder:

- Pioneered stoichiometry (the "recipe book" of chemistry)
- Advanced thermodynamics (how elements behave under heat pressure)
- Solution studies (why salt makes pasta water boil faster)

The ultimate flex? His periodic law became chemistry's grammar rules—proving elements don't just exist; they converse.

The Purple Accident That Rewrote Science (And Why Luck Matters More Than Genius)

Let's be real: If **William Perkins** were alive today, he'd be that kid in a garage startup, chugging energy drinks and ignoring his professor's advice. Because here's the thing—no serious chemist in 1856 thought some teenage amateur would crack synthetic dye. Yet, while trying (and spectacularly failing) to make artificial quinine, Perkins' flask spat out a purplish gloop that would make him filthy rich and upset every natural-dye merchant in Europe. History's best punches are always unexpected, aren't they?

Now, let's talk about why this "glorp" (as I imagine he called it) was revolutionary. Before mauveine, purple dye came from rotting sea snails—12,000 snails for one gram, to be exact. Yes, you read that right. The stench was so vile that ancient dye workshops were built *downwind* of cities. Then Perkin waltzes in with his coal-tar sludge, and suddenly, purple goes from "royal luxury" to "mass-market must-have." The original disruptive innovation.

But wait—there's more! Perkins' goo didn't just change fashion. It exposed a truth that still rattles scientists: waste is just unmade treasure. Coal tar, that greasy byproduct of gaslight factories, became the 19th-century equivalent of Silicon Valley's "big data." Aniline dyes? Check. Synthetic drugs? Oh yeah. Germany's entire chemical industry? Basically built on Perkins' "oops." And let's not forget the Perkin reaction—the 1868 chemical shortcut that's still saving grad students from thesis meltdowns today.

Here's my hot take: Perkin's story isn't about genius. It's about curiosity meeting chaos—and having the guts to bottle the results. (Literally.) In an era obsessed with "methodical science," his legacy screams: "Break stuff. Keep the interesting bits." Makes you wonder what we're *still* throwing away as "failed" today...

The X-Ray Files: How a "Glowing Mistake" Exposed Our Bones (and Egos)

Every time you complain about airport security scanners, blame **Wilhelm Röntgen** (1845-1923) —the German physicist who literally exposed humanity's insides in 1895. (Side note: Imagine being his wife, Anna Bertha, the first person to see her skeleton and *not* scream like a horror-movie victim. "I have witnessed my demise!" is arguably the most dramatic lab note in history. Must buy Anna flowers.)

Röntgen's discovery was not a mere coincidence, though picture this: A stubborn, detail-obsessed scientist (aren't they all?) tinkering with vacuum tubes in a pitch-black lab. He'd rigged up a Crookes-Hittorf tube—basically a Victorian lightbulb on steroids—wrapped in cardboard to block all light. But then… a faint glow flickered from a bench across the room—cue record scratch.

Here's where it gets wild: That glow came from a screen coated in barium platinocyanide (try saying that three times fast). Röntgen, being a pragmatist, slapped the label "X-rays" on his mystery rays—scientist code for *"No clue what this is, but it's cool."* Six weeks later, he's taking the world's first creepypasta selfie: his wife's skeletal hand, wedding ring dangling like a ghostly accessory. (Question: Would *you* let your spouse X-ray you as a "fun experiment"? Didn't think so.)

The Aftermath:

- Doctors lost their minds. For the first time, you could see broken bones without slicing someone open. (*Take that, medieval medicine!*)
- IUPAC immortalised him in 2004 by naming element 111 *roentgenium*—a radioactive flex for the ages.
- His Nobel Prize in 1901 was the **first** ever awarded… and honestly, who else could've claimed it? *"Sorry, Alfred Nobel, but we're busy staring at our own ribs."*

My hot take: Röntgen's story proves science thrives on stubborn curiosity—and the willingness to chase a glow everyone else would've ignored. Modern lesson? Next time your experiment "fails," ask: *"Am I annoyed... or on the verge of a Nobel Prize?"*

Edison: The Accidental Showman Who Lit Up the World (and Stole a Few Ideas)

Let's clarify something: **Thomas Edison** (1847 -1931) wasn't just an inventor—he was a 19th-century hype man with a knack for turning lab accidents into headlines. (His first "big win," the quadruplex telegraph, wasn't even his idea—he just improved others' work. *Sound familiar, Silicon Valley?*)

Picture Menlo Park in 1877: A chaotic lab where Edison's team played with electricity like kids with a new toy. When he wasn't "borrowing" Bell's telephone design (his "improved" version just shouted louder), he was busy inventing the phonograph by accidentally recording his voice on tinfoil. (Question: Why "Mary Had a Little Lamb"? Was he too embarrassed to curse into his machine?)

But here's the real drama: After the phonograph flopped (*shocking—who needed replayable sound in 1878?*), Edison pivoted harder than a startup chasing VC cash. Enter: the light bulb.

The Great Light Bulb Grind (1878-1879):

- Investors threw money at "Edison Electric Light Co." like it was **Bitcoin in 2017**.
- His team tested 6,000+ materials for the filament (including beard hair?!). The winner? Carbonised bamboo—because, of course, it was.
- On New Year's Eve 1879, he turned Menlo Park into a disco for nerds, dazzling crowds with glowing bulbs. (*Imagine explaining to those farmers: "No, it's not magic—just controlled lightning."*)

The Dark Side of the Glow:

- That "improved" carbon microphone? Edison sniped it from Western Union, then tweaked it just enough to patent. (Hot take: The OG "move fast and break things" guy.)
- By 1890, his tech was everywhere—and stayed relevant until the *1980s*. (*Let that sink in: your grandma's rotary phone used Edison's tech.*)

Love him or hate him, the man knew how to sell progress. Whether by luck, theft, or sheer stubbornness (**cough* 10,000 failed bulb attempts **cough*), he turned inventions into cultural earthquakes. Modern lesson? Innovation isn't about being first—it's about making people *believe* you were.

Luther Burbank: The Green-Thumbed Maverick Who Fed America (One Odd Potato at a Time)

A teenage boy with dirt under his nails, obsessively breeding plants in his mother's garden, armed with nothing but curiosity and a dog-eared copy of Darwin's *Variation of Animals and Plants*. Sounds like the origin story of a superhero? In a way, it was—because that kid, **Luther Burbank** (1849-1926), would go on to reshape American agriculture with freakishly productive potatoes, spineless cacti (*yes, really*), and flowers pretty enough to make your grandma swoon.

The Potato That Started It All: In 1871, Burbank—a college dropout with a plant addiction—stumbled onto his first hit: the Burbank potato. By crossbreeding a random garden seedling, he created a spud so tough it thrived during the Irish Potato Famine. (Question: How's that for beginner's luck?) He sold the rights for $150 (about $3,800 today)—just enough to fund his escape to Santa Rosa, California. Why Santa Rosa? Simple: its climate was "plant kink-shaming-free"—perfect for his wild breeding experiments.

From Backyard Hobby to Agricultural Revolution Once settled, Burbank went full "mad botanist":

- Shasta Daisies: He mixed four daisy species like a floral DJ, creating the polar bear of flowers—big, white, and indestructible.
- 100+ Plum Varieties: The Santa Rosa plum? That's him. The Wickson plum? Also him. (These plums are *still* supermarket staples today.)
- Spineless Cacti: Because even cows hate prickly food. Burbank's version was a drought-resistant snack for livestock.
- The Russet Burbank Potato: The MVP of French fries—denser, drier, and crispier than its ancestors. (*Next time you eat McDonald's fries, thank Luther.*)

But wait—there's more! Freestone peaches. Juicy nectarines. Apples that didn't bruise like a peach. He even gentrified walnuts.

And let's not forget his decorative lilies and poppies, which turned gardens into botanical rock concerts.

Burbank was the Steve Jobs of plants—part genius, part stubborn visionary. He didn't just grow food; he redesigned nature itself to feed (and beautify) the world. Modern lesson? Sometimes, the biggest innovations sprout from a kid playing in the dirt.

Pavlov's Dogs (And How They Trained Us Instead)

Let's be truthful: When you hear "Pavlov," you picture a drooling dog. But **Ivan Petrovich Pavlov** (1846-1936) was far more than the "Bell Guy"—he was a stubborn Russian physiologist who accidentally discovered psychology while just trying to study spit. (Fun fact: He hated being called a psychologist. *"I'm a physiologist!"* he'd snap. *Tell that to every Psych 101 textbook, Ivan.*)

The Drool That Changed Science: 1890s Russia. Pavlov, a man so meticulous he made lab coats look tense, is studying dog digestion by creating miniature stomachs (yes, really). But his "aha!" moment came when he noticed something weird: the dogs started drooling *before* food arrived—just from hearing the lab assistants' footsteps.

Cue the world's most famous bell.

Pavlov's genius wasn't just proving dogs could associate bells with food (though let's be real—those pups were basically furry lab techs by now). It was realizing this "conditioned reflex" revealed how *all* brains learn—human or hound. Nobel Prize in 1904? Well deserved. (Question: Why do we remember the dogs but forget his actual prize was for *digestion* research? Typical.)

From Spit to Psychotherapy

- By 1930, Pavlov had turned saliva into the OG biometric data, using drool to measure "mental activity." (*Take that, Fitbit!*)

- Sir Charles Sherrington later connected these reflexes to spinal nerves, but Pavlov one-upped him by proving the *brain* was pulling the strings—with cortical drama, sleep disruptions, and even neuroses.
- Today? Every behaviour therapist owes him. Phobias, addictions, even that weird anxiety you get when your phone pings? Thank (or blame) Pavlov.

My Take: Pavlov would hate that his dogs overshadowed his digestive work. But here's the irony: his accidental discovery conditioned us to see behaviour differently. Modern lesson? Sometimes the biggest breakthroughs come from noticing what's dripping right in front of you.

The Accidental Invention That Sparked the Electronic Age (Literally)

It's 1904 in smoky London labs, where **John Ambrose Fleming** (1859-1914)—a moustachioed British engineer with Victorian flair—is tinkering with glass bulbs and frustrated by radio's unreliable signals. Then *bam*: he accidentally creates the first electronic device in history. (This "thermionic valve" was the grandfather of every gadget in your pocket today—though Fleming probably couldn't imagine we'd use his tech to watch cat videos.)

How the "Magic Bulb" Worked (Yes, It Was Wizardry):

- Inside a glass bulb: a cathode filament (translation: hot wire) and a metal plate anode (fancy term for a metal sheet).
- Apply positive voltage? Electrons party from filament to plate (AC → DC conversion).
- Negative voltage? Electrons sulk in the corner (current stops).
- Result: A one-way electron bouncer that tamed wild alternating current into obedient direct current. (Question: Why

does this matter? Try powering your laptop with raw AC and *see what happens*.)

But Wait—There's More Drama! Fleming didn't just invent a bulb. He helped Marconi shout across the Atlantic with a 25,000-watt spark transmitter (think: lightning in a box). That first transatlantic radio signal in 1901? Fleming's tech was the muscle behind the magic.

The Bittersweet Twist: Within 50 years, his glorious glass valves were dethroned by tiny transistors—proving even the brightest inventions eventually become "old-school cool." (Hot take: Silicon Valley's chip giants owe Fleming a *massive* royalty check.)

Why Fleming Still Matters: Without his "accidental" valve, we'd have no radios, no early computers, and definitely no Spotify playlists. Modern lesson? Sometimes the biggest revolutions begin with a frustrated engineer and a lucky glass tube.

Becquerel's Happy Accident: How Uranium Ghosted Its Way Into History

Let's set the scene: Paris, 1896. Physics is buzzing after Röntgen's X-ray discovery, and **Antoine Henri Becquerel** (1852 -1908)—a third-generation scientist with uranium salts in his pockets—is determined to one-up the Germans. His hypothesis? That uranium could "recharge" sunlight into X-rays. (He was spectacularly wrong… but stumbled on something far cooler.)

The "Oops" That Changed Science:

- Becquerel's plan: Wrap uranium salts in black paper (the 19th-century version of duct tape), place them on photographic plates, and wait for magic.
- First attempt: Sunny day = success! Uranium left shadowy imprints on the plates. *"Genius!"* he thinks.
- Then… disaster. Paris clouds over for days. Frustrated, he dumps the experiment in a drawer… only to find later that

the uranium *had burned its ghostly image onto the plates anyway*. Cue record scratch.

The Revelation: No sunlight? No problem. The uranium was spitting out radiation autonomously—no external energy needed. (Question: How many grad students today would've just tossed those "failed" plates in the trash?) This was radioactivity—nature's version of a perpetual motion machine.

Legacy of a Glowing Mistake:

- The Becquerel (Bq) became radioactivity's SI unit—fitting, since his career peaked by ignoring his experiment.
- His "failure" birthed nuclear physics, radiotherapy, and yes, atomic bombs. (Dark twist: He died in 1908, blissfully unaware his discovery would shake the world decades later.)

Becquerel proves science's best discoveries happen when plan A flops. Modern lesson? Next time your experiment "fails," ask: *"Am I incompetent... or about to rename a fundamental force of nature?"*

The Experiment That Killed the Ether (And Why It Still Matters Today)

It's 1887, and two American scientists - **Albert Michelson** (the perfectionist) and **Edward Morley** (the patient one) - are about to destroy one of science's most beloved theories. Everyone "knew" light needed the luminous ether to travel through space - an invisible cosmic jelly that filled the universe. But what if it didn't exist?

The Michelson-Morley Death Blow to Ether:

- Their genius setup: Compare the speed of light in different directions. If ether existed, light would travel faster "with the current" than against it.
- The shocking result: No matter which way they turned their equipment, the light stubbornly kept the same speed. The ether was a no-show.

*(Their measurements were so precise they'd make a Swiss watchmaker jealous - accurate to within *4 km/s* of today's value!)*

Wait - Why Should You Care?

This "failed" experiment became the rocket fuel for Einstein's special relativity. As Michelson himself said: *"The more important fundamental laws will be found through stubborn precision rather than philosophical speculation."*

Michelson's Other Brilliant Toy: The Interferometer

This wasn't just some lab curiosity - it became science's ultimate reality-check machine:

1. Split light into two beams
2. Send them on different paths
3. Watch the light waves gossip when they reunite (that's the interference pattern)

- First achievement? Measuring Betelgeuse's diameter - proving stars weren't just twinkly dots
- Ultimate flex? Detecting gravitational waves in 2015, precisely 100 years after Einstein predicted them

The Punchline: That same interferometer design that Michelson created in the 1880s? It's now hunting black hole collisions across the universe with 4 km-long arms. Not bad for a gadget built initially to kill off imaginary ether!

My Take: Michelson and Morley proved that sometimes, the most revolutionary discoveries come from proving something *isn't* there. Their stubborn precision changed physics forever - and their tools are still making breakthroughs today. Who needs ether when you've got interferometers?

The Curious Case of the Cathode Ray and the Birth of the Electron

It's 1897 in a dim Cambridge lab, where **Joseph John Thomson**—a man with a moustache so Victorian it could've had its own PhD—is zapping glass tubes with electricity. Suddenly, he spots something weird: mysterious rays bending under magnets. Little did he know, he'd just discovered the electron—and physics would never be the same.

From "Electric Charge" to Actual Particle:

- Irish physicist George Stoney had *theorised* the electron in 1891 (naming it from the Greek *"elektron"* for amber). But Thomson? He *caught* the little bugger.
- Using cathode-ray tubes (think: great-grandpa of your TV), he found rays bent toward positive charges—proof they were *negative* particles.
- The kicker? These particles were 2,000 times tinier than hydrogen atoms. (*Cue physicists everywhere screaming:* "Atoms aren't indivisible?!")

Thomson's Quirky Legacy:

- The "Plum Pudding" Model: His theory that atoms were "positive goo with electron raisins" (officially: a positive sphere with embedded electrons) was wrong… but *deliciously* creative. (Side note: Rutherford later proved atoms are mostly empty space—way less tasty.)
- Isotopes & Mass Spec: He invented tools to weigh atoms and discovered isotopes—basically, atomic siblings with different weights.
- The Ultimate Flex: His students included Niels Bohr and Ernest Rutherford—meaning he taught *the guys who proved him wrong*. (Lesson: Great scientists raise greater successors.)

Remember, every smartphone, MRI machine, and that static shock you get from socks? All possible because Thomson poked at glowing tubes. Not bad for a 19th-century guy who never saw a microchip!

In my opinion, Thomson's story proves science advances through equal parts rigour and whimsy (plum pudding atoms, really?). Sometimes you need to embrace the wrong ideas to find the right ones.

Planck's Quantum Leap: How a Physics Rebellion Changed Everything

It's 1900, and **Max Planck** (1858- 1947)—a stiff-collared German physicist—is staring at a math problem that won't behave. Classical physics says energy flows like a smooth river, but its calculations keep screaming that heated objects should blast infinite UV energy (the so-called "ultraviolet catastrophe"). Ever seen a glowing toaster emit X-rays? Exactly. Something was *very* wrong.

The Moment Physics Broke:

- Planck, ever the rule-follower, hated his solution: maybe energy *wasn't* continuous. Perhaps it came in tiny, stubborn chunks—"quanta."
- His equation E=hv was the ultimate mic drop:
  - h (Planck's constant): The universe's smallest price tag for energy (*6.626×10⁻³⁴ Js*—basically the atomic version of pocket change)
  - ν (frequency): Higher frequency = pricier energy packets

Planck himself called this a "desperate act." (Translation: "This makes no sense... but the math works!")

Why This Was Revolutionary:

- Einstein ran with it (photoelectric effect, 1905), proving light itself was quantised. Take that, Newton!

- Suddenly, the atomic world wasn't a gentle classical waltz—it was a glitchy quantum rave.
- 1918 Nobel Prize? Well-earned, though Planck probably still muttered about "temporary fixes" on his deathbed.

Planck was the reluctant rebel of physics. His "quantum" idea—meant to *save* classical theory—ended up torching it entirely. Sometimes the biggest breakthroughs come from admitting your favourite theory is wrong.

Nettie Stevens: The Chromosome Detective Who Cracked Nature's Gender Code

It's 1905, and **Nettie Stevens**—a stubborn American biologist with microscope calluses on her eyes—is peering at mealworm cells when she spots something odd. The males consistently exhibit mismatched chromosomes (XY), whereas females have perfect pairs (XX). Boom. In that moment, she solves one of biology's oldest mysteries: how sex is determined. (*Take that, Aristotle and your "heat theory" of gender!*)

After grinding through Stanford physiology and a Bryn Mawr PhD (1903), Stevens became obsessed with chromosomes—back when most scientists thought they were just cellular spaghetti. She worked through cancer treatments, making her discoveries while fighting for her life. (Question: How many of us skip work with a *headache*?). Her tools? A microscope, mealworms, and sheer bloody-minded patience.

The Big Discovery (With Mealworm Drama):

- XX = Female | XY = Male: Stevens proved it wasn't environment or "vital heat" but chromosomal roulette that decided gender.
- The kicker? The Y chromosome was the tiny but mighty decider—like a genetic light switch. (*Funny how something so small causes so many arguments, huh?*)

- Bonus: She invented modern cytology by treating chromosomes like biological treasure maps.

Why Stevens Got Robbed (My Pet Rant):

- Her male colleague (Edmund Wilson) published similar findings *weeks later*—yet history often credits him more. (Typical.)
- Died of breast cancer at just 50, cutting short a career that could've reshaped genetics even earlier.
- Today? Her XY system is taught in every biology class... while her name gathers dust in footnotes.

Stevens was the Sherlock Holmes of chromosomes—solving cases others didn't even know existed. Modern lesson? Next time you see an XX or XY, remember: a sick, underpaid woman in a lab coat cracked nature's code first.

The Curie Family: How a Glowing Obsession Changed Medicine Forever

Paris, 1898. A young Polish scientist named **Marie Curie** (1867-1934)—working in what historians generously call a "shed" (read: leaky, unheated shack)—is stirring a vat of pitchblende with an iron rod bigger than she is. Why? Because she's convinced there's something strange and radiant hiding in the ore. (She was right—and it would eventually kill her.)

The Glowing Discoveries:

- After Becquerel's uranium rays baffled the science world, Marie and her husband Pierre became radioactivity's first power couple.
- They discovered polonium (named after Marie's homeland, because patriotism burns bright) and radium (so radioactive it *glowed blue* in the dark).

- It took 4 tons of pitchblende to extract *1 gram* of radium. (*Try explaining that to your PhD advisor today.*)

Science as a Family Business:

- Their daughter Irène later won her *own* Nobel Prize—making the Curies the only family with three Nobels. *(Question: How's your family reunion going?)*
- Even Pierre, the quiet engineer, got dragged into the spotlight. (*"Mon amour, hold this uranium sample while I take notes..."*)

When Theory Met Tragedy (and Triumph):

- WWI's "petites Curies": Marie strapped X-ray machines to cars, creating mobile units that saved countless soldiers' lives. (*Take that, trench warfare!*)
- The dark side: Those same radium cures gave Marie terminal anaemia—yet she kept her vials of radium by her bed like nightlights. (*Scientists: brilliant yet terrible at self-preservation.*)

The Curies weren't just studying radioactivity—they lived it. Modern lesson? Next time you complain about lab work, remember: Marie hand-stirred toxic sludge for four years, to name an element.

The Human Computer Who Measured the Universe (While Nobody Was Looking)

It's 1908 at Harvard Observatory. **Henrietta Leavitt** (1864-1932) —a "computer" paid 30 cents an hour (less than the telescope cleaners)—is squinting at photographic plates of stars. Suddenly, she notices something extraordinary: certain stars pulse like cosmic lighthouses, and their rhythm reveals their true brightness. This quiet discovery would soon become astronomy's most powerful yardstick.

The Breakthrough Everyone Almost Missed: Leavitt studied Cepheid variables—stars that brighten and dim with clockwork regularity. In the Small Magellanic Cloud (a dwarf galaxy), she found that the longer the pulse, the brighter the star. (*Think of it like fireflies: the ones with slower flashes are actually bigger.*). Her "Period-Luminosity Relation" (aka Leavitt's Law) became the Rosetta Stone of cosmic distances. (Question: How many galaxies has Hubble measured using her rule? *Almost all of them.*)

Why This Was Revolutionary:

- Before Leavitt, astronomers were literally lost in space. Her law let them calculate distances to galaxies without guessing.
- Edwin Hubble used it to prove Andromeda was another galaxy—smashing the idea that the Milky Way was the entire universe.
- Fun fact: Her law works up to 50 million light-years—far enough to map our cosmic neighbourhood. (*Beyond that? Even Leavitt would need glasses.*)

The Bittersweet Part:

- As a woman, she wasn't allowed to operate telescopes. Her title? "Human computer."
- She died at 53, never knowing her work would redefine cosmology. (My take: If Leavitt were alive today, she'd deserve a Nobel—and back pay.)

Modern Reality Check:

Yes, her law has limits:

- Works only where we can spot Cepheids (cosmic breadcrumbs).
- Needs calibration using nearby stars (thank you, parallax method).
- Beyond 100 million light-years, we switch to redshift. (*Even geniuses need backup plans.*)

Next time you see a Hubble deep-field image, remember—an underpaid woman with a magnifying glass made it possible.

Rutherford: The Bull in Nature's China Shop Who Redefined the Atom

It's 1899 in Montreal, and a loud, brash New Zealander (think: a rugby player who wandered into a lab) is poking at uranium like it owes him money. Suddenly—*BAM*—he discovers two types of radiation. Naming them? Simple: alpha (the shy one) and beta (the troublemaker). Little did **Ernest Rutherford** (1871—1937) know that he'd just kicked open the door to the atomic age.

From Backwater Labs to Gold Foil Fame: After J.J. Thomson "discovered" electrons (*cough* plum pudding model *cough*), Rutherford took one look and said, "Nope." His 1907 gold foil experiment was the ultimate mic drop: He fired alpha particles at gold foil. *Most sailed through* (expected). *Some bounced back like they'd hit a wall.*

Conclusion? Atoms are mostly empty space with a tiny, dense nucleus—basically a mosquito in a cathedral.

Nuclear Physics' Greatest Hits (Rutherford Edition):

1. Radioactive Decay: Proved atoms could morph into other elements (take *that*, alchemy).
2. First Nuclear Reaction (1919): Shot alpha particles at nitrogen and—*surprise!*—made protons fly out. (Scientist equivalent of hitting a piñata and getting cash.)
3. Predicted Neutrons (1920): Like a boss, he called their existence before Chadwick found them in 1932.

The Cavendish Circus:

As head of Cambridge's Cavendish Lab, Rutherford ran what might be history's most productive madhouse:

- Discovered fusion (1934) by smashing deuterium nuclei (*"Let's play atomic bumper cars!"*)
- Trained 17 future Nobel winners (because he was also a talent whisperer)

Rutherford treated atoms like they'd insulted his mother—bullying them into revealing their secrets. Modern physics? Built on his "hold my beer" approach to experimentation.

Next time you hear "nuclear," thank the loud Kiwi who proved even tiny things can explode your worldview.

Lise Meitner: The Physics Rebel Who Split the Atom (And Got Written Out of History)

Imagine this: Berlin, 1938. A Jewish woman physicist (already a rarity) flees Nazi Germany with just 10 marks in her pocket. Weeks later, she cracks one of nature's biggest secrets—nuclear fission—using pencil and paper from exile. Yet when the Nobel Prize came, they gave it to her male lab partner. Sound unfair? That's because it was.

The Atomic Detective Story:

- Meitner (1878-1968) and chemist Otto Hahn had been bullying uranium with neutrons for years, trying to make heavier elements.
- Then boom—Hahn found barium (element 56) in what should've been uranium (element 92). *"This makes no sense!"* he wrote to Meitner. (Understatement of the century.)
- Over Christmas in Sweden, Meitner and her nephew Otto Frisch did the math:
    - The nucleus had split like an overfilled water balloon
    - The energy released matched Einstein's $E=mc^2$ (turns out, the old man was right)
    - They called it "fission"—borrowing from biology's term for cell division

Why This Was Revolutionary:

- One uranium fission releases 200 MeV—50 million times more energy than burning carbon. (*Your car's gas tank? Pathetic by comparison.*)
- Meitner instantly saw the dual potential: limitless energy or unthinkable weapons

The first person to suggest fission (Ida Noddack in 1934) was ignored. (Science moves fast... unless you're a woman.)

The Injustice Files:

- The 1944 Nobel Prize in Chemistry went to… Otto Hahn alone. (*Cue record scratch.*)
- Meitner? She got a consolation footnote in history as the "mother of nuclear power"

My take: This wasn't just sexism—it was theft. Her physics explanation was what made the discovery meaningful.

Later Years (The Bittersweet Part):

- Refused to work on the atomic bomb (take that, Manhattan Project)
- Retired to Cambridge, where colleagues finally called her "the German Marie Curie"
- Died in 1968, her gravestone reading: "Lise Meitner: a physicist who never lost her humanity"

*Next time you hear "nuclear energy," remember—it was a **fleeing Jewish woman** who unlocked it, not just the men who took the credit.*

Einstein: The Patent Clerk Who Outsmarted Newton (With Help From His Friends)

It's 1905 in Bern, Switzerland. A 26-year-old patent clerk with unruly hair is scribbling equations while reviewing patent applications for electromagnetic gadgets. His "office"? The Olympia

Academy—a glorified book club with Maurice and Conrad, where they debated physics over cheap wine. Little did they know that their chats would birth $E=mc^2$, relativity, and quantum theory. (Take that, stuffy university professors!)

The Genius Borrowed (Before He Became Einstein™)

1. Maxwell's Electromagnetic Gift

- James Clerk Maxwell's equations were the OG physics mixtape—proving light was an electromagnetic wave and carrying energy.

Without Maxwell, Einstein might've been stuck explaining why compass needles wiggle instead of revolutionising physics.

2. The Almost-Einsteins

- Hasenöhrl (1904): Got *close* to $E=mc^2$ but fumbled the math (like forgetting to carry the 1 in cosmic calculus).
- De Pretto (1903): Guessed $E=mc^2$ but had zero proof (*the 1900s equivalent of a Reddit physics hot take*).
- Lorentz & Poincaré: Built the math elevator… but Einstein pushed the "relativity" button.

Question: Why do we remember Einstein and not them? Because he connected the dots—mass, energy, light—into one earth-shattering framework.

1905: Einstein's Miracle Year (Or How to Win Physics Bingo)

1. Photoelectric Effect – The Quantum Side Hustle

- Hertz and Lenard saw light kicking electrons off metals, but were utterly confused why blue light worked better than red.
- Einstein's fix? Light comes in chunks (photons)!
    - Equation: $E=h\nu$ (where h is Planck's constant, and ν is frequency)

    - K.E. = hν - ϕ (ϕ = work function, aka the metal's "electron clinginess")
- Legacy: Proved light is both wave AND particle—upsetting physicists almost as much as his hair upset barbers.

2. Special Relativity – Bye-Bye, Newton's Absolute Time

- Einstein's upgrades to Lorentz's math:
    - Ditched the ether (because ghostly space jelly was so 1899)
    - Made light speed the universe's speed limit (sorry, NASCAR)
    - Revealed time is a personal experience (*your GPS agrees—thanks, time dilation!*)

3. E=mc² – The Ultimate Flex

- Matter and energy are the same thing in different outfits.
- 1 gram of mass = 90,000,000,000,000 joules (enough to power 30,000 homes for a year).
- Hot take: The equation's simplicity is deceptive—it hides the chaos of nuclear bombs and stars.

General Relativity: When Einstein Bent the Universe

- Gravity isn't a force—it's spacetime's curvy dance floor.
    - Proof #1: Eddington's 1919 eclipse photos showing starlight bending like a drunk photon.
    - Proof #2: GPS satellites gain 38 microseconds/day because time runs faster farther from Earth.
    - Proof #3: LIGO's gravitational waves—ripples in spacetime from black holes tangoing.

My Final Thought: Einstein stood on giants' shoulders… then leapt into the cosmos. Next time your phone's GPS works, thank the patent clerk who rewrote reality between coffee breaks.

The Mouldy Petri Dish That Changed Medicine Forever

September 1928. A messy Scottish lab at St. Mary's Hospital, where Alexander Fleming (1881-1995)—a man who never cleaned his workspace—returns from vacation to find a science fair project gone wrong. A mouldy Petri dish sits forgotten, its bacterial colonies mysteriously dying around a blue-green intruder. Most scientists would've tossed it. Fleming? He saw a medical revolution amidst the chaos.

The Accidental Discovery (Thanks to Bad Housekeeping):

- The mould was *Penicillium notatum*—nature's tiny antibiotic factory.
- It created clear "death zones" around itself where bacteria dared not grow. (*Take that, staphylococci!*)
- Fun fact: This wasn't even Fleming's first antibacterial find—he'd previously discovered lysozyme in snot and tears. (Question: How many researchers would proudly publish a paper titled *"My Nasal Mucus Kills Bacteria"**?*)

Why This Was Revolutionary:

1. First true antibiotic that killed pathogens without harming human cells (unlike arsenic or mercury "cures").
2. Proved nature makes better chemists than humans (*eat your heart out, Big Pharma*).
3. WWII miracle: Florey's team later turned it into a mass-produced lifesaver, sparing countless soldiers from gangrene and sepsis.

The Bittersweet Part:

- Fleming couldn't purify penicillin himself (lab techs: the unsung heroes of science).
- He shared the 1945 Nobel Prize... but history remembers him as the "mould guy" while Florey got the production glory.

- My take: Science needs both—the observant slob who spots miracles in messes *and* the meticulous teams who make them usable.

Next time you take antibiotics, thank a forgetful Scot and his pet mould. Modern medicine owes more to accidents and oddballs than we admit.

Bohr: The Quantum Rule-Breaker Who Made Atoms Make Sense

1913, Manchester. A 28-year-old Danish physicist stares at Rutherford's atomic model—a tiny nucleus with electrons buzzing around like confused bees. "This makes no sense!", Neil Bohr (1885-1962) mutters. "Electrons can't just orbit anywhere they please!" And with that outburst, quantum mechanics was born.

The Atomic Revolution (With Danish Flair):

- Bohr's big idea? Electrons ride fixed orbits like cosmic trams—no in-between stops allowed.
- Jump to a higher orbit? Absorb a photon snack.
- Fall back down? Burp out light at specific wavelengths.
- Suddenly, hydrogen's rainbow-like emission spectrum finally made sense—no more "magic wavelengths."

Bohr's model worked perfectly... for hydrogen. Other atoms? "We'll fix that later," he shrugged. (They're still working on it.)

Quantum Drama at the Solvay Conference:

- Einstein: "God doesn't play dice with the universe!"
- Bohr: "Stop telling God what to do!"
- Their legendary debates birthed the Principle of Complementarity:
    - Electrons are particles AND waves (just not at the same time)

- Reality depends on how you look at it (*philosophy majors felt vindicated*)

The Bohr Effect (Beyond Physics):

- Mentored Heisenberg (uncertainty principle) and Pauli (exclusion principle)—basically, the godfather of quantum rebels.
- Fled Nazis in WWII with atomic secrets hidden in beer bottles (true story).
- My perspective: Bohr was the Yoda of physics—his Copenhagen Interpretation became quantum gospel.

Schrödinger: The Quantum Poet Who Put Physics in a Box

Imagine this: 1926, Zurich. A 40-year-old Austrian physicist with a fondness for mountain hikes and romantic poetry stares at his notes. Suddenly, inspiration strikes—not with a lab experiment, but with an equation so elegant they'd later carve it on his tombstone. Little did Erwin Schrödinger (1887-1961) know that his "wave equation" would make electrons dance and cats become famously undead.

The Equation That Made Particles Wavy:

- Schrödinger's $i\hbar\partial\psi = H\psi$ became the quantum rulebook:
    - ψ (psi): Not a particle, but a "probability wave" (think: electron as a cloud of maybes)
    - H: The Hamiltonian—basically, the quantum bouncer deciding where ψ can go
- Overnight, electrons went from being tiny billiard balls to mysterious smears of potential

The equation works so well that we now use it to design everything from lasers to MRI machines

Schrödinger's Cat: Physics's Most Infamous Pet

In 1935, tired of quantum weirdness, Schrödinger devised a thought experiment so savage it's still debated today:

1. Take one cat (preferably imaginary)
2. Add radioactive atom + poison vial + quantum uncertainty
3. Seal box. Now the cat is simultaneously alive AND dead
    - His point? "This Copenhagen Interpretation nonsense leads to absurdity!"
    - Irony? The paradox became the poster child of quantum theory, and he was criticising

Dublin's Hidden Legacy: From Physics to DNA

During WWII exile in Ireland, Schrödinger wrote *"What is Life?"*—a physics book that accidentally inspired biology:

- Proposed genes were "aperiodic crystals" storing code (basically predicting DNA)
- Gave Watson & Crick the quantum push to discover DNA's structure

My take: Schrödinger was the original interdisciplinary rebel—proving you don't need a lab coat to change science.

Hubble: The Stargazer Who Stretched the Universe

1924, Mount Wilson Observatory. A former boxer-turned-astronomer (yes, really!) peers through the world's largest telescope and makes an impossible discovery—the Milky Way isn't alone. Edwin Hubble (1889-1953), the man who would smash our cosmic ego, was about to prove the universe was far bigger... and stranger... than anyone dreamed.

The Discovery That Shrank Humanity:

- Using Cepheid stars as cosmic yardsticks (their pulse = their brightness), Hubble proved:
  - Those "nebulae" weren't clouds—they were entire galaxies millions of light-years away
  - The Milky Way? Just one greasy spoon in a cosmic food court

When Hubble presented his findings, senior astronomers literally gasped. One muttered: "This destroys my life's work." (Tough day at the office!)

The Even Bigger Bombshell: The Runaway Universe

- Hubble noticed galaxies were redshifted—their light stretched like taffy as they fled
- The farther the galaxy, the faster it ran (Hubble's Law)
- Mind-blowing implication: The universe itself was stretching like a cosmic balloon
- Question: How would YOU react if someone told you space itself was growing? (*Most 1920s astronomers: "Pass the whiskey."*)

The Importance of His Role Today

- Hubble's work became the smoking gun for the Big Bang
- His constant (H_0) still fuels debates—is it 67 or 73 km/s/Mpc? (Astronomers: still fighting)
- My viewpoint: Hubble did for cosmology what Columbus did for geography—proved we'd been living in a tiny corner of something vast

Next time you feel important, remember—we're all specks on a speck, orbiting a speck, in an ever-fleeing cosmic neighbourhood. Thanks, Edwin.

Watson-Watt: The Scottish Scientist Who Saw War Coming (Literally)

1935, rural England. A moustachioed Scotsman stands in a field, staring at a jumble of radio equipment. The British Air Ministry had asked him to build a "death ray" to zap enemy planes from the sky. His response? *"That's daft... but I can* hear *them coming instead."* And with that, radar was born—just in time to save Britain from the Blitz.

From Thunderstorms to Thunderbolts (of War): Young Watson-Watt cut his teeth tracking lightning with radio waves (because even storms can't hide from Scottish ingenuity). His key insight? Metal planes reflect radio waves just like lightning disturbs them (*nature's cheat code for detection*).

His first successful test in 1935 detected a bomber 15 miles away—using equipment so jury-rigged it looked like "a mad inventor's garage sale"

How Radar Changed Everything:

1. Chain Home Network: By WWII, his towers dotted Britain's coast, spotting Luftwaffe raids while German pilots wondered, *"how do they always see us coming?"*
2. Civilian Spin-offs: Today, it guides planes through fog, tracks storms, and even catches you speeding (*thanks, Robert*)
3. The Ultimate Flex: Proved you don't need death rays when you've got clever physics and Scottish stubbornness

The Man Behind the Magic:

- Started as a meteorology nerd tracking lightning (*"Aye, that cloud's looking shifty..."*)
- Turned wartime panic into one of history's most effective defence systems

My take: Watson-Watt was the MacGyver of WWII—he saved lives with radio parts and big ideas

Remember, next time your flight lands safely in fog, thank the thrifty Scot who taught us to "see" with radio waves.

Compton: The Physicist Who Made Light Behave Badly

1923, St. Louis. A 31-year-old professor is blasting X-rays at electrons like a cosmic game of pool. When the numbers come in, Arthur Compton (1892-1962) realises something shocking—the X-rays are changing their tune after collisions. This wasn't just scattering; this was the Compton Effect, and it was about to break physics.

The Discovery That Shook Up Light: Compton proved X-rays lose energy when they smack into electrons (like a cue ball slowing after a hard break). The result? The X-rays' wavelength stretched out—direct evidence that light behaves as particles with momentum.

Medical imaging: Suddenly, doctors understood why X-rays scatter in tissues (*your chest X-ray thanks him*)—quantum revolution: Gave Einstein's photons street cred alongside his $E=mc^2$ fame. Materials science: Explained why some materials glow under X-rays (*turns out electrons are terrible at keeping secrets*)

The Man Behind the Effect: Started as a lightbulb engineer during WWI (*yes, really*). Became the first to "see" quantum mechanics in action

The Curie Legacy Continues: Irène's Radioactive Love Story

Paris, 1925. A 28-year-old woman with a famous last name stares at a piece of aluminium foil being zapped with alpha particles. The lab notebook beside her reads: *"If Mom could turn pitchblende into radium, why can't I make new elements?"* This was Irène Joliot-Curie(1897-1956) - not just Marie's daughter, but a scientific force in her own right.

From Battlefield to Breakthroughs: Started as a teenage X-ray tech in WWI trenches (most kids her age were worrying about algebra tests). Married her lab partner Frédéric (scientific romance goals) - their wedding rings were probably slightly radioactive

Their discovery of artificial radioactivity was so unexpected that other scientists initially thought it was "a Curie family trick"

The Discovery That Changed Medicine:

When they bombarded aluminium with alpha particles:

1. Created the first **man-made radioactive element** (phosphorus-30)
2. Discovered positron emission - where protons turn into neutrons while spitting out antimatter
3. Medical revolution: Suddenly, hospitals could make their radioactive tracers (*no more hauling radium from mines!*)

Why This Matters Today:

- PET scans? Thank the Joliot-Curies
- Cancer treatments? Their discovery paved the way

SUMMARY

The Century That Rewrote Reality: When Science Grew Up

Let's be honest - the 1800s were supposed to be about steam engines and top hats, but a handful of stubborn minds completely redrew humanity's understanding of existence. This was the century when Darwin turned biology upside down (yes, we're *related to bananas*). Mendel's peas proved inheritance had rules (take that, aristocrats!). Pasteur made microbes public enemy #1 (while inventing vaccines in his spare time)

The Lightbulb Moments That Lit Up the 20th Century: Röntgen's accidental "ghost photos" (X-rays) - the original medical magic trick. Marie Curie - who carried radium in her pockets (safety protocols? *Never heard of them*). Maxwell's equations - the invisible rules that make your smartphone possible. Einstein's famous equations, Planck's quantum leap - proving even physics has trust issues ("*But can we really observe it?*")

The Overshadowed Geniuses We Owe Apologies To: Lise Meitner (nuclear fission's brains) - Nobel committee's greatest snub. Ada Lovelace wrote the first computer code when "computer" meant *a person who computes*. Hubble - who found the universe was expanding (while most astronomers were still mapping constellations)

This was the era when science stopped being gentlemen in wool coats arguing and started saving lives, splitting atoms, and questioning reality itself. Not bad for a pre-Internet century!

Coming Next: How the 1900s turned these discoveries into nuclear power, space travel, and the digital age (with twice the drama).

CHAPTER 6

The Age of Modern Science 20th Century (1901-)

The Moving Target of "Modern" Science: Ever noticed how "modern" science keeps changing its address? What Newton called cutting-edge in 1687 would barely register on today's scientific radar. That's the funny thing about progress - today's revolution becomes tomorrow's textbook footnote.

So what made 20th-century science special? Three words: Quantum. Transistors. DNA. Quantum Physics: The moment scientists realised particles could be *two places at once* (and still be late for dinner). Without it? No transistors. No smartphones. No Netflix binge-watching at 2 AM. The Transistor Revolution: These tiny switches shrunk room-sized computers into pocket devices. The device you're reading this on contains *billions* of them - each smaller than a red blood cell. Cracking Life's Code: DNA went from mysterious "nuclein" to the blueprint of life itself. Now we're editing genes like text documents (*What would Darwin say?*)

And let's not forget AI - our newest scientific child that's already:

- ✓ Beating chess grandmasters
- ✓ Writing (mediocre) poetry
- ✓ Making us question what "intelligence" really means

Here's my take: The 20th century didn't just advance science - it rewrote the rules of discovery itself. And if history's any guide, our "modern" science will look just as quaint to 2100's researchers. We'll explore how these quantum quirks and silicon chips built the world you live in today.

Linus Pauling: The Quantum Chemist Who Fought for Peace

1931, California. A 30-year-old chemist with a cowboy hat (yes, really!) stares at chalkboards covered in quantum equations. Most chemists were still thinking in straight lines and right angles—but Linus Pauling (1901-1994) saw molecules dancing in 3D. His secret? Treating chemical bonds like quantum mechanical handshakes.

The Bond Whisperer: Revolutionised chemistry by proving atoms don't just "stick"—they hybridise their orbitals (think: atomic identity crisis). Explained why methane is tetrahedral and benzene rings are flat—solving puzzles that baffled chemists for decades. He wrote *"The Nature of the Chemical Bond"*—the chemistry bible that's still dog-eared in labs today.

Cracked protein structures using X-rays and quantum math (because why choose one superpower?). Discovered the alpha helix—nature's favourite protein curl. His work directly inspired Watson & Crick's DNA model (*though they never gave him proper credit—typical!*)

This is the Scientist Who Said "No" to Nukes. After mastering molecules, Pauling took on world peace. His 1963 Nuclear Test Ban Treaty proved scientists could change history beyond the lab. Only person ever to win two unshared Nobels, Chemistry (1954), Peace (1962).

If more scientists had his conscience, we'd live in a very different world. Next time you see a protein diagram or hear about nuclear disarmament, remember the cowboy-hat-wearing genius who taught atoms to dance and politicians to think.

Enrico Fermi: The Nuclear Maestro Who Played With Atoms

December 1942, Chicago. A 41-year-old Italian physicist stands atop a pile of uranium and graphite, about to conduct the world's first nuclear chain reaction. No safety gear, no panic - just Fermi (1901-1954) calmly calculating with slide rules as his team sweats bullets. *"Don't worry,"* he assures them, *"the reaction will self-regulate."* And just like that, the Atomic Age was born in a squash court.

From Pisa to Plutonium: Started as a prodigy studying X-rays (yawn). He revolutionised physics by creating Fermi-Dirac statistics (because even particles need social distancing rules). Predicting neutrinos - the universe's most elusive ghosts and inventing weak interaction theory (nature's most awkward handshake).

The "Oops" That Changed History: He thought he'd discovered new elements (transuranics). Split the atom without realising it (*Whoops!*). His "failed" experiment became the blueprint for every nuclear reactor today.

Chicago Pile-1: The World's Most Dangerous Science Fair Project

- Built under a football stadium (because why not?)
- Used wooden control rods (the 1940s version of "hold my beer")
- Proved chain reactions could be controlled - or, as Fermi called it, "Tuesday"

Legacy of the Nuclear Architect:

- Won 1938 Nobel Prize (just in time to flee Mussolini)
- Mentored six future Nobel winners

Fermi proved brilliance means both changing science AND surviving your own experiments.

Next time you flip a light switch powered by nuclear energy, thank the Italian maestro who turned atomic chaos into clean energy... and lived to tell the tale.

Heisenberg's Uncertainty Principle: The Universe's Built-in Fog Machine

1927, Germany. A 26-year-old physicist named Werner Heisenberg (1901-1976) stares at his equations, realising something unsettling - *the universe doesn't want to be spied on.* His discovery? The ultimate cosmic "mind your own business" rule - the Uncertainty Principle.

The Equation That Broke Physics:

$\Delta x \Delta p \geq h/4\pi$(Translation: *"The more you know where a particle is, the less you know where it's going... and vice versa"*)

Why This Shook Scientists:

- Proved the universe isn't just unpredictable - it's *fundamentally fuzzy* at quantum scales
- Electrons aren't tiny planets - they're existence probability clouds

The Principle in Plain English:

1. Try to pin down an electron's location? Its speed becomes unknowable
2. Want to measure its momentum perfectly? Say goodbye to knowing its position
3. It's not our tools' fault - nature itself wears a blurry mask

My Favourite Mind-Bender:

This applies to *everything* in the quantum realm:

- Energy vs. Time
- Angular momentum components

- Even quantum love affairs (entangled particles break all the rules)

Heisenberg's Legacy:

- Forced physicists to accept probability over certainty
- Inspired countless bad Breaking Bad references

Barbara McClintock (1902–1992): The Maverick Who Discovered "Jumping Genes"

Ever heard of genetic instructions that don't stay put? It sounds like science fiction, but American scientist Barbara McClintock proved it's real. While mid-20th-century genetics clung to the idea of static DNA, she uncovered something radical: mobile genetic elements called transposons—genes that switch physical traits on and off. Imagine the audacity of suggesting genes could "jump" in an era when chromosomes were seen as unshakable rulebooks!

What drove her? After earning a Ph.D. in botany, McClintock didn't just study corn chromosomes—she obsessed over them. Using painstaking microscopy and staining techniques, she tracked every twist and turn of maise DNA. Why corn? Its kernels offered a visual roadmap of genetic chaos, with colour variations that defied Mendel's tidy rules. And then came her eureka moment: By linking pigment quirks to chromosomal breaks, she spotted two rogue genes—dubbed "controlling elements"—that didn't just sit quietly but shuffled along chromosomes, scrambling nearby genes like a molecular game of musical chairs. She called them "transposable elements." (Sound familiar? Today, we know them as transposons.)

McClintock argued these hopping genes could explain a paradox—how can a heart cell and a brain cell, with identical DNA, behave so differently? Her answer: dynamic gene regulation. This blew apart the dogma of genomes as static heirlooms passed unchanged to offspring. Yet for decades, few believed her. *(Funny how often pioneers are dismissed until technology catches up.)*

Now, of course, we know transposons aren't genetic glitches—they're evolutionary engines, shaping everything from antibiotic resistance in bacteria to human immune responses. McClintock's "wild" ideas earned her a Nobel Prize in 1983... and forever changed how we see life's code.

The Transistor Revolution: How Quantum Physics Shrank the World

Think about it: What invention changed the modern world more than the transistor? Just as the printing press exploded access to knowledge in the 15th century, the tiny transistor became the unsung hero of the 20th century—the "Gutenberg moment" of technology. Without it, your smartphone would be a room-sized machine, and global communication would still rely on crackling radio towers. But here's the twist: this revolution began with a quantum physics puzzle and three stubborn scientists at Bell Labs.

The Problem: Fragile Valves and a Quantum Leap

Before transistors, we had clunky thermionic valves—glass tubes that amplified signals but broke like lightbulbs. Imagine a world where computers needed 18,000 of these temperamental valves (like the ENIAC did)! By the 1940s, Bell Labs was desperate for something better: a solid-state amplifier that wouldn't shatter or overheat. Enter the dream team:

1. Walter Brattain (1902 -1987)—a hands-on experimenter who studied how electrons danced on mercury's surface.
2. John Bardeen (1908 – 1991)—a quantum physics wizard (and future two-time Nobel laureate).
3. William Shockley (1910 – 1989)—their brilliant but abrasive leader, obsessed with semiconductors.

Funny enough, their "Eureka!" moment came from a failure. Shockley's initial design—using an electric field to control conductivity in germanium—flopped spectacularly. Why? Quantum mechanics threw a curveball: surface states (defects trapping electrons) acted like a shield, blocking the field. *(Ever tried tuning a radio through a wall? Same idea.)*

The Breakthrough: Point Contacts and Minority Carriers

So what saved them? Bardeen's genius hunch: if electric fields couldn't penetrate, maybe jabbing the germanium with metal contacts would inject charges directly. Brattain rigged up a makeshift device—two gold foil strips pressed onto germanium like a sandwich—and voilà! A small current at one contact ("emitter") magically amplified into a larger current at the other ("collector"). How?

- Injected minority carriers (electrons in p-type germanium) diffused through the crystal, boosted by germanium's quantum properties.
- This "current amplification" was the transistor's heartbeat—and it relied entirely on quantum physics.

Their first transistor (1947) was far from perfect—it hissed like a misbehaving microphone—but it birthed the digital age. By 1956, all three won Nobels. Not bad for a "failed" experiment!

Why This Matters Today: Without quantum mechanics, transistors wouldn't exist—and neither would Silicon Valley. Those early germanium quirks? They're why today's chips use silicon (better at taming surface states). Next time you video-call someone across the globe, thank Brattain's messy lab bench and Bardeen's quantum intuition.

From Vacuum Tubes to Compilers: The Unsung Heroes of Computing

Imagine a world where computers were rooms full of fragile glass tubes - hissing, overheating, and consuming enough electricity to power a small town. That was reality before the transistor revolution! But let's rewind further. Before even transistors, we had Charles Babbage's analytical engine - a mechanical marvel that was more steam-punk fantasy than a practical tool in its time (Swade, 2000).

So, how did we jump from gears and vacuum tubes to silicon chips?

The transistor was indeed the game-changer, but there's another hero in this story: Grace Hopper - the "Queen of Code", who taught computers to understand human language.

Grace Hopper: The Navy Officer Who Spoke Machine

A PhD mathematician and Navy rear admiral, Hopper (1906-1092) wasn't your typical programmer. Can you picture this: a woman in the 1940s writing assembly code for the hulking Harvard Mark I computer, its mechanical relays clattering like a room full of typewriters (Beyer, 2009)?

Her breakthrough? Realizing that "computers should understand English too" - a radical idea when everyone was writing in binary! In 1952, she created the A-0 System, the first compiler.

How did this "magic translator" work? Think of it like:

1. A chef (programmer) writes a recipe in simple English ("Bake cake")
2. The compiler translates this into precise machine instructions ("Preheat oven to 350°F...")
3. The computer (oven) executes it perfectly

The catch? The A-0 System didn't have pretty source code like today's Python or Java. It worked directly with magnetic tapes and punch cards, stitching together subroutines like a quilter assembling patches (Ceruzzi, 2003).

COBOL: The Language That Powered Business

Hopper's masterpiece was COBOL - the "business English" of programming. Ever wondered why your bank's ancient systems still work? Thank COBOL's natural language syntax:

COBOL

Copy

Download

```
DISPLAY "Hello World!"
COMPUTE TAX = AMOUNT * 0.07
```

Simple enough for accountants to read! This philosophy made COBOL the backbone of financial systems for decades (Sammet, 1981).

Maria Goeppert Mayer: The Woman Who Cracked the Nucleus' Secret Code

It's 1948, and physicists are utterly baffled. Why do certain atomic nuclei behave like perfect spheres while others wobble like unbalanced tops? The answer came from an unlikely source - a German-American woman working part-time at the University of Chicago's nuclear physics lab.

Maria Goeppert Mayer (1906-1972), a brilliant theorist who'd been relegated to unpaid research positions for most of her career (can you believe that?), made one of the most beautiful discoveries in nuclear physics. She realised that the nucleus isn't just a messy soup of protons and neutrons - it has an elegant shell structure, much like electrons orbiting an atom.

The "Magic Numbers" That Changed Physics: Her eureka moment came when she noticed something peculiar: nuclei with certain numbers of protons or neutrons (2, 8, 20, 28, 50, 82, 126) were remarkably stable. These weren't random digits - they were nuclear magic numbers, the atomic equivalent of completing an electron shell.

Think of it like building blocks:

- Just as atoms with full electron shells (noble gases) won't react
- Nuclei with full proton/neutron shells won't decay easily

This explained why lead-208 (with 82 protons and 126 neutrons) is so stable it's practically immortal!

An Idea So Good, It Was Discovered Twice: Here's the kicker - across the Atlantic, German physicist Hans Jensen had the same insight independently. When they learned of each other's work, rather than competing, they collaborated on the Nuclear Shell Model. Their theory is finally explained:

- Why some isotopes are more common than others
- How nuclear binding energy works
- What makes specific nuclei exceptionally stable

The ultimate validation? Sharing the 1963 Nobel Prize in Physics (with Eugene Wigner) - making Mayer only the second woman ever to win the physics Nobel.

A Legacy Beyond Nuclear Physics: What's truly remarkable is how Mayer's work anticipated future technologies. Her understanding of energy levels in nuclei directly influenced:

1. Laser development (through similar quantum principles)
2. Nonlinear optics (via analogous energy transitions)
3. Modern nuclear medicine (explaining isotope stability)

How many other scientific breakthroughs might be waiting in the notebooks of underappreciated researchers today?

Dorothy Hodgkin: The X-Ray Visionary Who Saved Millions

Imagine trying to solve a 3D puzzle with no picture on the box—and each piece is the size of an atom. That's essentially what Dorothy Hodgkin (1910-1994) did when she revolutionised X-ray crystallography, a technique so powerful it lets us "see" molecules atom by atom. Born in Egypt to British parents in 1910, Hodgkin would become one of science's unsung heroes, cracking the chemical codes of life-saving medicines.

Penicillin: The War-Time Breakthrough

During World War II, while men fought on battlefields, Hodgkin waged her own war against disease. Using X-ray crystallography, she mapped **penicillin's molecular structure**—a feat many thought impossible at the time. **Why does this matter?** Because understanding its shape allowed mass production of the antibiotic, saving countless soldiers from infections.

Vitamin B12: The Puzzle That Won a Nobel Prize

Hodgkin's next challenge was Vitamin B12, a monstrously complex molecule with over 100 atoms. For years, colleagues doubted it could ever be deciphered. But in 1956, after grinding through millions of X-ray diffraction patterns, Hodgkin triumphed. Her reward? The 1964 Nobel Prize in Chemistry—only the third woman ever to win it solo (Nobel Prize Committee, 1964).

Insulin: A 34-Year Labour of Love

Here's where Hodgkin's story gets personal. She began studying **insulin** in 1934, but the technology of the era was like "trying to read a book through a fogged-up window".

What changed?

1. Computers arrived: 1960s-era machines finally crunched the mountains of data.
2. Her team grew crystals so pure they diffracted X-rays like diamonds.

The result? In 1969, Hodgkin revealed insulin's intricate structure—a blueprint that transformed diabetes treatment. Today, her work underpins:

- Synthetic insulin for Type 1 diabetics
- Advanced drug designs for Type 2 therapies

Jacques Cousteau: The Man Who Gave Us Gills

France, 1943. A young naval officer with a broken body and an unbroken spirit stares at the Mediterranean. The ocean taunts him—its secrets locked away behind the icy barrier of human limitation. This was Jacques Cousteau's (1910-1997) reality after a near-fatal car crash. But what if I told you that this accident gave birth to modern diving?

From Broken Bones to Breaking Barriers: Cousteau's rehabilitation swimming sessions revealed a truth as cold as the water: existing diving gear was clunky, dangerous, and about as graceful as a sinking anchor. Most would've accepted this. Not Cousteau. With the same stubbornness that got him through physical therapy, he asked: *"Why can't we breathe underwater as easily as fish?"*

Enter Emile Gagnan—a gas equipment wizard. Together during WWII's chaos, they crafted the aqualung (1943), a device so revolutionary it:

- Freed divers from surface air hoses
- Allowed deeper/longer exploration
- Essentially invented scuba diving as we know it

The Calypso Years: Science Meets Showmanship: Ever the visionary, Cousteau transformed a rusty minesweeper into RV Calypso—a floating lab that became as iconic as his red beanie. His 1953 book *The Silent World* didn't just document marine life; it made millions fall in love with the ocean's "inner space."

Then came his masterstroke: *The Undersea World of Jacques Cousteau* (1966-1976). This TV series did what no textbook could:

- Showed whales singing
- Revealed coral reefs in living colour
- Made oceanography as exciting as space exploration

Think about it: Before Cousteau, marine biology was stuffy labs and specimen jars. He turned it into an adventure we all wanted to join.

Legacy: More Than Just a Diver

Cousteau wasn't perfect (his early films harmed some ecosystems), but his true gift was making us see the ocean as:

1. A frontier to explore
2. A treasure to protect
3. Our planet's beating blue heart

Next time you strap on a scuba tank or see a BBC ocean documentary, remember—it all traces back to one Frenchman's refusal to let gravity win.

Richard Feynman: The Jazz-Playing Physicist Who Made Quantum Physics Fun

What do bongo drums, topless bars, and quantum electrodynamics have in common? They were all passions of **Richard Feynman** (1918-1988) - perhaps the most colourful Nobel laureate in history. As someone who's devoured his lectures, I'm constantly amazed how he could make the most complex physics concepts feel like sharing stories at a dinner party.

The Man Who Doodled His Way to a Nobel Prize

Feynman's approach to quantum mechanics was as unconventional as his personality. While other physicists buried their ideas in dense equations, Feynman drew his insights. His famous Feynman diagrams - those playful squiggles representing particle interactions - revolutionised how we visualise quantum events (Feynman, 1949).

"If you can't explain it simply, you don't understand it well enough," he often said. This philosophy led to his groundbreaking work on Quantum Electrodynamics (QED), for which he earned the 1965 Nobel Prize alongside Schwinger and Tomonaga (Nobel Foundation, 1965). But true to form, Feynman nearly declined the honour, quipping that awards distracted from the real joy of discovery.

From Los Alamos to the Classroom

During the Manhattan Project, while other scientists stressed over nuclear calculations, Feynman relieved tension by picking classified safes - not to steal secrets, but to expose security flaws. Later at Caltech, his legendary Feynman Lectures on Physics became the gold standard for physics education. Who else could explain quantum spin by comparing it to a spinning plate in zero gravity?

The Ice Water That Shook NASA

Feynman's most dramatic public moment came during the 1986 Challenger disaster investigation. In a stunning live demonstration, he dropped a rubber O-ring into ice water (-1°C, the launch temperature) and showed how it lost elasticity (Rogers Commission Report, 1986). His simple experiment exposed NASA's fatal oversight and cemented his famous warning:

"For a successful technology, reality must take precedence over public relations, for nature cannot be fooled."

This moment perfectly captured Feynman's core belief: Truth should be so clear it fits on a cocktail napkin.

Legacy: The Joy of Finding Things Out

What makes Feynman endure isn't just his science - it's his infectious curiosity. Whether explaining why trains wobble or how rubber bands stretch, he showed that physics wasn't about memorising formulas but about falling in love with the world's beautiful complexity.

Frederick Sanger: The Quiet Revolutionary Who Decoded Life's Blueprint Twice

Imagine winning one Nobel Prize - now picture doing it twice in the same field! That's the extraordinary legacy of Frederick Sanger (1918-2013), the unassuming British biochemist from

Gloucestershire who cracked two of biology's greatest puzzles: protein sequences and DNA. What's most remarkable? He did it with homemade tools and relentless patience when most scientists thought these feats were impossible.

The Insulin Detective Work (1940s-1950s)

In post-war Cambridge, while others focused on flashier research, Sanger patiently unravelled insulin's structure like a molecular Sherlock Holmes. Using paper chromatography (imagine sophisticated coffee filter chemistry) and chemical degradation, he spent a decade piecing together insulin's 51-amino acid sequence.

"Why does this matter?" you might ask. Before Sanger:

- Proteins were mysterious macromolecules
- We didn't understand how sequence determines function
- Diabetes treatment relied on crude animal insulin extracts

His 1958 Nobel Prize wasn't just an award - it proved life's machinery follows a precise chemical code (Nobel Foundation, 1958).

From Proteins to DNA: The Sequencing Revolution (1970s)

Just when colleagues thought he'd retire on his laurels, Sanger turned to DNA. His ingenious dideoxy method (later called Sanger sequencing) worked like molecular scissors:

1. Create DNA fragments that stop at each base (A, C, G, T)
2. Separate them by size using electrophoresis
3. Read the genetic code like a ladder's rungs

The result? In 1977, his team sequenced φX174 bacteriophage - all 5,386 bases of it. This earned him a second Nobel in 1980, making him one of only four double laureates in history.

Legacy: The Tools That Built Modern Biology

Sanger's quiet persistence gave science two foundational tools:

1. Protein sequencing → Enabled engineered insulin (saving millions of diabetics)
2. DNA sequencing → Made the Human Genome Project possible

He famously declined knighthood, saying, *"I don't want to be different"*. Yet his methods changed biology forever.

Rosalind Franklin: The Overlooked Architect of DNA's Double Helix

How does science remember its pioneers? All too often, it's like watching a play where the stagehands never take a bow. This was the fate of **Rosalind Franklin** (1920-1958), the brilliant London-born chemist whose X-ray images revealed DNA's structure, yet who watched from the wings as Watson, Crick, and Wilkins accepted the Nobel Prize for her work.

Photo 51: The Shot That Changed Biology (But Stole Her Credit)

At King's College London, Franklin perfected X-ray crystallography like no one before her. Her student Raymond Gosling captured the now-legendary Photo 51 in 1952 - an X-ray diffraction image so clear it practically screamed "double helix!".

But here's the bitter twist: Without her knowledge or consent, Maurice Wilkins showed this image to James Watson. Like seeing the final puzzle piece, Watson immediately recognized its significance. Within weeks, he and Crick published their famous DNA model in *Nature* (1953) - with only a passing mention of Franklin's "unpublished work".

"Why does this still sting?", because Franklin's meticulous measurements (showing DNA's 20Å diameter and 3.4Å helix turns)

were the backbone of their theory - yet she never received proper credit during her lifetime.

From DNA to Viruses: A Legacy Cut Short

After this betrayal, Franklin moved to Birkbeck College, where she:

- Mapped the tobacco mosaic virus (TMV) structure
- Revealed how RNA winds within viruses
- Mentored future Nobel laureate Aaron Klug, who openly credited her methods (Klug, 1968)

Tragically, ovarian cancer claimed her at just 37 - four years before the Nobel Prize was awarded for "her" discovery. Even in death, the committee ignored her, honouring only the men (Nobel Foundation, 1962).

Posthumous Justice: The Franklin Effect

Today, we know the truth:

1. Her notebooks prove she deduced DNA's helical symmetry first (Elkin, 2003)
2. Modern re-enactments show Photo 51 alone was enough to solve the structure
3. Laboratories worldwide now teach the "Franklin Method" of crystallography

Perhaps Franklin's greatest legacy? A cautionary tale about how prejudice can blind even science - and a reminder that credit, like DNA, sometimes takes decades to unwind properly.

Rosalyn Yalow: The Nuclear Physicist Who Turned Radiation Into Life-Saving Medicine

What if the same atomic science that built bombs could cure disease? This was the radical question driving **Rosalyn Yalow** (1921-

2011), a Bronx-born physicist who transformed nuclear physics into a medical superpower. In an era when women were expected to be secretaries or schoolteachers, Yalow fought her way into the Manhattan Project's labs - only to later ask: *"Could radioisotopes diagnose rather than destroy?"*

From Atomic Bombs to Diabetes Breakthroughs

After WWII, while most nuclear researchers chased bigger explosions, Yalow partnered with Dr. Solomon Berson to explore a revolutionary idea: **using radioactive tracers as medical detectives**. Their target? Insulin - the hormone that diabetes patients desperately needed to understand.

Here's how their "Radioimmunoassay" (RIA) worked:

1. Tag insulin with radioactive iodine-125 (like putting a GPS tracker on a molecule)
2. Mix it with blood samples and antibodies
3. Measure the radiation to detect insulin levels a million times smaller than ever before

"Why does this matter?" Because for the first time, doctors could:

- Diagnose type 2 diabetes years earlier
- Prove that insulin resistance was real
- Personalise treatment doses (Nobel Foundation, 1977)

The Bittersweet Nobel

When Yalow won the 1977 Nobel Prize in Physiology or Medicine, it was historic:

✓ First American-born woman to win in this category

✓ Developed entirely outside major research institutions

✓ Proved that nuclear physics could heal rather than harm

Yet there was tragedy too - her partner Berson had died years earlier and couldn't share the honour.

RIA's Legacy: From Dominance to Niche

Like vinyl records in the Spotify era, RIA was eventually replaced by safer ELISA tests. But don't be fooled - this pioneer still shines where it counts:

- RIA's sensitivity remains unmatched for rare hormones
- It paved the way for every modern blood test
- Proved that cross-disciplinary science (physics + medicine) saves lives

Next time you get a blood test, remember Yalow - the woman who saw radiation's healing light when everyone else only saw its destructive flash.

Har Gobind Khorana: The Molecule Architect Who Cracked Life's Alphabet

What if you could write in the language of life itself? This wasn't just a thought experiment for Har Gobind Khorana (1922-2011) - the Punjab-born scientist who went from herding cattle in rural India to literally spelling out the genetic code in a Wisconsin lab. His story proves that scientific genius can bloom anywhere, even when you start with nothing but curiosity.

From Humble Beginnings to Genetic Breakthroughs

Khorana's journey was anything but ordinary. After earning his PhD in organic chemistry (against all odds in colonial India), he asked a revolutionary question: *"If DNA is life's instruction manual, can we learn to read - and write - its sentences?"*.

His approach was brilliantly straightforward:

1. Build RNA words - He chemically synthesized short RNA strands with specific codon sequences (like "ACU" for threonine)
2. Decode their meaning - By observing which amino acids they produced in cell-free systems
3. Verify the dictionary - Confirming that 64 possible codons specify 20 amino acids

Why does this matter? Before Khorana, we knew DNA carried information - but he gave us the Rosetta Stone to read it.

The Ultimate Test: Writing Genes From Scratch

Not content with just reading nature's code, Khorana aimed to write it. In 1970, his team:

- ✓ Created the first synthetic gene (a yeast tRNA)
- ✓ Successfully inserted it into living bacteria
- ✓ Proved artificial genes could function like natural ones

This was biological alchemy - turning chemicals into working genetic material.

A Legacy That Still Replicates Today

Khorana's phosphodiester bond technique became the foundation for:

- Automated DNA synthesizers (now used in every biotech lab)
- Gene editing technologies like CRISPR
- The entire synthetic biology field

When he shared the 1968 Nobel Prize with Holley and Nirenberg, it wasn't just for cracking the genetic code - but for giving us the tools to rewrite it.

Next time you hear about synthetic life or gene therapy, remember Khorana - the boy from a small Indian village who taught us to speak DNA's language.

Tsung-Dao Lee and the Mirror Universe That Wasn't: How Physics Lost Its Symmetry

What if the universe had a favourite hand? That's the earth-shattering question **Tsung-Dao Lee** (1926-2024) and Chen-Ning Yang dared to ask in the 1950s, challenging one of physics' most sacred cows: parity conservation. It was as radical as suggesting gravity might sometimes push instead of pull.

The Mirror That Lied

Imagine brushing your teeth left-handed in a mirror world. Parity conservation claimed the physics should feel identical - but Lee and Yang suspected nature might be right-handed (or left-handed) in certain situations.

"Why did everyone believe this symmetry was absolute?" Because it held perfectly for:

- Gravity (Newton's apple falls the same way in any mirror)
- Electromagnetism (light behaves identically in reflection) But the weak force? That was another story.

The Experiment That Shook Physics

Enter Chien-Shiung Wu - "the First Lady of Physics" - who designed an experiment more elegant than a Swiss watch:

1. Supercooled cobalt-60 atoms to near absolute zero
2. Aligned their spins like compass needles with a magnetic field
3. Observed beta particles fleeing preferentially opposite the spin direction

The result? A cosmic left-handed preference so clear it made physicists gasp. As Freeman Dyson later quipped: *"The mirror wasn't broken - it never existed to begin with."*

Nobel Glory and Glaring Omissions

While Lee and Yang won the 1957 Nobel Prize (the fastest awarded in physics history), Wu was conspicuously absent from the podium - a snub still debated today. Her meticulous experiment:

- ✓ Confirmed parity violation conclusively
- ✓ Opened doors to CP violation studies
- ✓ Explained why the universe favors matter over antimatter

Ironically, the same bias Wu exposed in nature (left vs. right) mirrored academia's bias against women scientists.

Legacy: The Crooked Universe

This discovery didn't just break symmetry - it shattered paradigms:

1. **Electroweak unification** became possible
2. **Standard Model** gained critical validation
3. **Modern particle accelerators** trace their lineage to Wu's cobalt experiment

As Lee himself reflected: *"Sometimes to find truth, you must first lose symmetry."* A lesson both profound and painfully human.

James Dewey Watson (1928-), **Francis Harry Compton Crick** (1916-2004), **Maurie Wilkins** (1916-2004)

When it comes to the discovery of the double helix structure of DNA, four people were involved in the success of the finding. Nobel prizes went to James Dewey Watson, Francis Harry Compton Crick and Maurice Wilkins, leaving out Roslyn Elsie Franklin, who deserved the most. Watson and the team used X-ray data available from Franklin to introduce DNA's molecular structure model.

DNA consists of two twisted strands forming a double helix. Each strand has a sugar-phosphate backbone made of deoxyribose and phosphate groups arranged in opposing directions (antiparallel orientation). Nitrogenous bases attached to the sugar molecules function as the information carriers of the DNA molecule. The four bases in DNA are adenine, cytosine, guanine, and thymine.

The double helix configuration of DNA, featuring its unique base-pairing rules and antiparallel strands, guarantees that genetic data is preserved precisely and can be duplicated consistently. This graceful design is essential to every living being.

Stephen Hawking: The Cosmic Rebel Who Gave Black Holes an Expiration Date

What happens when a brilliant mind gets trapped in a failing body? Stephen Hawking (1948-2016) answered this question spectacularly - by setting his intellect free to roam the cosmos. Diagnosed with ALS at 21 and given just years to live, this Cambridge physicist would go on to revolutionise our understanding of black holes and the birth of the universe, all while becoming the most recognisable scientist since Einstein.

The Discovery That Shook Astrophysics

In 1974, Hawking dropped a bombshell: *"Black holes aren't so black after all!"* His theory of Hawking radiation revealed that:

- Due to quantum fluctuations at the event horizon, black holes slowly leak energy
- They can eventually evaporate completely
- This created the "information paradox" that still puzzles physicists today

Imagine that - the universe's ultimate vacuum cleaners actually have a slow leak! This groundbreaking work married Einstein's relativity with quantum mechanics in ways nobody had dreamed possible.

From Big Bang to No Boundaries

With Roger Penrose, Hawking proved that:

- ✓ The universe must have begun as a singularity
- ✓ Black holes inevitably form singularities
- ✓ Time itself began at the Big Bang

Later, he proposed the mind-bending "no-boundary" hypothesis with James Hartle - suggesting the universe is like the surface of a sphere: finite but without edges. "What came before the Big Bang?" becomes as meaningless as asking "What's north of the North Pole?"

The Pop Culture Physicist

Despite his debilitating disease, Hawking:

- Wrote *A Brief History of Time* (1988), which sold over 25 million copies
- Voiced himself on *The Simpsons* and *Star Trek*
- Inspired millions with his wit and perseverance

His quest for a Theory of Everything remains unfulfilled, but as he often said: *"Remember to look up at the stars, not down at your feet."* (Hawking, 2013).

Peter Higgs: The Quiet Genius Who Gave Mass to the Universe

What gives everything in the universe its weight? This deceptively simple question haunted physicists for decades until Peter Higgs (1929-2024), a modest British theorist, proposed a revolutionary answer in 1964 - one so bold even his peers initially rejected it (Higgs, 1964). Little did they know this soft-spoken professor from Edinburgh was about to rewrite the rules of particle physics.

The "Eureka" Moment That Almost Wasn't

Picture Edinburgh, 1964: Higgs scribbles equations that suggest an invisible field permeates the cosmos like cosmic molasses. But here's the twist - when he first submitted his paper to Physics Letters, it was rejected as "of no obvious relevance to physics". Talk about scientific irony!

His theory proposed that:

- Particles gain mass by interacting with what we now call the Higgs field
- The stronger the interaction, the heavier the particle
- This happens through exchanges with Higgs bosons - the field's quantum manifestations

"Why does this matter?" Because without this mechanism:

✓ Electrons wouldn't orbit atoms

✓ Stars couldn't ignite

✓ You literally wouldn't exist

The Long Wait for Validation

For nearly 50 years, Higgs' theory remained just that - a theory. Then, on July 4, 2012, CERN announced the unthinkable: they'd found the Higgs boson (ATLAS Collaboration, 2012). The detection required:

- A 27km underground particle collider
- Temperatures colder than outer space
- Data equivalent to stacking CDs from Earth to Neptune and back 7 times

When the news broke, Higgs famously wiped a tear from his eye - the ultimate "I told you so" moment in scientific history.

Legacy: The Universe's Weight Watchers

Higgs' work completed the Standard Model like the final piece of a cosmic jigsaw puzzle. Yet true to form, when asked about his Nobel Prize (2013), he quipped: *"It's been a long time coming... and I'm glad it's over."* (Nobel Foundation, 2013).

Next time you step on a scale, remember - you're not just measuring your weight, but your interaction with an invisible quantum field predicted by a humble British physicist.

Roger Penrose: The Maverick Who Saw Infinity (And Tried to Tile It)

What happens when a mathematician stares into a black hole and sees art? You get **Sir Roger Penrose** (1931-) - the brilliant British physicist who proved Einstein right about singularities, then went on to challenge everything we know about consciousness. I've watched most of his interviews (he gives them reluctantly, like a cat being petted), and what strikes me most is how he sees the universe differently - literally.

The Man Who Mathematically Proved Black Holes Are Real

In 1965, while others debated whether singularities were mathematical quirks, Penrose did something extraordinary: **he proved they were inevitable**. His singularity theorem showed that when massive stars collapse, they don't just form black holes - they create regions where:

- Density becomes infinite
- Space and time curve beyond recognition
- Physics as we know it stops working (Penrose, 1965)

"Why does this matter?" Because it was the first rigorous proof that Einstein's wildest predictions weren't just fantasy - and it paved the way for Hawking's groundbreaking work

A Geometer's Playground

Penrose's genius isn't confined to black holes. He's also the mind behind:

- **Penrose diagrams**: The "Google Maps" of spacetime that help physicists navigate cosmic monsters
- **Penrose tiles**: Mathematical patterns that never repeat, yet cover infinite planes perfectly
- **Twistor theory**: A radical approach that replaces coordinates with complex geometry

Here's the kicker: His tiles were considered pure mathematical play until 1984, when quasicrystals were discovered - materials with those exact non-repeating patterns. Sometimes, reality catches up with genius.

The Consciousness Crusade

Never one to shy away from controversy, Penrose ventured where most physicists fear to tread: **the human mind**. His Orch-OR theory with Hameroff proposes:

- ✓ Consciousness arises from quantum vibrations in microtubules
- ✓ The brain might be a quantum computer
- ✓ Current AI can never achieve true awareness

The establishment scoffs, but as Penrose quips: *"If you're not offending somebody, you're probably not saying anything interesting."* (Penrose, 1994).

Nobel Glory and Beyond

When he won the 2020 Nobel Prize at 89, it was for work done in the 1960s - proving that good science ages like fine wine. Yet true to form, he's still working on his cyclical universe theory (CCC), suggesting:

- The Big Bang was preceded by another universe
- Time is infinite but broken into "aeons"
- Black holes hold clues to the next cosmic cycle

Final thought: In an era of hyperspecialisation, Penrose reminds us that the most exciting ideas often live at the boundaries - between physics and art, between the very large and very small, between what we know and what we dare to imagine.

J. Craig Venter: The Maverick Who Cracked Life's Code (And Rode the Storm)

What happens when a Vietnam medic-turned-scientist decides to sequence the human genome against all odds? You get **J. Craig Venter (1946 -),** the brash, brilliant, and often controversial figure who turned biology upside down. Love him or loathe him, this is the man who raced the US government to map human DNA... and won.

From Battlefields to Genetic Frontiers

Venter's journey reads like a Hollywood script:

- Dropped out of high school to surf
- Served as a Navy corpsman in Vietnam (where he nearly drowned)
- Earned his PhD studying adrenaline receptors

The Genome Wars

In the 1990s, while the $3 billion Human Genome Project plodded along, Venter dropped a bombshell: **shotgun sequencing**. Imagine shredding millions of DNA copies into pieces, then having a supercomputer reassemble them like a cosmic jigsaw puzzle.

The establishment scoffed. *"It'll never work!"* they said. But Venter's startup Celera Genomics:

- ✓ Sequenced the human genome in just 3 years (vs. the projected 15)
- ✓ Forced the public project to accelerate
- ✓ Published simultaneously with NIH in 2001

The irony? The "outsider" had beaten the system at its own game.

Creating Life 2.0

Never one to rest, Venter then:

- Built the first synthetic organism (Mycoplasma laboratorium) in 2010
- Designed Syn 3.0 - a minimal genome with just 473 genes
- Encoded secret messages in DNA like a molecular Banksy

His 2014 venture Human Longevity Inc. asks perhaps the ultimate question: *"What if we could read our DNA like a medical crystal ball?"*

The Legacy of a Scientific Rebel

Venter embodies the tension between:

- Open science vs. commercialisation
- Individual brilliance vs. institutional research
- Breakthrough speed vs. careful validation

As he famously said: *"I don't want to die without doing something important first."* (Venter, 2007). Given he sequenced his own genome and founded over a dozen companies, it's safe to say mission accomplished.

Sir Tim Berners-Lee (1955 -): The Accidental Revolutionary Who Wove Our Digital World

What were you doing in 1989? While most of us were listening to Walkmans or watching the Berlin Wall fall, an unassuming British physicist at CERN was quietly inventing something that would change civilisation more than any political event - the World Wide Web. And the most remarkable part? He gave it away for free.

From Scrapheap Computer to Digital Revolution

Picture a young Tim Berners-Lee at Oxford in the 1970s, soldering together a computer from spare parts - a fitting metaphor for how he'd later assemble the web from existing technologies (Gillies & Cailliau, 2000). His background was perfect for the challenge:

- Parents worked on Britain's first commercial computer
- Physics degree gave him systems-thinking skills
- CERN's chaotic information needs provided the perfect laboratory

"Why did this particular scientist succeed where others failed?" Perhaps because he saw the problem differently - not as a technology challenge, but as a human one.

The Birth of the Web: A Story in Three Acts

1. The Spark (1980): His early program "Enquire" (named after a Victorian etiquette book!) linked ideas randomly - like a primitive Wikipedia (Berners-Lee, 1989 proposal)
2. The Breakthrough (1989-91): Working on a sleek NeXT computer (Steve Jobs' pet project), he created:
    - HTML: The skeleton of web pages
    - HTTP: The nervous system
    - URLs: The global addressing system

3. The Gift (1991): He released it all - no patents, no royalties. *"What if he'd charged just 1% royalty?"* He'd be the richest person alive today.

The Web's Midlife Crisis

Today, Sir Tim fights for the web's soul through:

- W3C: Guarding open standards since 1994
- Solid Project: His plan to break up Big Tech's data monopolies (Berners-Lee, 2021 TED Talk)
- Web Foundation: Advocating for digital human rights

The first website (info.cern.ch) is still online - a digital museum piece!

Why This Matters More Than Ever

As we wrestle with misinformation and privacy concerns, Berners-Lee's original vision shines brighter:

✓ **Openness** over walled gardens

✓ **Decentralisation** over monopolies

✓ **Utility** over exploitation

His knighthood and Turing Award (2016) honour not just technical brilliance, but profound humanity. In an age of tech billionaires, he remains that rare inventor who valued impact over income.

SUMMARY

The 20th Century: When Humans Cracked the Cosmic Codebook

What an extraordinary century to be alive! The 1900s weren't just about world wars and rock music - they were the time when our species finally began to decipher nature's secret languages. From the atom's heart to DNA's double helix, we went from tinkering with steam engines to holding the blueprints of life itself. Let's take a victory lap through these game-changing discoveries:

The Nuclear Paradox: Power and Peril in One Package

Remember that famous Chicago football game they never finished? On December 2, 1942, under those same bleachers, Enrico Fermi's team achieved something far more monumental - the first controlled nuclear chain reaction. Talk about a double-edged sword! This breakthrough gave us:

- Clean energy potential
- Devastating weapons
- The sobering realisation that excellent knowledge brings great responsibility

The Tiny Switch That Changed Everything

While nuclear physics made headlines, three quiet geniuses (Bardeen, Brattain, and Shockley) were cooking up something equally revolutionary in a Bell Labs basement - the humble transistor. *"Why care about a microscopic switch?"* Because without it, you wouldn't be reading this on your phone/laptop/tablet right now! Their 1947 invention became the Lego blocks of the Digital Age.

The DNA Decoders

Then came biology's big bang:

- Feynman gave us quantum doodles (those delightful diagrams)
- Sanger invented genetic "reading" (sequencing life's alphabet)
- Watson & Co. revealed DNA's elegant spiral staircase
- Venter turbocharged genomics like a biological Steve Jobs

The human genome contains about 3 billion base pairs - if printed as text, it would fill 200 Manhattan phone books (Venter, 2007)!

Penrose: Mapping the Mind-Bending Universe

And let's not forget Sir Roger, who:

- Proved black holes weren't sci-fi
- Created mathematical art (those Penrose tiles)
- Dared to ask if quantum physics explains consciousness

All these breakthroughs happened within just 60 years - barely a cosmic blink!

Next Stop: The 21st Century Frontier

Hold onto your lab coats, because in our next chapter, we're diving into:

- CRISPR gene editing
- Quantum computing
- Climate
- AI revolutions
- And who knows what else!

If the 20th century taught us anything, it's that human curiosity knows no bounds. The real question is - what will we discover next?

CHAPTER 7

The 21st Century and the Future of Science

7.1 CRISPR: The Bacterial Superpower That Revolutionised Genetic Engineering

What if I told you the most powerful gene-editing tool was stolen from bacteria? That's exactly what happened when Emmanuelle Charpentier and Jennifer Doudna cracked nature's genetic cut-and-paste system in 2012, earning them the Nobel Prize in Chemistry (2020). But like all great discoveries, this story has many heroes.

The Accidental Discovery That Changed Everything

Decades before CRISPR became a household name, scientists like Francisco Mojica were puzzling over strange repeating sequences in bacterial DNA. Mojica, studying salt-loving microbes in Spain, realized these CRISPR sequences were essentially "mugshots" of past viral invaders - a bacterial immune system (Mojica et al., 2005).

"Why didn't bacteria get Nobel Prizes for inventing this first?" you might ask. Because it took Charpentier and Doudna's brilliance to realise we could hijack this system to edit any organism's DNA.

How CRISPR Works: Nature's Genetic Swiss Army Knife

Imagine you're a bacterium under viral attack. Your CRISPR system works like this:

1. Memory bank: Stores snippets of viral DNA in CRISPR arrays ("genetic wanted posters")
2. GPS-guided scissors: Uses guide RNA to lead Cas9 enzymes to matching viral DNA
3. Cut!: Slices the invader's DNA like molecular scissors

Charpentier and Doudna's genius was realising we could:

✓ Design custom guide RNAs to target any gene

✓ Use this in plants, animals, and even human cells

✓ Edit DNA with precision never before possible

Designing a CRISPR experiment is now so simple, undergrads can do it - a far cry from the painstaking gene-editing methods of the past!

The CRISPR Revolution: From Lab to Clinic

This technology is already changing lives:

- **Cancer treatment**: Engineered immune cells hunting down tumours
- **Genetic diseases**: Fixing mutations causing sickle cell anaemia
- **Agriculture**: Creating disease-resistant crops without GMO fears

But with great power comes great responsibility. When Chinese scientist He Jiankui created the first CRISPR-edited babies in 2018, the world gasped. *"Have we gone too far?"* The ethical debate rages on.

What's Next?

As we stand at this genetic crossroads, one thing's clear: CRISPR has given us unprecedented control over life's code. The question isn't *can we* edit genes, but *should we* - and how wisely we'll use this extraordinary tool.

7.2 Quantum Computing: The Spooky Science That Could Change Everything

What if your computer could be in two places at once? Welcome to the bizarre world of quantum computing, where the standard rules of physics take a coffee break. While your laptop struggles with spreadsheets, quantum computers harness the strangest phenomena in physics to solve problems we once thought impossible.

The Quantum Difference: Why This Isn't Just a Faster Computer

Imagine flipping a coin. In our everyday world, it's either heads or tails. But in the quantum realm, that coin is spinning so fast it's somehow both at once - this is superposition, the first trick up quantum computing's sleeve.

Now, picture two coins spinning in perfect sync across the universe - change one, and the other instantly changes too. This entanglement (which Einstein called "spooky action at a distance") lets qubits communicate faster than light.

Finally, think of these quantum states as ripples in a pond. When they overlap just right (interference), they can amplify the right answers and cancel out the wrong ones. Together, these phenomena let quantum computers explore millions of solutions simultaneously. Crack problems that would take regular computers millennia. Potentially revolutionise fields from medicine to finance

"But why isn't my laptop quantum yet?" you might ask. Well...

From Theory to (Almost) Reality: A Quantum Timeline

The quantum computing story reads like scientific drama:

- **1980s**: Richard Feynman, ever the visionary, suggests quantum systems could simulate nature better than classical computers (Feynman, 1982)
- **1994**: Peter Shor drops a bombshell - quantum computers could break modern encryption (Shor, 1994)
- **2019**: Google's Sycamore processor completes in 200 seconds what they claim would take a supercomputer 10,000 years (though IBM argues it's more like 2.5 days) (Arute et al., 2019)
- **Today**: We're in the "Noisy Intermediate-Scale Quantum" (NISQ) era - think of it as the Wright brothers phase of quantum flight

Current quantum computers are so delicate that they operate at temperatures colder than outer space to prevent quantum decoherence (basically, quantum stage fright).

The Quantum Future: Hype or Hope?

While your quantum smartphone isn't coming tomorrow, the potential is staggering:

- Medicine: Simulating drug interactions atom-by-atom could slash development time from years to days
- Climate Science: Modelling complex weather patterns with unprecedented accuracy
- Finance: Optimising global markets in real-time
- AI: Training neural networks on datasets we can't currently handle

But here's the catch - quantum computers won't replace classical ones. They're more like specialised power tools for specific jobs.

And yes, they could break current encryption... but they'll also create unhackable quantum encryption in return.

The bottom line? We're witnessing the birth of an entirely new form of computation. It's messy, it's exciting, and it might just change everything.

7.3 Our Climate Crossroads: How Science Can Help Heal the Planet

What if I told you we've known about climate change for nearly 200 years? The story of our climate crisis reads like a slow-motion car crash we saw coming but couldn't stop. From 19th-century scientists connecting the dots to today's desperate race for solutions, this is humanity's most significant test - and our most urgent opportunity.

The Ghosts of Climate Science Past

The climate warning signs were there all along:

- **1824**: French physicist Joseph Fourier does the math and realises Earth should be an ice ball. His "greenhouse effect" theory suggests our atmosphere acts like a cosy blanket (Fourier, 1824).
- **1859**: Irish scientist John Tyndall identifies the culprits - CO_2 and water vapour - calling them "heat-trapping gases" (Tyndall, 1861).
- **1896**: Svante Arrhenius calculates that doubling CO_2 could raise global temps by 5-6°C. He ironically thought this might prevent future ice ages (Arrhenius, 1896)!

"Why didn't we listen?" Perhaps because these warnings came decades before the first Model T rolled off Ford's assembly line.

The Smoking Gun: Keeling's Curve

Enter Charles Keeling in 1958, meticulously measuring CO_2 atop Mauna Loa. His now-iconic curve shows:

- Pre-industrial CO_2: 280 ppm
- 2020 levels: 420 ppm (highest in 3 million years)
- Annual increase: 2-3 ppm - like adding another layer to that atmospheric blanket each year (Keeling et al., 1976)

The numbers don't lie:

+1.2°C since 1880

Oceans have been rising 20cm since 1900

Last decade: hottest on record

Renewable Revolution: Our Best Shot

Here's the good news - we have the tools to change course:

1. **Solar Power**: Enough sunlight hits Earth in 90 minutes to power humanity for a year (Lewis, 2007)
2. **Wind Energy**: Modern turbines can power 2,000 homes each
3. **Nuclear**: Despite fears, it's our most reliable zero-carbon baseload (MIT, 2018)
4. **Emerging Tech**: From green hydrogen to fusion, the pipeline looks promising

But here's the catch: We're in a race against physics. Every 0.1°C matters, and as climate scientist Katharine Hayhoe says, *"The most important thing you can do is talk about climate change."*

Our Karma, Our Choice

The science is precise, the solutions exist - what's missing is collective will. As the IPCC warns, we have perhaps until 2030 to make a dramatic change in course (IPCC, 2021). The question isn't whether we can solve this, but whether we'll choose to.

Final thought: Future generations won't care about our excuses - only whether we left them a livable world.

7.4 Future of Science

For me, the "**Before the Big Bang**" Question is the most challenging subject to answer. I will leave it to the next generation to accomplish, if possible, with evidence to support it. One of my insights is that there is some form of cyclic process involved for the Universe to exist. Roger Penrose's Conformal Cyclic Cosmology (CCC) is a mostly ambitious and speculative theory that proposes the universe undergoes an infinite sequence of cycles, or "aeons." Each aeon begins with a Big Bang, expands, and eventually becomes dominated by massless particles (like photons and gravitons) as all massive particles decay (including protons and electrons, which is a significant point of contention with the Standard Model). In this infinitely expanded, massless state, the universe becomes conformally smooth, allowing its future conformal infinity to be identified with the Big Bang of the next aeon.

Here's how future science might address CCC, along with the challenges and potential evidence:

How Future Science Will Address CCC

Future scientific endeavours will likely focus on:

1. **Observational Evidence from the Cosmic Microwave Background (CMB):**
    - **Hawking Points:** Penrose and his collaborators have claimed to find "Hawking points" in the CMB, which are anomalous spots of unusually high or low temperature. These are hypothesized to be the residual radiation from the evaporation of supermassive black holes in the previous aeon that crossed over into our current aeon.

- **Concentric Circles:** Another predicted signature is the presence of concentric circular patterns in the CMB, which could arise from the gravitational radiation emitted by collisions of supermassive black holes in the preceding aeon.
- **Future CMB Missions:** More precise and higher-resolution CMB data from future missions could either confirm these faint signals or definitively rule them out. The current consensus among most cosmologists is that the claimed signals are not statistically significant and can be explained by random fluctuations within the standard inflationary model, once the "look-elsewhere effect" is accounted for (An et al., 2020; Bodnia et al., 2022). Future missions will need to overcome these challenges and provide irrefutable evidence.

2. **Particle Physics and Fundamental Laws:**
    - **Proton and Electron Decay:** A cornerstone of CCC is the requirement that all massive particles, including protons and electrons, must eventually decay or become massless. While proton decay is hypothesized in some speculative extensions of the Standard Model (e.g., Grand Unified Theories), it has never been observed, and the predicted lifetimes are extremely long (far beyond the current age of the universe). Electron decay or loss of mass is even more problematic and not predicted by conventional particle physics.
    - **Neutrino Mass:** Penrose has nuanced his earlier strong requirement for *no* mass, allowing some massive particles as long as their contribution is insignificant and energy is dominated by kinetic energy in a conformal geometry (Penrose, 2020 Nobel Prize Lecture). However, the implications of neutrino mass for the "smoothing out" process between aeons still need to be rigorously addressed.

- **Experimental Verification:** Future particle physics experiments, such as those searching for proton decay, could directly test this crucial assumption of CCC. If protons are found to be absolutely stable, it would be a severe blow to the theory.

3. **Theoretical Refinements and Alternatives:**
   - **Mathematical Rigor:** While CCC is mathematically elegant, especially concerning conformal geometry, the physical mechanisms for the "crossover" between aeons need more detailed explanation. Recent work by Meissner and Penrose attempts to provide a more detailed description of this crossover through a "gravitational wave epoch" (Meissner & Penrose, 2025).
   - **Information Paradox:** CCC offers a potential solution to the black hole information paradox by suggesting that fermions are irreversibly converted into radiation during black hole evaporation, preserving the smoothness of the boundary between aeons. Future developments in quantum gravity and black hole thermodynamics could shed light on this aspect.
   - **Comparison with Inflationary Cosmology:** CCC provides an alternative to cosmic inflation for explaining the initial low entropy of the universe and the near scale-invariance of CMB fluctuations. Future theoretical work will continue to compare the explanatory power and predictive capabilities of CCC against inflationary models, as well as other cyclic or bounce cosmologies.
4. **Gravitational Wave Astronomy:**
   - **Primordial Gravitational Waves:** CCC predicts that a certain amount of gravitational radiation should be preserved across the boundary between aeons. This "extra" gravitational radiation could potentially explain the observed cosmic acceleration without resorting to dark

energy. Future gravitational wave detectors (e.g., LIGO/Virgo upgrades, LISA) might be sensitive enough to detect such relic gravitational waves, providing a unique observational test.

Challenges and Criticisms

CCC faces significant challenges and is not widely accepted by the cosmological community. Key criticisms include:

- **Lack of Conclusive Observational Evidence:** The claimed CMB anomalies have not been independently reproduced with statistical significance. Many argue that they are consistent with random fluctuations or foreground contamination (Hajian, 2011; Jow & Scott, 2020; Bodnia et al., 2022).
- **Fundamental Particle Physics Assumptions:** The requirement for all massive particles (especially electrons) to eventually lose their mass or decay contradicts the current Standard Model of particle physics, for which there is strong experimental support.
- **The Borde-Guth-Vilenkin Theorem:** This theorem suggests that expanding universes (under certain energy conditions) must have an absolute beginning. Penrose's model attempts to circumvent this by assuming an infinitely large universe in the infinite past, which some find philosophically problematic.
- **The Nature of the Crossover:** While mathematically elegant, the physical mechanism for how a universe with infinite spatial extent and extreme dilution at the end of one aeon seamlessly transitions into a hot, dense singularity at the beginning of the next, while preserving physical laws, remains a point of contention and requires further detailed physical justification.

Citations and References

- Primary Source: Penrose's ideas on CCC are extensively discussed in his book "Cycles of Time: An Extraordinary New View of the Universe."

Key Papers and Discussions:

- Penrose, R. (2006). "Conformal Cyclic Cosmology." *AIP Conference Proceedings*, 957(1), 1-13. (While an early presentation, subsequent work has developed the theory further).
- Gurzadyan, V. G., & Penrose, R. (2010). "Concentric circles in WMAP data may provide evidence of pre-Big Bang activity." *arXiv preprint arXiv:1011.3706*. (This paper made the initial claims about CMB anomalies).
- Hajian, A. (2011). "The search for concentric circles in the cosmic microwave background." *Physical Review Letters*, 107(15), 151301. (One of the early papers refuting the statistical significance of the claimed circles).
- An, T., Meissner, K. A., Nurowski, P., & Penrose, R. (2020). "Apparent Anomalies in the CMB, and Hawking Points." *Monthly Notices of the Royal Astronomical Society*, 496(2), 2291-2300. (Further claims of Hawking points and associated analysis).
- Jow, D., & Scott, D. (2020). "Concentric circles in the cosmic microwave background revisited." *Monthly Notices of the Royal Astronomical Society*, 497(3), 3290-3298. (Another paper challenging the claims of CMB anomalies).
- Bodnia, E., Isenbaev, V., Colburn, K., Swearngin, J., & Bouwmeester, D. (2022). "The quest for CMB signatures of Conformal Cyclic Cosmology." *arXiv preprint arXiv:2208.06021*. (A comprehensive search for CCC signatures, finding no statistically significant evidence after accounting for unusual spots).

- Meissner, K. A., & Penrose, R. (2025). "The Physics of Conformal Cyclic Cosmology." *arXiv preprint arXiv:2503.24263*. (Recent work attempting to provide more detail on the crossover).

In summary, future science will continue to scrutinise CCC through precise CMB observations, advancements in particle physics (especially searches for proton and electron decay), and theoretical developments in quantum gravity. The current scientific consensus remains sceptical due to the lack of robust observational evidence and its reliance on unproven particle physics assumptions. Still, the elegance of Penrose's mathematical framework ensures that it continues to attract interest and investigation.

CHAPTER 8

8.1 Artificial Intelligence & Stewardship

Would AI be a conscious being one day? First, describe how AI comes into the world. Second part, what is consciousness?

Famous quote from René Descartes: "I think, therefore I am"

For AI, "I compute, therefore I am".

Roger Penrose explains that consciousness is not purely computational, whereas AI is fundamentally based on computation. A computer operates according to Turing machine logic. A Turing machine is a theoretical and abstract computing device introduced by Alan Turing in 1936. It manipulates symbols on an infinite tape according to a finite set of rules. This concept laid the groundwork for computer algorithms and the theory of computability.

What is understanding? Is it following the rules? Is it an algorithm? No, it does not follow an algorithm. What is it then? Thinking is a conscious process. Without qualia (subjective experience), there is no true consciousness. And qualia can't be computed—only simulated. Computation can model the behaviour of a mind, but not its being. But—Are Humans Fully Non-Computational? Here's the counterpoint often made by AI theorists: What if all human cognition, including your experience of being you, is emergent from complex computation? Maybe we just haven't found an algorithm that feels like a soul. In this view, consciousness is computational, but radically complex and embodied. Roger Penrose would disagree, but this is where mainstream AI research often tends to lean.

Let's examine AI first, and then we will cover consciousness and its connection to humans in later chapters. Before discussing the advantages and disadvantages of AI, let's examine how it has become an integral part of our lives. Initially, we will explore the emergence of computing power and the factors that contributed to advancements in artificial intelligence.

Charles Babbage's concepts of a general-purpose computer influenced later pioneers like Alan Turing and John von Neumann. His work inspired a new way of thinking about machines, ultimately leading to the development of modern computing technology. A Turing machine is a theoretical, abstract computing device that manipulates symbols on a potentially infinite tape according to a finite set of rules. It formed the foundation for computer algorithms and computability theory. If we consider the computer processing unit (CPU) as Charles Babbage proposed, the subsequent modification is not far from its original design.

To gain a basic understanding of computational systems, we can examine some of their components and functions related to processing. The basic CPU consists of the program counter, memory address register (MAR), memory contents, Instruction register, accumulator register, sum register, ALU (arithmetic logic unit) and input-output device connections. It functions as follows: The program counter sends the memory address to the MAR through the bus connection to fetch the opcode. Then MAR fetches the opcode and data from the memory location and sends them to the instruction register (IR). IR is then sent to the accumulator to store and perform the next operation. The result will be output to a display.

What makes the processor intelligent is the JMP (jump) instruction, which jumps into another location in memory to execute the program from there. This is a powerful feature in the CPU for executing programs. In high-level languages, we apply it in a manner akin to IF statements. Without the IF statements, the CPU cannot perform clever program executions. Jump instructions can be used to build intelligence. Without jumps, a computer marches forward like a zombie. With jumps, it starts to choose what to do. This is the key part played in the AI revolution of programming. **Remember,**

the conditional jump based on CPU flags, such as carry and zero, makes it possible for AI programs to make intelligent decisions, which is purely computational.

At the most fundamental level, intelligent behaviour in artificial systems emerges from the interplay of low-level machine flags and control flow. Based on flags like the carry and zero bits, conditional jumps form the foundation of all decision-making logic — the spark from which all AI cognition arises.

Let's investigate how AI is built from scratch, from logic gates to intelligence. Logic gates are made of transistors that turn on or off to represent 1s and 0s. They are wired together to create logic gates such as AND, OR, NOT, XOR, NAND, etc. These gates are atoms of digital logic. Gates are combined into circuits like adders, multipliers, and comparators, which live inside a CPU's ALU (arithmetic logic unit). When the ALU runs calculations, it sets status flags. (Zero, Carry, Negative). When JUMP instructions are set in the CPU, decision-making begins. Here's where we get actual control flow. JZ (Jump if Zero) → Go somewhere only if the result is zero. JC (Jump if Carry) → Go somewhere if we overflow. JMP (Jump always) → Go anywhere unconditionally. If-Else logic, For/While loops, Function calls, and recursions form the backbone of the algorithms of programming of AI. Allow me to present an example of an assembler program, which is as follows.

```
Loop:
  LOAD A, [i]
  CMP A, 0
  JZ End
  INC i
  JMP Loop
End:
```

Now, the machine can reason in steps, not just in a straight line. Any software developed by people or any software that can create programs employs the same logical steps demonstrated above in any computer processing unit. Neural networks are built on Math and logic. We use math circuits to simulate a neuron.

Output = activation (w1∗x1+w2∗x2+...+b)

Multipliers → weight (w1) * input(x1)

Adders → sum them up

Comparator + Jump → apply activation function (like Relu or Sigmoid)

Relu – (Rectified Linear Unit) is a popular activation function in neural networks.

Sigmoid -- is a logistic curve plot of the error function.

RELU in logic:

```
CMP A, 0

JL SetZero

JMP Continue

SetZero:

LOAD A, 0

Continue:
```

So even the fancy neural net... is just math + jumps and surely physics in future. Neural Net Layer Execution is each neuron's process: Multiply inputs × weights, add bias, apply activation (via conditional jump), and pass output to next layer. Each layer = more math + more flags + more jumps. Thousands of neurons running in parallel = pattern recognition engine. For example, "Is this a dog?" becomes: "If activation in neuron #392 > 0.8, then activate neuron #412…", a conditional logic outcome.

Now we investigate AI Models' training and Inference. Training = Loops of error calculation + weight updates (via math + control flow). Inference = Just running the network forward, many neurons deep. Each decision? It still boils down to comparing values, setting flags, and making jumps. For example, A GPT (Generative Pre-trained Transformer) prediction: "Given the word 'The', what word is likely next?" Internally, Softmax activation (built with math + logic) chooses the highest probability via comparison and jumps to that output. Intelligent Output by your AI chatbot replies: "The cat sat on the mat." But under the hood: Billions of instructions ran, Millions of comparisons made, Millions of flags set, Millions of jumps taken, all from transistors flipping based on rules we built.

To illustrate how an 8-bit computer simplifies logic operations inside a CPU, reference is made in **Appendix 4**. If you are feeling **adventurous**, please explore Appendix 4 for a detailed explanation of the CPU's workings of JMP instructions with flags. Modern processing units operate on the same principle, with added features that incorporate computational logic. The first processor was the 4-bit 4004 processor by Intel, introduced in 1971, and has evolved into today's high-end processors with multiple cores. Now we have GPUs (Graphics Processing Units), TPUs (Tensor Processing Units), FPGAs (Field-Programmable Gate Arrays), and NPUs (Neural Processing Units). Each is designed for different computing tasks. The underlying factor is that no matter how advanced we are with transistor technology, the logic behind the enormous power of current computing technology is based on logic, thus **computational**.

The Double-Edged Sword of AI: Promise and Peril

Imagine a tool so powerful it could cure cancer or start wars - that's AI today. We're standing at a technological crossroads where artificial intelligence could either become humanity's greatest ally or its most dangerous invention. Let's weigh both sides honestly.

The Bright Side: AI as Humanity's Helper

I've been amazed watching AI transform fields that once seemed untouchable by technology:

- Healthcare revolution: AI diagnostics can spot tumours in X-rays faster than any human radiologist.

- Research accelerator: While we struggle to remember what we ate for breakfast, AI systems can digest millions of research papers overnight
- Everyday magic: From predicting weather patterns to optimising traffic flow, AI quietly improves lives daily

The most exciting part? We're just scratching the surface. With quantum computing on the horizon, AI might solve problems we can't even conceptualise yet.

The Dark Side: Risks We Can't Ignore

Yet, as a technologist who's worked in this field, I lose sleep over three big concerns:

1. The control problem: Like giving a child a nuclear codes - what happens when AI systems become more intelligent than their creators?
2. Weaponisation potential: Autonomous drones making life-or-death decisions should terrify anyone
3. The black box problem: Even developers often can't explain why advanced AI makes certain decisions

"But couldn't AI just... turn evil?" Here's why I'm cautiously optimistic: current AI has about as much simulated consciousness as your toaster. Those sci-fi scenarios? Pure fantasy with today's technology.

The Consciousness Debate: Why AI Isn't Alive

After countless late-night debates with colleagues, here's where I land:

- Consciousness isn't just complex computation - it's biological, messy, and deeply personal
- My daughter's first laugh contained more genuine experience than any AI could simulate

- Even if we someday create synthetic consciousness (doubtful), it would be alien to human experience

The Path Forward: Guardrails, Not Gates

Rather than halting progress, we need smart regulations:

- Transparency laws: No more secret algorithms making important decisions
- Ethical review boards: Like we have for human medical trials
- International cooperation: Because AI doesn't respect borders

The bottom line? AI is neither saviour nor destroyer - it's a mirror reflecting our own choices. Handle with care, but **don't fear progress.**

8.2 Stewardship in the Age of Intelligence

AI, Ethics, and the Future of Human Control

"What we create may one day outpace our understanding. The true challenge is not invention, but stewardship."

Throughout the journey of science, every significant discovery—fire, writing, the wheel, printing presses, engines, and electricity—has expanded humanity's reach across the physical world. Today, in the age of artificial intelligence and self-evolving systems, we are expanding into something new: the realm of cognition itself. We have created machines that can predict, generate, and even simulate forms of thought. But with this astonishing capability comes an urgent question: Can humanity maintain ethical control over the forces it has unleashed?

This chapter examines the crucial role of stewardship, which involves the active, responsible guidance of powerful technologies to ensure that intelligence without consciousness does not result in innovation, ethics, or progress devoid of humanity. The future will be shaped by what we invent and how we choose to lead what we have created.

"We must not only create but also care for what we create." The 5000-year arc of science has always been defined by innovation, but its future will be determined by stewardship.

8.3 The Rise of Uncontrollable Technologies

For millennia, human creativity concentrated on conquering the outside world. We developed instruments to enhance our capabilities, broaden our perspective, increase efficiency, and expedite communication. Our creations, from the bronze sword to the steam engine, stayed under our control throughout history. They needed human hands to function, human intellect to lead, and human determination to steer their aim. Currently, that equilibrium is changing. We are developing technologies that are not just tools but systems that can learn, adapt, and evolve in ways that have become difficult for us to predict or control (Bostrom, 2014). Artificial intelligence, synthetic biology, autonomous systems, and self-replicating algorithms signify an innovation category.

These systems can change and improve themselves without direct human programming. Once developed, they can be copied, shared, and modified almost instantly worldwide. Unlike factories or power plants, they operate across global networks, independent of national borders (Schwab, 2016). This transformation marks a historic break from the past. It raises a profound new challenge: How do we steward creations that may evolve beyond the intentions of their creators?

Past technological revolutions, such as steam engines, nuclear reactors, and even early computers, were highly centralised and physically constrained. Steam engines require coal, metal, water, and a vast array of mechanical components. Nuclear technology demanded vast infrastructure, rare materials, and centralised regulation (Mokyr, 1990). By contrast, today's AI systems and genetic engineering platforms can operate on personal devices, in cloud computing platforms, through open-source codebases shared worldwide. Knowledge has become democratised, and innovation has become decentralised (Benkler, 2006). This makes technological progress faster, but control vastly harder.

The Case of Artificial Intelligence (AI) epitomises this shift. Modern AI systems train themselves on vast datasets, and machine learning algorithms find patterns without being explicitly programmed to do so (Russell, 2019). Generative AI models can create new content, strategies, and even code, some of which their developers do not fully understand. This unpredictability is not a flaw; it is the very design of modern AI. It is why these systems are so powerful—and so difficult to foresee, govern, or limit. In short, AI is no longer simply a tool we wield. It is a force we must guide (Amodei et al., 2016).

In synthetic biology, parallel transformations occur. Gene editing tools, such as CRISPR (Clustered Regularly Interspaced Short Palindromic Repeats), enable precise modifications to DNA at a low cost and with high accessibility (Doudna & Charpentier, 2014). Synthetic organisms can now be engineered to perform new functions—producing chemicals, breaking down waste, or even evolving in controlled environments. The line between the natural and the artificial is becoming increasingly blurred. We are not just observing evolution; we are directing it (Church & Regis, 2012).

Why Uncontrollable Technologies Are Different: These technologies differ from past inventions in several critical ways:

- **Speed:** They improve and adapt faster than regulatory bodies can respond (Tegmark, 2017).
- **Scale:** They can affect millions—or billions—of people without centralised deployment (Brynjolfsson & McAfee, 2014).
- **Accessibility:** They are becoming available to individuals and small groups, not just governments or large corporations (Zuboff, 2019).

- **Opacity:** Their inner workings (especially in deep learning) are often complex for experts to interpret fully (Marcus, 2018).

These characteristics create a technological environment where emergent behaviours, unexpected failures, and runaway impacts become plausible—and perhaps inevitable (Yudkowsky, 2008). And, as with AI. The danger is not malevolence—it is unpredictability. A genetic change intended to solve a problem could create unintended consequences that cascade beyond control (Esvelt, 2018).

The New Challenge: Not Just Invention, but Stewardship

In every previous era, the responsibility of innovation was simple: build better tools. Today, the responsibility has expanded to develop better tools *and* create systems to guide, monitor, and ethically govern them (Floridi, 2013). The rise of uncontrollable technologies demands a new philosophy: a shift from command and control to care and guidance, a mindset of stewardship, not just mastery.

We are at the dawn of an era where our creations possess agency of a kind—adapting, replicating, and influencing. Our choices will determine whether these forces augment human potential or erode it (Harari, 2016). The question is no longer whether we can build intelligent, evolving systems. We already have. The question is whether we can guide them wisely, before their evolution outpaces our ability to lead.

Intelligence Without Insight: Why Machines Can Solve Problems but Cannot Understand Them

The rise of artificial intelligence has stunned the world with its fluency, speed, and apparent creativity. AI can now write essays, compose symphonies, drive cars, diagnose diseases, and design products (Marcus & Davis, 2019). It can beat human champions at chess, Go, and video games, which were once considered bastions of intuition and foresight (Silver et al., 2018). It can predict financial trends, generate scientific hypotheses, and simulate realistic human conversations (Brown et al., 2020). And yet, behind this astonishing capability lies a profound absence: Artificial intelligence does not understand what it is doing. It computes, predicts, optimises—but does not reflect, feel, or know. Modern AI is powerful, but it is still intelligence without insight—calculation without comprehension (Searle, 1980).

What AI Does (and Doesn't Do)

At their core, today's AI systems—especially large language models and deep learning networks—function through pattern recognition and statistical association (LeCun et al., 2015). They work by analysing vast amounts of data, learning probabilistic relationships between elements (e.g., words, images, behaviours), and generating outputs that fit the expected patterns statistically. What they do not do is:

- Understand meaning (Harnad, 1990)
- Possess goals or emotions (Damasio, 1999)
- Form subjective experiences (Chalmers, 1995)
- Reflect on their actions (Dennett, 1991)
- Grasp context beyond correlations (Lake et al., 2017)

In other words, AI knows what to say, but not why it matters.

Optimisation Without Understanding

AI excels at optimising for objectives but does so without comprehending the larger systems or ethical frameworks in which it operates.

Examples:

- A recommendation algorithm maximises watch time, but may amplify polarisation and undermine public trust (Pariser, 2011).

- A content generator optimises for engagement, but may produce misinformation or plagiarism (O'Neil, 2016).
- A trading algorithm maximises profits—but may trigger market instability (Taleb, 2007).

In each case, the machine achieves its narrow goal but fails to grasp the broader consequences of its success. This is the hallmark of intelligence without insight: Solving the immediate problem and missing the more profound meaning (Bostrom, 2014).

Case Studies: When AI Gets It "Right" for the Wrong Reasons

- **Image Recognition:** An AI trained to distinguish between wolves and huskies correctly classifies them, but upon inspection, it turns out the model was simply recognising snow in the background rather than features of the animals themselves (Ribeiro et al., 2016).
- **Language Models:** A chatbot can fluently discuss moral philosophy, but it has no internal beliefs, no values, and no comprehension of what morality is (Bender et al., 2021).
- **Medical Diagnostics:** An AI model trained to detect pneumonia on chest X-rays performed extremely well until researchers realised it was cheating by learning to recognise hospital-specific markings instead of medical features (Zech et al., 2018).

Each example shows how AI can achieve correct outcomes for incorrect, fragile, or meaningless reasons.

The Risk of Misaligned Intelligence

When systems without insight optimise objectives, small misalignments can lead to massive consequences (Russell, 2019). A content generator could flood the internet with synthetic disinformation (Chesney & Citron, 2019). An autonomous system could prioritise a measurable metric while ignoring human values (Amodei et al.,

2016). Given the wrong goal, a superintelligent AI could relentlessly pursue it without understanding the harm caused (Yudkowsky, 2008). This phenomenon is known as the **alignment problem**—one of the most urgent challenges in AI safety research.

Without understanding, even the most intelligent machines cannot distinguish:

- Efficiency from harm
- Cleverness from cruelty
- Productivity from purpose (Bostrom, 2014)

Why Human Insight Still Matters

In a world of increasingly intelligent machines, human insight becomes more, not less, important. Insight provides:

- **Ethical judgment:** seeing beyond immediate outcomes to long-term impacts (Floridi, 2013).
- **Empathy:** understanding the lived experiences of others (Hoffman, 2000).
- **Wisdom:** balancing competing goods, making complex trade-offs with care (Maxwell, 2007).
- **Contextual thinking:** seeing patterns across disciplines, histories, and cultures (Gardner, 2006).

These qualities cannot be reduced to algorithms or optimised through data alone. They are the heart of ethical civilisation, and they are uniquely human.

A machine can predict the future, but a human must choose what future is worth creating. In the coming age, intelligence without insight may build robust systems, but insight without intelligence will lead them wisely (Harari, 2016).

8.4 The New Ethical Dilemmas

When Intelligence Grows Faster Than Wisdom

Throughout history, every major technological breakthrough has created new ethical questions. However, the rise of artificial intelligence and self-adapting technologies is different. For the first time, we face inventions that can act, learn, and influence without human oversight at every step (Bostrom, 2014). Without proper understanding or empathy, we create systems that can make decisions, shape behaviour, and affect millions. This raises a series of urgent, complex, and unprecedented ethical dilemmas. They are not theoretical concerns for the future. They are unfolding now—in courts, hospitals, markets, and city streets (Zuboff, 2019).

The Core Ethical Dilemmas of Intelligent Systems

1. Bias and Fairness

AI systems learn from data, and all data reflect the biases of the societies that produced it (O'Neil, 2016). Hiring algorithms may reinforce racial or gender discrimination (Bolukbasi et al., 2016). Predictive policing tools may disproportionately target marginalised communities (Benjamin, 2019). Facial recognition systems have been shown to perform far worse on people of colour than on white faces (Buolamwini & Gebru, 2018). The challenge: How do we prevent AI from replicating and amplifying historical injustices? Bias is not just a technical flaw—it is an ethical failure that can perpetuate inequality on a massive scale (Noble, 2018).

2. Transparency and Accountability

Many modern AI systems—especially deep learning networks—are black boxes: We can see their inputs and outputs, but we often cannot explain how they arrived at a particular decision (Marcus, 2018). When an AI system denies a loan, recommends a prison sentence, or diagnoses an illness, who is responsible if it makes a mistake? How can the affected person contest the decision if they cannot understand it? Transparency—the ability to explain and audit AI decisions—is not just good practice. It is essential for justice, trust, and democratic governance (Wachter et al., 2017).

3. Privacy and Surveillance

AI thrives on data. The more it knows, the better it predicts. But this hunger for data raises critical questions: How much personal information should AI systems be allowed to collect? Who controls this information? What safeguards protect individuals from surveillance, manipulation, or exploitation? Without strong privacy protections, the same technologies that empower connection can also enable mass surveillance and behaviour control at an unprecedented scale (Zuboff, 2019). Privacy is not merely a technical issue. It is about the dignity and freedom of individuals in the digital age (Solove, 2013).

4. Autonomy and Human Agency

Many AI systems are designed to nudge, persuade, or optimise human behaviour. Recommendation engines guide what we watch, read, and buy (Pariser, 2011). Navigation systems suggest where we go and how we get there. Even dating apps influence who we meet (Hancock et al., 2020). The danger is subtle but profound: If machines increasingly shape our decisions, are we still fully autonomous? Protecting human agency—the freedom to make meaningful choices—must be a central goal in the design and governance of intelligent systems (Floridi, 2013).

5. Existential Risk: Superintelligence and the Alignment Problem

Looking further ahead, many thinkers warn of a deeper, existential concern: If we eventually create artificial general intelligence (AGI) systems that surpass human intelligence across domains, how do we ensure their goals align with human values? The alignment problem asks: Can we design systems that achieve goals efficiently *and* understand, respect, and prioritise human ethics (Russell, 2019)? If we fail, the consequences could be catastrophic—not because of evil intent, but because of misaligned optimisation at superhuman speed (Yudkowsky, 2008). In this sense, the challenge of AI ethics is not just about preventing individual harms. It is about preserving humanity's future (Bostrom, 2014).

The Need for New Ethical Frameworks

The ethical traditions humanity developed over millennia—religious teachings, moral philosophy, human rights—remain invaluable. But they must now be adapted and expanded to meet the scale and speed of the technologies we have unleashed (Floridi, 2013). This means:

- **Embedding ethics into the design process**—not as an afterthought, but as a foundational principle (Mittelstadt et al., 2016).
- **Creating multidisciplinary collaborations** between technologists, philosophers, ethicists, policymakers, and citizens (Jobin et al., 2019).
- **Recognising that no single culture, nation, or company** can define the ethics of global technologies alone (Whittlestone et al., 2019).

Ethics must evolve as dynamically as the technologies they seek to guide.

Conclusion

Technology expands our power, and ethics must expand our vision. Humanity's task is straightforward in a world of machines that can act without insight: We must be the conscience of our creations and ensure that we do not lose wisdom in the race to build intelligence (Harari, 2016).

8.5 Stewardship: Guiding the Forces We Have Unleashed

From Mastery to Responsibility in the Age of Intelligence

For most of human history, the relationship between humanity and its inventions has been one of command and control. We built machines to serve our needs, shaped matter to our will, and extended our reach over nature through force and ingenuity (Mitcham, 1994). Today, we face a new reality: We have created forces—artificial intelligence, synthetic biology, autonomous systems—that can act beyond direct human command (Bostrom, 2014). These forces are not malevolent. They are not conscious. But they are powerful, fast, self-adapting, and potentially indifferent to human intentions if left unguided (Russell, 2019). The era of simple mastery is ending. The era of stewardship must begin.

What Is Stewardship?

Stewardship is not about domination; it is about care, responsibility, foresight, and ethical leadership (Block, 2013). A steward nurtures what is powerful instead of exploiting it recklessly. A steward guides forces with wisdom rather than commanding them through brute authority (Kim & Mauborgne, 2014). A steward recognizes that creation brings obligation (Jonas, 1984).

In the context of today's technologies, stewardship means ensuring that AI, genetic engineering, and other transformative innovations are:

- Aligned with human values (Gabriel, 2020)
- Monitored for unintended consequences (Taleb, 2007)
- Adapted wisely as they evolve (Tegmark, 2017)

This perspective requires us to move from viewing technologies merely as tools to understanding them as dynamic ecosystems that require constant tending, adjustment, and care (Floridi, 2013).

Three Pillars of Stewardship

1. Governance and Global Collaboration

No single nation, company, or institution can manage the challenges of powerful, unbounded technologies alone (Bremmer, 2020). Stewardship requires coordinated, flexible, and adaptive governance. This includes:

- International agreements on AI safety and ethical standards (Jobin et al., 2019)
- Regulatory bodies to oversee high-risk technologies (Cath et al., 2018)
- Shared norms across cultures about acceptable risks (Whittlestone et al., 2019)

Governance must move at the speed of innovation, not lag decades behind it (Zuboff, 2019). If the future is global, stewardship must also be global (Risse, 2019).

2. Technical Safeguards and Value Alignment

Stewardship begins at the design stage—inside the technology itself (Amodei et al., 2016). Engineers must embed:

- Explainable AI: Systems that articulate their decisions (Doshi-Velez & Kim, 2017)
- Robust Alignment: Models trained on broad human values (Gabriel, 2020)
- Fail-Safes: Mechanisms for human override (Russell, 2019)

Good stewardship means building technologies that are resilient, transparent, and human-centred by default (Mittelstadt et al., 2016).

3. Cultural Adaptation and Education

Stewardship is a cultural transformation. Societies must:

- Educate citizens about emerging technologies (Reynolds & Bird, 2020)

- Promote public debate on ethical values (Floridi, 2018)
- Empower diverse voices in shaping technology (Benjamin, 2019)

Just as literacy became universal in the age of printing, technological literacy must become a civic skill in the age of intelligence (UNESCO, 2021).

The Difficulties of Stewardship

Stewardship is more complex than command for several reasons:

- Complexity: Technologies outpace simple regulations (Tegmark, 2017)
- Speed: Evolution exceeds legal adaptation (Zuboff, 2019)
- Diffusion: Power is decentralized (Benkler, 2006)
- Incentives: Short-term profit often overrides ethics (Susskind, 2022)

Stewardship demands foresight over greed, collaboration over competition, and patience over impulse (Harari, 2016). It requires leadership rooted in both humility and ambition (Schwartz, 2021).

Conclusion

We have crossed the threshold from building machines to building forces. From now on, invention without stewardship is not progress but peril (Bostrom, 2014). Those who invent the most powerful tools will not shape the future. It will be shaped by those who guide them wisely (Russell, 2019). Stewardship is not optional. It is the price of continuing the human journey that began with the first spark of imagination (Harari, 2015).

8.6 Futures at the Crossroads

Choosing Between Empowerment and Erosion in the Age of Intelligence

Humanity now stands at one of the most consequential crossroads in its 5000-year journey of science and innovation. (Harari, 2015). Never before have the tools we created been so powerful, far-reaching, and independent of our direct control (Bostrom, 2014). The rise of artificial intelligence, synthetic biology, and autonomous systems presents an extraordinary opportunity to amplify human potential—and an equally profound risk of diminishing human agency (Zuboff, 2019). The future is not inevitable. It will be shaped by the decisions we make now (Tegmark, 2017). We are no longer simply discovering the future. We are engineering it.

"The future we live in depends on how wisely and quickly we embrace the responsibility of stewardship."
—Floridi (2013, p. 154)

The Threshold of Stewardship

Throughout history, the relationship between humanity and its creations has largely been one of command and mastery (Mitcham, 1994). From flint hand axes to steam engines, technologies obeyed human will without adaptation (Mokyr, 1990). Today, AI, biotechnology, and autonomous systems learn, adapt, and act unpredictably (Russell, 2019). This shift demands a new philosophy:

- **Stewardship over control**: Guidance through "care, vigilance, and ethical imagination" (Jonas, 1984, p. 22)
- **Responsibility for evolution**: Shaping trajectories, not just inventions (Stilgoe et al., 2013)
- **Alignment with human values**: Ensuring technologies respect dignity (Gabriel, 2020)

The AI Paradox: Intelligence Without Insight

Artificial intelligence epitomises this challenge:

Capability	Limitation	Risk
Superhuman optimization(Silver et al., 2018)	No comprehension (Searle, 1980)	Misaligned goals(Bostrom, 2014)
Bias amplification (Bolukbasi et al., 2016)	No ethical reasoning(Binns, 2018)	Entrenched inequality(Noble, 2018)
Autonomous action (Amodei et al., 2016)	No accountability (Wachter et al., 2017)	Erosion of agency(Floridi, 2018)

Table 1. The dual nature of AI's impact

Two Paths Forward

1. Empowerment Scenario

- Medical breakthroughs (Topol, 2019)
- Personalised education (Luckin, 2018)
- Sustainable technologies (Cowls et al., 2021)

2. Erosion Scenario

- Algorithmic manipulation (Chesney & Citron, 2019)
- Mass surveillance (Zuboff, 2019)
- Existential misalignment (Yudkowsky, 2008)

The difference lies in governance choices:

"Technological power requires ethical scaffolding that evolves as fast as innovation itself."

—Whittlestone et al. (2019, p. 12)

The Stewardship Imperative

Five critical tasks for the 21st century:

1. **Dynamic Governance**
    - International AI treaties (Cath et al., 2018)
    - Adaptive regulatory frameworks (Rahwan, 2018)
2. **Value-Sensitive Design**
    - Explainable AI (Doshi-Velez & Kim, 2017)
    - Fail-safe mechanisms (Amodei et al., 2016)
3. **Cultural Transformation**
    - Technological literacy (UNESCO, 2021)
    - Multistakeholder deliberation (Jobin et al., 2019)
4. **Alignment Research**
    - Reward modeling (Leike et al., 2018)
    - Ethics as a system requirement (Gabriel, 2020)
5. **Distributed Responsibility**
    - Beyond "move fast and break things" (Brooks, 2020)
    - Long-term thinking over short-term profit (Susskind, 2022)

Conclusion: The Unwritten Future

As Jonas (1984) warned, our new powers demand a new ethic of responsibility. The age of intelligence will be judged not by computational prowess but by:

- **Wisdom** to balance innovation with precaution (Tegmark, 2017)

- **Courage** to confront unintended consequences (Taleb, 2012)
- **Imagination** to centre human flourishing (Sen, 1999)

"The greatest achievement may not be invention itself, but the wisdom to guide it."

CHAPTER 9

Consciousness

The Affective Survival Theory of Consciousness (AST)

Why Do We Feel?

Why does pain hurt? Why does love matter? Why do we grieve the dead, shiver at the edge of cliffs, or seek beauty in music and meaning in suffering?

These are not just philosophical questions; they are scientific ones. Today, we know more than ever about the brain—its neurons, networks, and neurotransmitters. We can scan its activity, simulate its computations, and trace its evolutionary lineage. And yet one question remains unanswered:

Why does any of this feel like something?

Why does neural activity not simply compute in silence? Why is it accompanied by joy, fear, sorrow, or awe? This mystery—why physical processes in the brain give rise to conscious feeling—is what philosopher David Chalmers famously called the "hard problem of consciousness" (Chalmers, 1995). Cognitive science and neurobiology can often explain how we respond to stimuli, make decisions, or learn from experience. But they cannot yet explain why those experiences feel the way they do—or why they feel at all. This Chapter proposes a new evolutionary answer. **The Affective Survival Theory of Consciousness**

The theory I present in this Chapter—Affective Survival Theory (AST)—argues that consciousness evolved not to think, but to feel. Conscious feeling is not a side effect of cognition or a philosophical puzzle detached from biology. It is an evolved mechanism—A system refined by natural selection to aid organisms in remembering, prioritising, and acting in ways that enhance survival and reproduction. In the AST framework, emotion is not the opposite of intelligence; it is its evolutionary foundation.

We feel the need to survive.

We survive by remembering what felt good, what hurt, what threatened, and what saved us.

"**Consciousness is an evolved, emergent property of living systems—engineered by evolution as a felt system of survival intelligence**."

From this perspective, consciousness is not a blank mirror reflecting the world, but a value-based filter. It colours perception with urgency. It stores experience in memory according to emotional salience. And it modulates behaviour in real time to enhance life-preserving choices. How was consciousness selected for in evolution?

Affective Survival Theory (AST) offers a direct evolutionary answer: Consciousness was selected because affective experiences, such as pain, fear, hunger, and desire, enabled organisms to make real-time survival-relevant decisions, with greater precision, learning capacity, and behavioural flexibility than reflexes or hardwired programs alone.

Definition of Affective Survival Theory (AST): Affective Survival Theory proposes that consciousness evolved to provide organisms with a survival advantage by emotionally tagging experiences with functional value, thereby enabling better memory, decision-making, and adaptive behaviour.

Darwin, Emotion, and the Mind

AST builds directly on Charles Darwin‘s evolutionary insights. In *The Expression of the Emotions in Man and Animals* (1872), Darwin proposed that emotional expression—like bodily form—evolved through natural selection. He viewed emotions like fear, grief, joy, and anger not as immaterial abstractions, but as adaptive behaviours inherited from our evolutionary ancestors. He wrote:

> *"The same state of mind is expressed throughout the world with remarkable uniformity; and this fact is interesting, as evidence of how small the differences are between the races of man."*
> — Darwin (1872, p. 366)

Darwin suggested that emotions provided fitness advantages, motivating behaviours that protected the organism, reinforced social bonds, and guided decision-making. AST takes this idea further by proposing that the subjective *feeling* of emotion, not just the behaviour, was selected for. In other words, the capacity to feel evolved because it helped organisms learn, adapt, and act more effectively in uncertain environments.

Feeling as Nature's Memory System

One of AST's central claims is that consciousness evolved to serve as a felt memory system. Pain teaches us what to avoid. Pleasure encourages repetition. Fear heightens attention. Love fosters loyalty. These are not accidental sensations—they are evolutionary bookmarks. Feeling tags experience with meaning, making it more likely to be stored, retrieved, and acted upon in the future.

This view is supported by neuroscience. Studies show that emotionally salient experiences are more likely to be remembered than neutral ones (Phelps, 2004). The amygdala, a brain region central to emotion processing, plays a critical role in linking feeling to memory, especially in response to danger, reward, and social stimuli (LeDoux, 1996; Damasio, 1999). These findings suggest that emotion is not peripheral to learning and intelligence—it is fundamental.

Beyond Reflex: The Evolution of Anticipation

Unlike simple reflexes, feelings allow organisms to anticipate rather than merely react. A reflex withdraws your hand from a flame. But fear helps you avoid the fire next time. A reflex flinches. A feeling remembers.

This anticipatory power is central to AST. Consciousness allows organisms to construct emotional simulations—imagining potential outcomes and making decisions based on their feelings. This emotional forecast, rooted in experience, enables behavioural flexibility, the evolutionary crown jewel of sentient life.

A Bridge to Quantum Biology

While AST is primarily a biological theory, it does not exclude more profound questions about the substrate of consciousness. Recent research in quantum biology suggests that specific life processes—including photosynthesis, bird navigation, and possibly neural computation—may exploit quantum phenomena like entanglement and coherence (Engel et al., 2007; Hameroff & Penrose, 2014).

AST is compatible with these models. If quantum processes underlie the *how* of consciousness, as in the Orchestrated Objective Reduction (Orch OR) theory, then AST addresses the *why*: why evolution retained and refined conscious awareness as a felt guide to life. The two theories, though distinct in level, may be complementary.

Scope and Purpose of This Book

This book is a journey through the lived architecture of consciousness. It traces the evolution of feeling across domains of experience:

- Fear, hunger, and pain as primal survival signals
- Touch, intimacy, and social pain as bonding tools

- The five senses as emotionally charged interfaces
- Memory, imagination, and planning as emotional simulations
- Reasoning, morality, and art as higher-order affective adaptations
- Self-awareness and spirituality as extensions of affective survival

Each chapter explores how a different human experience—emotional, sensory, or cognitive—can be understood as a survival-driven felt phenomenon, shaped by evolution and grounded in affect.

The goal is not to eliminate mystery but to reframe consciousness as something deeply biological, meaningful, and valuable—a tool life evolved to perceive, care, choose, and remember.

An Invitation

This section offers not a final theory but a new frame. It unites the brain and the body, instinct and memory, biology and awareness. One that starts with a simple idea:

Feeling is not the opposite of reason—it is the reason reason evolved.

At heart, the Affective Survival Theory is a theory of *value*, of how life learned to feel its way forward. If we wish to understand consciousness, we must understand why feeling matters.

Welcome to the science of survival through emotion.

PART I

Foundations — Life, Energy, and Evolutionary Imperatives

1: The Living Struggle — Life Against Entropy

1.1 What Is Entropy, and Why Is Life a Problem?

In physics, entropy is a measure of disorder or randomness. According to the Second Law of Thermodynamics, closed systems naturally evolve toward increasing entropy—gas spreads, heat dissipates, structure decays. And yet, life is *highly ordered.* A living cell maintains boundaries, regulates internal chemistry, and constructs intricate molecules like proteins and DNA. From the standpoint of physics, this seems improbable. How can matter spontaneously organise itself into such elaborate, low-entropy forms?

"Life seems to be 'working uphill' in a universe that prefers downhill processes."

— Erwin Schrödinger, What is Life? (1944)

AST begins with this paradox: **life is a thermodynamic rebellion.**

1.2 Schrödinger's Negative Entropy

Physicist Erwin Schrödinger, in his seminal lectures (*What is Life?*, 1944), suggested that organisms survive by feeding on negative entropy—that is, they import order from their environment by consuming energy-rich resources (like sunlight, sugar, or nutrients) and using them to maintain internal structure.

"Life feeds on negative entropy" (What Is Life?, 1944)

"It is by avoiding the rapid decay into the inert state of 'equilibrium' that an organism appears so enigmatic."
— *Schrödinger* (1944)

This insight reframes life as a thermodynamic system open to energy flow—it resists entropy *not by breaking physical laws*, but by mastering their constraints.

1.3 Life as Energy-Flow Management

All life depends on the capacity to:

- **Capture** energy from the environment (sunlight, chemical gradients)
- **Convert** that energy into a usable form (ATP, cellular metabolism)
- **Use** that energy to build, repair, and replicate complex structures

The second law of thermodynamics states that the total entropy of an isolated system can only increase over time. While life locally decreases entropy by creating order, it does so at the cost of increasing entropy in its surroundings. This describes that the increase in overall entropy is not something life tries to avoid; it's why life exists and persists. The flow of energy through living systems drives their organisation and complexity. Without the drive to dissipate energy gradients (and thus increase overall entropy), there would be no thermodynamic imperative for the emergence of such complex, energy-processing systems we call life.

"Life is a localised, self-sustaining reduction in entropy (achieved by energy dissipation) that maintains order within a system while increasing the total entropy of its surroundings."

Breakdown:

1. **Locally ordered**: Organisms maintain structure (low entropy).
2. **Globally costly**: Requires energy input, increasing environmental entropy (e.g., heat waste).
3. **Far-from-equilibrium**: Sustained by continuous energy flow (e.g., sunlight, food).

Biochemist **Nick Lane** argues that early life likely emerged around **alkaline hydrothermal vents**, where natural proton gradients offered a source of free energy. Primitive membranes harnessed these gradients, forming the first energy-hungry, entropy-resisting cells.

"Life arose as a way to dissipate energy gradients—not in spite of entropy, but because of it."
— *Lane, The Vital Question* (2015)

1.4 Homeostasis: The First Survival Strategy

The earliest cells not only existed, but they also had the ability to regulate themselves. They maintained stable internal pH and Controlled ion gradients across membranes. Regulated temperature and repaired damaged molecules. Reproduced when resources allowed. This process is known as homeostasis: the dynamic regulation of internal conditions despite external fluctuations. It represents the earliest form of survival intelligence.

"To live is to keep dying at bay."
— Antonio Damasio, 2010

In AST, homeostasis is where *affect begins*—not as conscious feeling but as *internal evaluations*: "too hot," "too acidic," "low energy." These binary value judgments were the foundation of future *subjective experiences*.

1.5 Autopoiesis: The Self-Making System

Chilean biologists Maturana and Varela introduced the concept of autopoiesis—a system capable of reproducing and maintaining itself. An autopoietic system:

- Is bounded (separates self from environment)
- Is self-regulating
- Is self-producing

This definition of life emphasises not DNA or replication but organisational closure—a system that defines internal rules about its environment.

"A living system is a network of processes that regenerate the very network."

— Maturana & Varela, 1980

In AST, autopoiesis is the *first form of selfhood*. The system doesn't just react—it *acts to preserve itself*. This behaviour is deeply affective in nature, even if it lacks consciousness.

1.6 From Survival to Evaluation

With energy flow and boundary maintenance came *valuation*:

- Is this environment safe or dangerous?
- Is this molecule helpful or harmful?
- Should I move toward or away?

These early evaluations did not have thoughts or symbols—just *preferences, gradients*, and *biases* encoded into molecular machinery.

Over time, these binary preferences became more complex:

- What used to be "acidic vs. safe" became *pain*
- What used to be "resource-rich vs. barren" became *hunger*
- What used to be "safe vs. threatening" became *fear*

AST Claim: The earliest form of cognition was *not symbolic* but *affective*: an embodied feeling of survival relevance.

1.7 Life's Thermodynamic Imperative and the Rise of Feeling

Thus, life is the story of managing *entropy through affective regulation*. Feeling evolved because:

- It prioritised actions essential to entropy resistance
- It created adaptive feedback loops
- It enabled complexity to persist across generations

Evolutionary processes can be seen through the lens of entropy. As species adapt and increase their biological complexity over generations, they achieve greater organisation while indirectly raising the overall entropy of their environments.

Far from being a late-emerging human trait, feeling is the *core biological solution to disorder*, and eventually gave rise to consciousness itself.

2: Autopoiesis and the Birth of the Self-System

2.1 The Problem of Defining Life

The definition of life has long challenged scientists and philosophers. Is it the ability to reproduce? To evolve? To metabolise? To move?

Modern biology offers a more elegant framework: life is a self-producing, self-maintaining process that persists far from equilibrium. Living systems are organised so that they constantly remake themselves, structurally and functionally, while exchanging energy and matter with their surroundings. This brings us to the concept of autopoiesis—life as a closed loop of recursive self-making.

2.2 What Is Autopoiesis?

Coined by biologists Humberto Maturana and Francisco Varela in the 1970s, autopoiesis (from the Greek *auto*, "self," and *poiesis*, "creation") refers to a system that continuously produces and maintains the components necessary for its organisation.

A system is autopoietic if it:

- Maintains a boundary separating it from its environment (e.g., a cell membrane)
- Continuously regenerates its parts using its internal processes
- Functions as a closed organisational loop (not closed to matter or energy, but to its identity structure)

"Living systems are machines organised as a network of processes of production... that continuously regenerate that network."
— Maturana & Varela, 1980

Autopoiesis = Organisational closure + Material openness.

2.3 The First "Self": From Molecules to Identity

Imagine a simple lipid vesicle floating in the primordial ocean. It absorbs nutrients, expels waste, repairs damage, and—if it's lucky—divides. It is not conscious but has a boundary and a persistence logic. It does not just exist—it *resists nonexistence.*

This is the origin of what AST calls the self-system:

- An entity with internal coherence
- Capable of self-regulation
- Driven by the imperative to persist

"The cell does not 'know' it is alive but acts as if it must remain so."
— De Duve, 2002

This "as-if-ness" is crucial. The system is not yet conscious but exhibits the preconditions for affect: a way to evaluate internal state changes as relevant to survival.

2.4 Organisational Closure vs. Mechanical Systems

Unlike machines built by humans (e.g., clocks, computers), which operate according to externally imposed rules, autopoietic systems:

- Generate their own rules
- Define their boundaries
- Reconfigure themselves in real time

This means their "behaviour" is not simply reactive but self-directed toward maintaining organisational integrity. In AST, this is when life stops being "just chemistry" and starts being subjectively organised—the first flicker of "for-the-self" processing.

2.5 Autopoiesis as the Proto-Architecture of Affect

In AST, autopoiesis is not merely a biological threshold—it is the first architecture capable of feeling, because:

- It differentiates internal vs. external
- It registers environmental changes in terms of self-relevance
- It generates internal feedback loops that simulate "evaluation"

For example:

- A drop in internal pH leads to compensatory mechanisms to neutralise it.
- An influx of nutrients triggers metabolic upregulation.
- A threat to membrane integrity prompts repair or apoptosis.

These are not "emotions," but value-laden states: certain conditions are *better or worse* for system continuity.

Thus, Autopoiesis enables a primitive form of "matter that cares."

2.6 From Structural Coupling to Adaptive Behaviour

Maturana and Varela also introduced the concept of structural coupling: the idea that a living system and its environment co-evolve. The system changes in ways that allow it to persist within its environment, and vice versa.

Example:

- A bacterium senses sugar in the environment, → it moves toward it.
- Over time, the bacterium's receptors become more finely tuned to sugar gradients.

This feedback between structure and behaviour is the evolutionary bridge between:

- Metabolism and motivation
- Boundary maintenance and behavioural adaptation
- Chemistry and proto-cognition

2.7 The Emergence of Agency

Autopoiesis eventually led to motility (movement), which introduced choice:

- Should the organism move toward light or away from heat?
- Should it divide now or conserve energy?

Each action had a survival cost or benefit. To manage this, organisms evolved internal decision-making systems—not yet conscious, but *functional*.

This is the soil from which agency and later intentionality grew. It is inseparable from affective evaluation because deciding implies valuing.

2.8 AST View: Autopoiesis as the Biological Root of Subjectivity

AST proposes:

- The *first-person perspective* did not begin with humans or even animals.
- It began with maintaining the self-system in the face of thermodynamic chaos.
- This self-system had to evaluate, react, and eventually feel to survive.

Thus, in AST:

Autopoiesis is the first scaffold of subjectivity, not in the sense of introspection but of persistent self-reference.

3: Natural Selection and Survival Valence

3.1 Beyond the Gene: Why Survival Requires Valuation

In Darwinian terms, evolution is driven by variation, selection, and inheritance. Genes that help organisms survive and reproduce become more common over generations.

But survival is not just about *mechanics*. It requires the capacity to:

- Detect relevant threats and opportunities
- Respond appropriately
- Prioritise one behaviour over another

This requires valuation—an internal system for assessing "good vs. bad," "helpful vs. harmful," or "more vs. less likely to support survival." AST refers to this as *survival valence*.

"Natural selection shaped minds not just to act, but to care about what they act upon."
— Friston et al., 2017

3.2 The Emergence of Selective Preference

Early life forms operated primarily through chemical interactions. But even simple organisms began showing selective behaviour:

- Bacteria exhibit chemotaxis—they move toward sugar and away from toxins.
- Protists like *Paramecium* can reverse direction when they bump into objects.
- These actions are not random—they are biased toward self-preserving outcomes.

This behavioural bias represents a primitive form of **affective evaluation**:

"This is better than that, and I will move accordingly."

It's not conscious, but it's *directional.* This directionality forms the evolutionary precursor to **feeling**.

3.3 Natural Selection as a Valuator

Natural selection works by eliminating systems that fail and preserving those that succeed—but only if the system can differentiate and respond.

The key insight of AST:

Feeling is evolution's internalisation of natural selection.

Whereas natural selection operates across generations, affective valence allows real-time selection within an individual's lifetime:

- "This hurts → avoid."
- "This feels good → repeat."
- "This frightens me → flee."

In this sense, affect is internalised evolutionary wisdom—a fast, embodied way to score survival outcomes without logic or foresight.

3.4 Fitness Landscapes and Affective Navigation

Biologists often describe evolution using the metaphor of fitness landscapes: hills and valleys represent different levels of adaptive success.

For simple organisms, climbing these fitness peaks requires:

- Sensing environmental variables
- Reacting based on internal drives
- Adjusting behaviour through feedback

Affect provides a kind of inner compass—a survival-based signal system that guides organisms through these landscapes by signalling which directions are worth pursuing.

"Valence is a biological tool for navigating complex environments."
— Friston, 2010

3.5 Behavioural Selection and Affective Filters

In higher organisms, natural selection shaped not just physiology, but behavioural tendencies:

- Approach behaviours (SEEKING, curiosity)
- Avoidance behaviours (FEAR, disgust)
- Bonding behaviours (CARE, GRIEF)

These evolved because they offered adaptive advantages. For example:

- An animal that fears snakes survives longer than one that doesn't.
- An infant that cries when separated from its mother is more likely to be protected.

These emotional tendencies were encoded into affective systems, forming what AST calls evolutionary affective filters—built-in shortcuts for evaluating survival relevance.

3.6 Learning from Feedback: Affect as a Teaching Tool

Affect enables **individual learning** through real-time feedback loops:

- Touch fire → pain → avoid fire next time.
- Eat sugary fruit → pleasure → seek it out again.

This mechanism is called reinforcement learning. It works best when the experience is felt—the stronger the emotional signal, the faster the learning.

Thus, affect serves as both a signal and a memory marker, strengthening or weakening synaptic connections depending on the survival outcome.

"Emotion turns experience into memory."
— McGaugh, 2003

3.7 Survival Valence and the Roots of Subjectivity

The ability to evaluate survival relevance marked the first steps toward subjective experience:

- The system is no longer reacting to inputs mechanically.
- It acts according to its needs, thresholds, and priorities.
- It has a point of view, even if unconscious.

AST Claim:

Survival valence serves as the biological foundation for subjectivity. When a system "cares" about its own state, it begins to experience feelings.

This doesn't require language or thoughts—it only requires that *some states are better than others for the system.*

3.8. Conclusion: Selection Focused Internally

Natural selection not only shaped the evolution of organisms, but it also shaped the architecture of experience. The emergence of affect was the evolutionary shift that allowed organisms to:

- To evaluate internal and external conditions
- To choose adaptive responses
- To learn and predict future outcomes

From bacteria to mammals, valuation systems evolved as survival tools. Eventually, these internal signals became felt. And from there, **consciousness was born**.

PART II

The Rise of Affective Processing

4: From Reaction to Feeling — The Affective Leap

4.1 Beyond Reflex: Why Reactions Weren't Enough

Early life could react, but it couldn't feel. Bacteria swim toward nutrients and away from toxins. Simple reflex arcs allow a sea slug to withdraw from touch. These mechanical reactions follow fixed patterns without evaluation, experience, or awareness. But as environments became more complex and survival pressures more dynamic, reflexes alone became insufficient:

- A rigid response might be too slow or too costly.
- Some threats required anticipation.
- Competing motivations (e.g. fear vs. hunger) required choice.

The evolutionary solution? Introduce affect—an internal experience of value, urgency, and motivation. Feeling was not just an added feature; it was a biological innovation.

"Affect is evolution's way of internalising significance."
— Panksepp, 1998

4.2 What Is a Reaction? What Is a Feeling?

Let's distinguish two core concepts:

Reaction	Feeling
Triggered directly by stimuli	Emerges from internal integration
Rigid and preprogrammed	Flexible and context-sensitive
Often unconscious (e.g. pupil dilation)	Often conscious (e.g. fear, desire)
Does not require memory or learning	Deeply shaped by learning and memory
Localised and limited	Holistic, involving body and brain

In AST, the affective leap occurs when reactions become centrally processed, integrated, and felt. Instead of just executing an action, the organism knows (in some form) how the situation relates to its survival.

4.3 The Need for Integration: From Sensors to Sentience

Reflexes are modular. Touch something hot, pull away—no thought required. But feelings emerge when multiple inputs are weighed and assessed:

- Internal signals (e.g., hunger, fatigue)
- External context (e.g., presence of predators or mates)
- Past experiences (e.g., memory of pain or pleasure)

This requires a centralised affective architecture, such as:

- Brainstem structures (e.g., periaqueductal gray)
- Limbic system (e.g., amygdala, hypothalamus)

- Midbrain dopaminergic systems
  (e.g., ventral tegmental area)

These systems don't simply process input—they evaluate, prioritise, and respond adaptively.

4.4 The Emergence of Valence: Good vs. Bad

Valence is the most fundamental affective quality: something feels *positive* or *negative, attractive* or *aversive.*

This simple binary creates an internal compass:

- Hunger = negative valence → seek food
- Warmth = positive valence → stay
- Pain = strong negative valence → withdraw

This is where the evolutionary role of affect becomes clear:

Feeling is how organisms come to "care" about their survival conditions.

Importantly, valence allows for motivation and agency: the organism doesn't just *do*—it *wants, avoids*, and *learns.*

4.5 Feeling as a Model of the Self-in-the-World

Feeling doesn't just report bodily states—it models them in the context of survival. Antonio Damasio described this as the proto-self: a constantly updated image of the organism's internal condition.

As feelings became more sophisticated, they gained:

- Temporal depth (e.g., anticipation of pain = anxiety)
- Social relevance (e.g., separation = loneliness)
- Narrative structure (e.g., "I am sad because…")

In AST, the transition from reaction to feeling is the **transition from external behaviour to internal experience**.

"Whereas reactions are about the world, feelings are about *how the world feels to me.*"
— *Seth, 2021*

4.6 Repetition, Learning, and Affective Memory

Once feelings evolved, they became central to learning and memory:

- Pain teaches avoidance.
- Pleasure teaches repetition.
- Fear encodes trauma for future caution.

This is called **affective learning**, and it is essential for long-term survival. Over time, evolution fine-tuned this process through **reinforcement learning circuits**, primarily involving:

- Dopamine (reward prediction)
- Norepinephrine (alertness, fear)
- Serotonin (mood and regulation)

Feeling became nature's way of assigning importance to events, thereby enabling memory formation and flexible decision-making.

4.7 The Affective Loop: From Input to Meaning

AST proposes the Affective Loop as the minimal architecture of feeling:

1. Sensation: External or internal change is detected.
2. Valence: The system tags the input as positive or negative.
3. Integration: Inputs are compared with bodily needs and goals.
4. Action tendency: The system prepares or initiates behaviour.
5. Feedback: The outcome modifies future expectations and feelings.

This loop exists even in animals without language or a cortex. What changes in higher animals is the richness, resolution, and recursion of the loop, eventually producing *emotion*, *self-reflection*, and *conscious experience*.

4.8 Conclusion: The Dawn of Feeling

The shift from reaction to feeling marks a turning point in the evolution of life. Where once systems blindly responded, they now valued. Where once behaviour was rigid, it now became adaptive and meaningful. The affective leap was:

An evolutionary shortcut to survival

A feedback system for learning

A proto-self-awareness mechanism

In AST, this leap is not peripheral to consciousness. It is its foundation.

"Feeling was evolution's first whisper of consciousness."
— *Affective Survival Theory (AST)*

5: The Seven Core Affective Systems

5.1 Introduction: The Blueprint for Survival Feeling

In mammals, emotion is not a vague psychological concept—it's rooted in neuroanatomy. Neuroscientist Jaak Panksepp (1998) identified seven evolutionarily conserved, subcortical neural systems that generate *primary emotional feelings* in mammals, including humans. These systems are:

1. SEEKING
2. FEAR
3. RAGE
4. LUST
5. CARE

6. GRIEF / PANIC
7. PLAY

These are not learned behaviours or culturally shaped emotions. They are hardwired affective systems, present even in animals with minimal cortical development.

> "These circuits are the ancient biological platforms for the construction of emotional experience."
> — *Panksepp, 1998*

5.2 SEEKING: The Engine of Curiosity and Motivation

- Function: Drives exploratory behaviour, goal pursuit, and reward anticipation.
- Neuroanatomy: Originates in the ventral tegmental area (VTA) and medial forebrain bundle, modulated by dopamine.
- Affective Tone: Energising, anticipatory, hopeful.

SEEKING evolved to solve the problem of finding resources—food, shelter, and mates. Without it, organisms would remain passive and die.

AST Insight: SEEKING is the neurobiological foundation of motivation, desire, and learning. It allows life to pursue rather than merely respond.

5.3 FEAR: The Guardian of Survival

- Function: Warns of danger, triggers avoidance, escape, or freezing.
- Neuroanatomy: Amygdala, periaqueductal gray (PAG), and hypothalamus.
- Affective Tone: Unease, dread, panic.

FEAR prepares the organism for threat response before danger is fully perceived. It is central to animal survival and memory formation.

AST Insight:

FEAR introduced anticipation into affective life. It was one of the first systems to operate prospectively—to feel before something happens.

5.4 RAGE: Boundary Defence and Frustration

- Function: Responds to restraint, frustration, or violation.
- Neuroanatomy: Medial amygdala, hypothalamus, PAG.
- Affective Tone: Anger, aggression, irritation.
- RAGE ensures survival when an animal is trapped, dominated, or blocked. It is both defensive and territorial.

AST Insight:

RAGE evolved as a **corrective force** to overcome obstruction and restore autonomy or control.

5.5 LUST: The Drive to Reproduce

- Function: Triggers reproductive behaviour and sexual attraction.
- Neuroanatomy: Hypothalamus, medial preoptic area (MPOA), and limbic structures.
- Affective Tone: Sexual arousal, pleasure, craving.

LUST supports gene propagation and species survival. It is modulated by testosterone, estrogen, and oxytocin.

AST Insight:

LUST is evolution's way of turning reproduction into a felt experience, ensuring it becomes a high-priority behaviour.

5.6 CARE: Nurturing and Attachment

- Function: Drives parental care, social bonding, and empathy.
- Neuroanatomy: Anterior cingulate cortex, hypothalamus, oxytocin pathways.
- Affective Tone: Warmth, protectiveness, tenderness.

CARE allows mammals to raise vulnerable offspring and form long-term bonds. It supports kin survival and group cohesion.

AST Insight:

CARE introduces other-oriented emotion and may be the evolutionary root of empathy and morality.

5.7 GRIEF / PANIC: The Pain of Separation

- Function: Signals social loss, abandonment, and distress.
- Neuroanatomy: Anterior cingulate cortex, PAG, and endogenous opioid systems.
- Affective Tone: Loneliness, sorrow, longing.

GRIEF/PANIC evolved to motivate reconnection, especially in infants separated from caregivers. It is tied to social dependence and attachment.

AST Insight:

This system reveals that emotional pain evolved from physical pain, highlighting the deep overlap between bodily and social survival.

5.8 PLAY: The Engine of Learning and Joy

- Function: Promotes learning, social skills, and behavioural flexibility.
- Neuroanatomy: Subcortical motor areas, thalamus, basal ganglia.
- Affective Tone: Joy, fun, curiosity.

PLAY is most prominent in mammals and some birds. It helps animals practice survival behaviours in a safe setting.

AST Insight:

PLAY reveals that affective systems are not just about *avoiding harm* but also optimizing future survival through positive emotion.

5.9 Why These Seven? And Why They Matter for Consciousness

These seven systems share five core features:

- Subcortical origin (not dependent on cortex)
- Cross-species presence in mammals and many birds
- Spontaneous activation under naturalistic conditions
- Subjective affective tone (i.e., they are *felt*, not just enacted)
- Adaptive function directly tied to survival

Together, they form a **primary affective architecture** that:

- Motivates behaviour
- Organises memory
- Signals priority
- Balances competing drives

AST Claim:

These seven systems are the **foundational "languages" of feeling**, shaping the entire structure of emotion, learning, selfhood, and consciousness.

6: Affect Before Cortex — Brainstem Consciousness

6.1 The Cortical Bias in Theories of Consciousness

Most modern theories of consciousness, especially in cognitive neuroscience, emphasize the cerebral cortex, particularly:

- The prefrontal cortex (planning, reflection)
- The temporal lobes (memory, language)
- The parietal cortex (spatial integration)

These regions support complex thought, language, and higher-order cognition. But are they required for consciousness itself?

According to Affective Survival Theory, the answer is no. Core consciousness—a basic, subjective feeling of existence—emerges from the brainstem, *not* the cortex.

6.2 Brainstem Function and Consciousness

The brainstem is evolutionarily ancient and regulates:

- Arousal (via the reticular activating system)
- Basic drives (hunger, thirst, fear, pain)
- Autonomic functions (breathing, heart rate)
- Emotion and affect (via the periaqueductal gray or PAG)

Key regions involved:

- Periaqueductal gray (PAG) — coordinates pain, fear, maternal care
- Reticular formation — controls wakefulness and alertness

- Parabrachial nucleus — relays visceral and emotional signals
- Nucleus tractus solitarius (NTS) — integrates interoceptive input

These areas are:

- Directly involved in generating affective states
- Active even in patients or animals with minimal cortical function
- Present in nearly all vertebrates

"Without the brainstem, you cannot be awake. Without the cortex, you can be awake and *still feel.*"
— *Damasio, 2010*

6.3 Merker's Evidence: Consciousness Without a Cortex

In a landmark paper, Björn Merker (2007) reviewed cases of children born with hydranencephaly—a condition in which the cerebral cortex is largely absent or non-functional. These children:

- Cry when hungry
- Smile and respond to music
- Prefer familiar faces
- Show signs of pain, pleasure, and emotional arousal

Similarly, decorticated animals (rats, cats) show:

- Exploratory behaviour
- Fear and rage responses
- Social bonding cues
- Play behaviour

These observations suggest that affective consciousness arises from subcortical systems, not cortical computation.

"The capacity for conscious experience is not restricted to cortical animals."
— *Merker, 2007*

6.4 Solms: The Brainstem as the "Feeling Organ"

Neuropsychologist Mark Solms argues that affect is the foundational level of consciousness and originates in brainstem homeostatic circuits. The brainstem does not just regulate the body—it monitors survival-related imbalances and produces:

- Hunger and thirst
- Pain and pleasure
- Comfort and distress

These are felt states—not mere signals.

"We don't feel our cortex; we feel our bodies... and the feelings come from the brainstem."
— *Solms, 2021*

Solms proposes that the brainstem enables:

- Sentience (basic feeling)
- Volition (urge to act)
- Awareness of bodily need

These components precede conceptual thinking and underlie core consciousness.

6.5 Affect vs. Cognition: Which Came First?

In the AST framework:

- Cognition is late, cortical, symbolic, and abstract
- Affect is early, subcortical, embodied, and direct

This reverses the standard model, which sees emotion as a by-product of thought. Instead:

"Thought is layered *on top of* feeling. Feeling is evolution's first and primary assessment system."

Evidence:

- Animals without a cortex show emotions
- Brainstem lesions abolish consciousness; cortical lesions do not
- Feelings like hunger, pain, and fear are present across species

This suggests that affective consciousness is older, more robust, and more widespread than cognitive awareness.

6.6 The Implications for AST and Beyond

If feeling can exist without thought:

- Then, consciousness is not defined by intelligence
- Then, many non-human animals are conscious in a meaningful sense
- Then AI without affective architecture may never become conscious

AST Claim:

Feeling is the minimal criterion for consciousness, not language, logic, or self-report.

AST connects consciousness to the core survival architecture of all complex life by locating feeling in the brainstem. Feeling is not a luxury but a life-detection system rooted in body-based regulation and valuation.

7: The Embodied Mind — Interoception and the Felt Self

7.1 Feeling from the Inside Out

Most traditional models of consciousness focus on the perception of the *external* world—sight, sound, touch. But in recent decades, neuroscience has uncovered something more foundational: the brain's moment-to-moment perception of the internal body.

This process is called interoception—the continuous sensing, modelling, and regulation of internal bodily states like:

- Heartbeat
- Breathing
- Gut sensations
- Temperature
- Hormonal changes
- Muscle tension

"The experience of being a self is rooted in the feeling of being a body."
— *Seth, 2021*

7.2 What Is Interoception?

Interoception is the sense of the body's internal physiological condition. It is not just a passive process but an active monitoring system that updates the brain's internal model of bodily needs.

Key interoceptive structures include:

- Insular cortex (especially the anterior insula)
- Anterior cingulate cortex (ACC)
- Brainstem nuclei (e.g., nucleus tractus solitarius)
- Hypothalamus (homeostatic regulation)

These areas:

- Receive visceral input from the body
- Integrate it with emotional and cognitive signals
- Generate the felt sense of "how I am right now"

7.3 Interoception as the Core of Feeling

Feeling is not an abstract mental state. It is an evaluation of bodily conditions for survival. Examples:

- A pounding heart = anxiety
- A warm belly = satiety
- Shivers = fear or cold

In AST, affect is not just *in* the brain—it is about the body. The felt self arises from the continuous interplay between:

- Internal sensing
- Homeostatic goals
- Affective valence

This is why you *feel hunger* as a bodily state, not just a thought. And why emotions like fear and love have clear somatic markers (e.g., tight chest, rapid breath, gut tension).

> "Emotions are perceptions of interoceptive changes that prepare the organism for adaptive action."
> — *Damasio, 1999*

7.4 The Insula: Where the Body Becomes Felt

The anterior insula is considered the central hub of interoceptive consciousness. It:

- Receives internal sensory input
- Integrates it with memory, context, and goals
- Generates the subjective sense of feeling

Studies show that insula activity correlates with:

- Pain and temperature awareness
- Emotional awareness
- Empathy and social emotion
- Self-recognition

Damage to the insula can impair bodily awareness and emotional experience, further supporting its role as a bridge between physiology and consciousness.

7.5 The Self as a Dynamic Body Model

AST aligns with theories that see the self not as a fixed thing, but as a dynamic process: an ever-updated model of the organism's state and survival priorities.

This process is often called the "body-brain loop", and it includes:

- Interoceptive input from the body
- Affective evaluation of bodily state
- Action to correct imbalance (e.g., eat, rest, flee)
- Feedback integration into memory and identity

"The self is not a static representation—it is the feeling of an organism striving to survive."
— *Damasio, 2010*

This means the "I" you feel is deeply linked to the biological imperative to maintain homeostasis.

7.6 Interoception and Core Consciousness

Antonio Damasio's model of core consciousness arises directly from the brain's mapping of:

- The body's current state

- Its affective salience
- The context in which it occurs

This bodily awareness provides the most basic sense of *being a self here and now*, before thoughts, language, or reflection. It is:

- Embodied
- Momentary
- Affective

This is not a high-level narrative, but a felt presence. AST places this as the origin point of all later forms of consciousness.

7.7 When Interoception Fails: Dissociation, Trauma, and Disorders

Disruptions to interoceptive signalling can lead to profound changes in self-awareness:

- Trauma: numbing or hypervigilance to internal signals
- Anxiety: misinterpretation of bodily signals as threats
- Depression: blunted interoceptive accuracy and affective response
- Depersonalization: loss of "ownership" of bodily experience

This suggests that the integrity of interoception is necessary for a coherent sense of self and feeling.

7.8 AST View: The Self Is a Survival Interface

In Affective Survival Theory, the felt self is not an illusion, but it is not fixed. It is an interface, constantly rebuilt in real time through:

- Affective evaluation of the body's state
- Modelling of threats, needs, and priorities
- Adjustment of action and behaviour

Consciousness emerges when this model of bodily self-in-relation-to-world becomes felt-that is, when it acquires valence, urgency, and direction.

"Consciousness is the body modelling itself in time, feeling its needs, and acting on them."
— *Affective Survival Theory*

8: Quantum Biology and the Fabric of Experience

8.1 Introduction: Beyond the Classical Brain

Neuroscience has long operated under the assumption that the brain functions as a classical biological machine—neurons firing, synapses wiring, information flowing in computational pathways. Yet despite vast progress in mapping the brain's structure and activity, the core mystery of consciousness remains unsolved.

We know what the brain *does*. But we do not understand how and why it feels like anything.

Traditional models fail to explain subjective experience—why we feel pain rather than withdraw, or why we suffer grief instead of merely recognising loss. This persistent enigma, often called the **"hard problem of consciousness"** (Chalmers, 1995), has prompted researchers to look beyond the purely classical view of biology.

One such frontier is quantum biology—the study of whether the principles of quantum physics, long thought too delicate to survive in the "warm and wet" conditions of living systems, may play a role in the fundamental processes of life.

This chapter explores how quantum biology may contribute to a new understanding of consciousness and how the Affective Survival Theory (AST) offers the evolutionary framework to explain why these processes would have been selected by nature.

8.2 Quantum Biology: When Life Goes Non-Classical

For decades, it was believed that quantum effects—such as superposition, coherence, entanglement, and tunnelling—could not survive in biological systems. Yet in recent years, a series of discoveries have challenged that view.

8.2.1 Photosynthesis and Coherence

In photosynthetic organisms, such as algae and plants, energy from sunlight is transferred through quantum coherence, enabling the system to explore all possible energy pathways simultaneously and select the most efficient route (Engel et al., 2007). This process cannot be explained using classical physics alone.

8.2.2 Bird Navigation and Entanglement

Migratory birds appear to detect Earth's magnetic field using quantum entanglement in cryptochrome proteins within their eyes—a process known as magnetoreception (Ritz et al., 2000). These proteins appear to rely on delicate quantum states to interpret spatial information.

8.2.3 Smell and Quantum Tunnelling

The human sense of smell may involve quantum tunnelling, in which electrons pass through molecular barriers to detect scent by vibrational frequency, not just molecular shape (Brookes et al., 2007).

These examples show that quantum effects not only survive in biology but they confer an evolutionary advantage. If quantum processes help organisms absorb energy, navigate, or sense their environment more accurately, then evolution would have selected for these systems.

8.3 Orch OR: A Quantum Theory of Consciousness

The idea that quantum biology might underlie consciousness is most famously proposed in the Orchestrated Objective Reduction (Orch OR) theory, developed by Roger Penrose, a physicist, and Stuart Hameroff, an anesthesiologist.

Their model suggests the following:

- Consciousness arises from quantum computations in microtubules, the structural scaffolding inside neurons.
- These quantum states exist in superposition until they collapse via a process called objective reduction (OR), proposed to be tied to the fabric of spacetime itself.
- Biological processes, such as neurotransmitter release or metabolic conditions, orchestrate the collapses.
- Each collapse produces a moment of conscious awareness.

OR is controversial, and many neuroscientists remain sceptical. However, it offers one of the few physical theories that explains how subjective experience could emerge from matter, not as a simulation, but as a fundamental process of the universe.

8.4 How Affective Survival Theory Complements Orch OR

While Orch OR aims to describe the substrate of consciousness, AST explains its purpose. The two theories address different questions:

- Orch OR: How might consciousness emerge from quantum events in the brain?
- AST: Why did consciousness evolve to feel?

Orch OR may explain *how awareness is physically instantiated* through quantum-level events in microtubules. AST explains *why evolution preserved and refined these experiences* because emotionally felt awareness helped organisms survive.

From this perspective, AST and Orch OR are mutually reinforcing:

- Orch OR provides the spark.
- AST explains why the spark became useful.

If quantum microtubules give rise to basic conscious events, evolution could have shaped those events into emotionally meaningful experiences—fear to avoid danger, pleasure to seek food, love to bond with offspring.

8.5 Emotion as Modulator of Quantum States?

Though speculative, some researchers propose that emotional states could influence quantum coherence. Neurotransmitters like dopamine and serotonin regulate intracellular environments, potentially modulating how long microtubules remain in coherent states or when reductions occur.

In AST, emotion is not just a product of consciousness but a driver of conscious prioritisation. If emotional valence affects neural architecture at the quantum level, the boundary between feeling and physics becomes intriguingly blurred.

This speculative synthesis does not require quantum mysticism—it simply opens the possibility that evolutionary biology and quantum physics may intersect to shape experience.

8.6 Why Would Quantum Consciousness Evolve?

Even if quantum coherence supports conscious moments, why would evolution retain such a fragile and energy-intensive mechanism?

AST provides the answer:

Because felt awareness conferred adaptive advantage.

If conscious feelings help organisms:

- Predict and avoid danger (fear),

- Seek resources (hunger, desire),
- Maintain relationships (affection, social pain),
- Reinforce survival memories (trauma, joy),

…then any biological system supporting those feelings—even at the quantum level—would be evolutionarily selected.

The survival benefits of affective experience justify the cost of maintaining conscious systems, whether classical or quantum.

8.7 Conclusion: From Substrate to Strategy

The challenge of consciousness requires both mechanistic and functional explanations.

- Orch OR offers a possible mechanism: quantum events in microtubules.
- AST offers a functional rationale: felt experience as an evolved memory and decision-making system.

In this view:

- Quantum biology provides the fabric.
- Affective survival weaves the pattern.

Consciousness is not an inexplicable miracle. It is a layered phenomenon—emerging from physical substrates, shaped by emotional salience, and honed by evolution to ensure life reacts, remembers, cares, and survives.

9: The Hard Advantage of Feeling: Reframing the Mystery of Consciousness

9.1 Introduction: From Mystery to Mechanism

For decades, the study of consciousness has been dominated by what philosopher David Chalmers (1995) called the "hard problem": *Why do physical processes in the brain give rise to subjective experience—why does it feel like anything at all?*

While this question has enriched philosophical discourse, it has also stalled progress by treating conscious feeling as an inexplicable anomaly. Affective Survival Theory (AST) offers a shift in perspective. It asks not *why* consciousness exists in metaphysical terms, but *what it evolved to do.*

This reframing introduces what we call the "hard advantage of feeling": the idea that consciousness was selected because subjective experience gave organisms a clear survival benefit. In this view, qualia—the felt qualities of experience—are not accidental; they are functional tags that guide adaptive behaviour.

9.2 Feeling as Function: The Role of Qualia

Qualia are often treated as mysterious, irreducible phenomena. However, their role becomes clear in the AST framework: they give experiences emotional weight. This emotional tagging system:

- Makes pain feel urgent and avoidable
- Makes pleasure feel worth pursuing
- Encourages social bonding through joy, guilt, pride, and shame
- Encodes affectively rich memory for future learning

Feeling itself motivates behaviour, not just the awareness of stimuli. Organisms that could *feel* their way through danger, nourishment, and social life were more likely to survive and pass on their genes.

9.3 The Evolutionary Logic of Emotionally Guided Consciousness

Consciousness is energetically expensive. **If it were not useful, evolution would have eliminated it**. AST offers a Darwinian rationale: consciousness emerged and persisted because it enabled organisms to emotionally evaluate, remember, and respond to their environment more effectively.

Emotionally felt experience provides:

- Behavioural flexibility in unpredictable environments
- Faster learning through emotionally charged events
- Enhanced social intelligence, bonding, and cooperation
- Planning and imagination, based on affectively weighted simulations

The survival advantage wasn't in complexity for its own sake but in adaptive emotional guidance.

9.4 Consciousness vs. Computation: Why Feeling Matters

Many artificial intelligence systems can process data, recognise patterns, and perform tasks once considered uniquely human. But they do not *feel*. They lack:

- Emotional urgency
- A sense of self
- The ability to care about outcomes

AST draws a crucial boundary: computation is not consciousness. The *hard advantage of feeling* lies in how emotion informs behaviour with meaning and memory, something no purely computational system can do.

Feeling, not just logic, is what nature selected to navigate a dangerous and complex world.

9.5 From "Hard Problem" to Researchable Hypothesis

By reframing the "hard problem" as the "hard advantage," AST turns an abstract mystery into a scientific and evolutionary hypothesis. It invites research questions like:

- Do affectively tagged memories enhance survival across species?
- Can affective disruption explain clinical deficits in decision-making and learning?
- Are there neural structures whose primary role is emotional prioritisation?

This shift grounds the study of consciousness in biology and behaviour, rather than philosophical paradox.

9.6 Conclusion: Feeling as the Spark of Survival

The traditional "hard problem" asked: Why does experience feel like anything at all?

AST answers: Because organisms that felt were more likely to survive.

This reframing doesn't trivialise consciousness—it honours its biological brilliance. Feeling is not noise in the system—it is the *signal* evolution selected. The "hard advantage of feeling" tells a story in Darwinian terms: Consciousness is nature's way of caring about danger, pleasure, memory, others, and self. Through this lens, the puzzle of consciousness becomes not a metaphysical riddle, but a testament to how life evolved to feel its way through the world.

"Affective Survival Theory doesn't deny the hard problem — it reframes it. If feeling evolved for survival, then the mystery is not why we feel, but how evolution came to make feeling the most efficient vehicle for biological intelligence."

PART III

The Emotional Compass: Survival Through Feeling

10: Fear: The Compass of Danger

10.1 Fear as the First Teacher

Fear is often regarded as the most primal of human emotions. It can immobilise us, sharpen our senses, flood our bodies with adrenaline, and etch memories so profoundly that they last a lifetime. But fear is more than a disruptive feeling—it is an evolved survival strategy that helped our ancestors and all sentient life avoid harm, preserve life, and adapt through learning.

In the Affective Survival Theory (AST) framework, fear is not merely a psychological phenomenon. It is a biological compass calibrated by evolution to signal danger and promote memory of threatening experiences. It motivates behaviour in proportion to the perceived risk, and—most importantly—it feels unpleasant, not by accident, but by design.

We remember what we fear. And what we remember, we survive.

10.2 Darwin and the Adaptive Role of Fear

Charles Darwin was one of the first to propose that fear has a functional evolutionary role. In *The Expression of the Emotions in*

Man and Animals (1872), he noted that facial expressions of fear—wide eyes, tense posture, open mouth—were universal across cultures and species. These reactions prepared the body to confront or flee danger, improving survival odds.

Darwin observed: "Even insects express fear and anger." This remark, though brief, signalled a crucial evolutionary insight: emotions are not abstract—they are inherited responses shaped by natural selection.

AST extends Darwin's logic: fear is not only a behaviour but an emotionally felt signal that helps organisms encode danger into memory, reinforcing future avoidance.

10.3 Neurobiology of Fear: The Amygdala Circuit

The amygdala, a small almond-shaped structure deep in the temporal lobe, is the brain's emotional sentinel. It rapidly assesses sensory information and assigns emotional salience, particularly to threats. Research by Joseph LeDoux has shown that the amygdala can respond to danger even before the cortex fully interprets the threat (LeDoux, 1996).

When activated, the amygdala initiates a cascade of physiological responses:

- Heart rate increases
- Pupils dilate
- Muscles tense
- The hypothalamus triggers the HPA axis to release cortisol and adrenaline

These changes prepare the organism for fight, flight, or freezing. The amygdala also signals the hippocampus to store emotionally relevant contextual memories. This fear conditioning allows organisms to learn quickly from dangerous experiences.

The emotional intensity of fear enhances memory consolidation, ensuring that the organism learns not just the facts but the feeling of the threat (Phelps, 2004).

10.4 Anticipation and the Evolution of Intelligence

A central tenet of AST is that feeling enables anticipatory behaviour. Unlike simple reflexes, fear allows organisms to simulate danger before it occurs. This mental time-travel—the ability to *feel what might happen*—is an evolutionary leap.

Consider:

- A rabbit avoids an open field where it once saw a predator.
- A child hesitates before touching a hot stove after being burned.
- A person declines a risky job offer because of remembered social rejection.

In all these cases, conscious fear allows the organism to adjust its behaviour in advance, conserving energy and reducing risk. This capacity for forecasted feeling, rooted in memory, is the foundation of intelligent survival.

10.5 Social Fear: Exclusion as Existential Risk

Social connection is key to survival in mammals, including humans. For our ancestors, being ostracised meant losing protection, resources, and mating opportunities. As such, the brain evolved to treat social rejection as a threat.

Studies by Naomi Eisenberger and Matthew Lieberman (2004) showed that social pain activates the same brain regions as physical pain, particularly the dorsal anterior cingulate cortex (dACC). This neural overlap suggests that the distress of exclusion is not metaphorical but neurologically real.

In AST, social fear—fear of rejection, embarrassment, shame, or loneliness—is understood as a refined emotional adaptation that motivates prosocial behaviour. It maintains group cohesion and promotes empathy, conformity, and cooperation.

Feeling excluded doesn't just hurt—it compels reconnection.

10.6 When Fear Overwhelms: Trauma and Maladaptive Learning

While fear is evolutionarily adaptive, it can become maladaptive when overgeneralised or poorly regulated. This is especially evident in post-traumatic stress disorder (PTSD).

In PTSD, individuals relive traumatic events in vivid emotional detail, often triggered by unrelated stimuli. The fear memory becomes over-encoded, and the brain fails to distinguish past from present. This is due to dysregulation in the amygdala, hippocampus, and prefrontal cortex (Shin & Liberzon, 2010).

From an AST perspective, PTSD represents a malfunction in the fear-memory learning system, where the adaptive purpose of fear (to teach avoidance) is compromised by its intensity.

Nonetheless, the very existence of trauma points to how deeply fear matters. Evolution would not have preserved such a potent emotional memory system unless it conferred significant survival benefits.

10.7 Fear Across Species: Affective Continuity in Nature

Fear is not uniquely human. It is observed across mammals, birds, reptiles, and even invertebrates. For example:

- Fish exhibit avoidance learning and stress responses.
- Rats freeze or flee when exposed to predator odours.
- Dogs show fear conditioning, memory, and even trauma.

This widespread presence suggests that fear evolved early in the evolutionary timeline. The basic circuitry for fear appears highly conserved, reflecting its central role in survival (Panksepp, 1998).

AST supports a continuity of consciousness across sentient life, not because all animals reason like humans, but because many can feel what matters to them and act on it.

10.8 Conclusion: Fear as the Root of Emotional Intelligence

Fear is often misunderstood as a primitive hindrance to rationality. In reality, it is one of evolution's most intelligent inventions. It prioritises attention, encodes urgent memory, and motivates life-preserving action. It is the first compass in the affective architecture of survival.

In the AST model:

- Fear is a biological signal rooted in adaptive emotion.
- It is remembered because it is felt.
- It shapes not only immediate responses, but future planning.

Far from being a flaw, fear is the foundation of emotionally guided intelligence.

To fear is to forecast.

To feel fear is to remember what nearly cost us everything.

11: Hunger: The Urge to Sustain

11.1 Introduction: The Pain That Drives Life

Hunger is more than a physiological state. It is an emotional signal—a sensation that rises into consciousness with urgency, discomfort, and often suffering. Hunger affects mood, cognition, social behaviour, and even moral judgment. It can drive invention, aggression, desperation, and solidarity.

But why does hunger **feel** like anything at all?

Why doesn't the brain register energy deficit as a silent background process, like liver function or blood filtration? Why do discomfort, irritability, and even obsession accompany it?

The answer, according to Affective Survival Theory (AST), is simple:

Because organisms that *felt* hungry survived better than those that didn't.

In AST, hunger is a felt evolutionary signal, not just a chemical one. It is an emotion that motivates life-sustaining behaviour, makes memories of deprivation more powerful, and influences risk-taking, planning, and social dynamics. Hunger is not merely about food but about feeling the need to persist.

11.2 The Evolutionary Roots of Hunger

Every living organism requires energy to survive. For multicellular animals, this means foraging, feeding, and balancing intake against expenditure. The early animal that could efficiently detect internal energy deficits and respond accordingly had a significant advantage.

Over time, those biological signals were shaped by natural selection to become felt experiences—aversive enough to spur action, and memorable enough to prevent recurrence.

In this view, hunger evolved as a metabolic alert and a motivational force. It pushes the organism into the world to search, risk, compete, and innovate.

Darwin did not focus extensively on hunger in his emotional work, but he did recognise its role as a driving biological instinct. In *The Descent of Man* (1871), he referred to appetite as a fundamental animal drive that shaped behaviour long before reason emerged.

"All animals feel hunger and strive to satisfy it."

AST extends this observation: the feeling of hunger was selected for, not just the behaviour it induced.

11.3 The Neurobiology of Hunger

Hunger is regulated by a complex interplay of brain regions, hormones, and neural circuits. Central to this system is the hypothalamus, which monitors the body's energy balance and orchestrates feeding behaviour.

Key hormonal signals include:

- Ghrelin: A "hunger hormone" secreted by the stomach, it stimulates appetite and increases food-seeking behaviour.
- Leptin: Produced by fat cells, it signals satiety and suppresses appetite.
- Insulin: Influences glucose metabolism and food cravings.

These hormonal messages converge in the arcuate nucleus of the hypothalamus, which then communicates with the dopaminergic reward system (ventral tegmental area and nucleus accumbens) to generate motivation.

But crucially, what transforms hunger from a signal into a survival-shaping experience is its emotional tone:

- The irritability of fasting
- The distraction of craving
- The desperation of prolonged deprivation

These are not just sensations—they are emotionally valenced states, and as AST argues, they are essential to the survival-learning mechanism.

11.4 Hunger as Emotional Motivation

Why does hunger cause discomfort? Because pain motivates. The unpleasantness of hunger forces prioritisation, ensuring the organism focuses on food acquisition. Studies have shown that hunger affects:

- Attention span and cognitive performance (Benau et al., 2014)
- Risk tolerance and decision-making (Symmonds et al., 2010)
- Emotional volatility (Swami et al., 2012)

The term "hangry" may be modern slang, but the biology is ancient: hunger disrupts homeostasis, which in turn mobilises emotional urgency. According to AST, this emotional urgency tags the hunger experience as salient—it enhances memory encoding and reinforces foraging behaviours that lead to satisfaction.

In hunter-gatherer contexts, this made survival sense: the emotionally charged memory of hunger—and the feeling of its relief—ensured that organisms learned where to find nourishment and avoided prolonged starvation.

11.5 Learning, Memory, and Food-Seeking Behaviour

Emotion plays a crucial role in learning what and where to eat. Animals that consume toxic or unpalatable food develop conditioned taste aversion, often after a single exposure. This is one of the strongest and fastest forms of learning, because the stakes are survival.

Research shows that:

- Hunger increases memory of food-relevant cues (Smeets et al., 2005)
- Food deprivation enhances attention to food images and smells
- Animals will take greater physical or cognitive effort to obtain food when hungry (Zhang et al., 2015)

In AST, hunger is the affective driver of nutritional memory. Its felt quality ensures organisms remember what they need, where they found it, and what strategies worked.

11.6 Hunger, Risk, and Innovation

Hunger also increases an organism's willingness to explore, compete, and innovate. In animals, hunger increases:

- Territorial range
- Predator risk tolerance
- Conflict with conspecifics

In humans, prolonged food insecurity has historically driven:

- Migration
- Technological adaptation
- Cultural development around agriculture

Anthropologist Richard Wrangham (2009) argues that cooking food, which made nutrients more digestible, was a pivotal moment in human evolution, perhaps driven by hunger-related innovation.

Under AST, the feeling of hunger was a selective pressure for creativity. It made trial-and-error exploration more urgent, emotionally reinforced successful behaviours, and catalysed the development of survival-enhancing technology.

11.7 Hunger as a Social and Moral Force

Hunger influences hierarchy, cooperation, and empathy in many social species. Primates share food to maintain alliances. Humans have built religious and ethical systems around feeding the poor or fasting in solidarity.

The emotional power of hunger extends beyond the individual—it can shape moral feeling, political action, and cultural meaning. Hunger drives compassion and cruelty alike. In this sense, it is a collective emotional engine, not just a personal need.

AST interprets this as further evidence that hunger is a socially encoded emotional experience, embedded in our brains, behaviours, and cultural evolution.

11.8 Conclusion: Feeling the Need to Live

Hunger is not simply a biological alarm bell—it is an emotionally intelligent signal, evolved to preserve life by motivating behaviour, enhancing memory, and guiding choice.

In the AST framework:

- Hunger is an adaptive affective state, not a neutral metric.
- Its unpleasantness makes it useful—it commands attention and action.
- Its resolution reinforces learning, attachment to resources, and cultural behaviours.

We hunger, therefore we plan.

We feel hungry. Therefore, we survive.

As with fear, hunger reveals the more profound logic of consciousness. Feeling is not optional—it is strategic. Hunger is one of nature's most ancient affective tools, and in its urgency lies the seed of everything from survival to civilisation.

12: Social Pain: The Cost of Disconnection

12.1 Introduction: The Hurt That Cannot Be Seen

Rejection, loneliness, abandonment, and exile are not just metaphors or emotional disappointments. They are deeply painful experiences, often described as worse than physical injury. In fact, studies show that social exclusion activates the same brain regions as physical pain, a discovery that has revolutionised our understanding of emotion, consciousness, and human evolution (Eisenberger & Lieberman, 2004).

According to Affective Survival Theory (AST), this is not a coincidence—it is biology. Social pain is not a psychological by-product of advanced cognition, but a primary evolutionary adaptation. It exists to protect one of our most important resources: social connection.

In the ancestral environment, to be excluded was to be endangered.

Social pain evolved as a survival signal—a way to register and remember isolation, motivate reconnection, and reinforce group cohesion. Just as hunger signals energy need, social pain signals the need for belonging.

12.2 Darwin and the Social Brain

Charles Darwin recognised that sociality was central to human and animal evolution. In *The Descent of Man* (1871), he emphasised that survival often depended not on brute strength but on cooperation, mutual aid, and emotional bonds. He wrote:

"Man is a social animal. … Selfish and contentious people will not cohere; nothing can be effected without coherence."

Group living brought survival benefits—protection from predators, shared food, child-rearing support—but also created a new kind of risk: social exclusion. AST builds on Darwin's insight by suggesting that the emotional pain of being excluded evolved as a warning system to keep individuals aligned with group norms, alliances, and status.

12.3 The Neuroscience of Social Pain

In a groundbreaking set of experiments, Naomi Eisenberger and Matthew Lieberman used functional MRI to study brain activity during experiences of social rejection. Participants played a virtual ball-tossing game (Cyberball) and were later excluded by the other players. The result?

- Exclusion activated the dorsal anterior cingulate cortex (dACC) and anterior insula—the same regions involved in physical pain processing (Eisenberger et al., 2003).

This neural overlap suggests that the brain does not distinguish between social and physical threats sharply. Pain is pain—whether from a burn or a breakup. From the AST perspective, this redundancy makes adaptive sense. If both types of pain threaten survival, both must be felt, remembered, and avoided.

12.4 Attachment, Loss, and the Need to Belong

Human infants are born helpless and depend entirely on caregivers for survival. This evolutionary dependency gave rise to the attachment system, a biologically hardwired emotional mechanism that ensures infants stay close to protectors and protest when separated (Bowlby, 1969).

Separation distress in infants triggers crying, seeking, and anxiety behaviours that recruit social support and increase chances of reconnection. In adults, similar mechanisms persist:

- Romantic heartbreak feels physically painful.
- Grief from losing a loved one can alter immune function and cognition.
- Social isolation increases mortality risk (Holt-Lunstad et al., 2015).

In AST, these phenomena are not side effects of complex brains—they are core features of emotionally encoded social intelligence. The feeling of loss is evolution's way of ensuring we value connection enough to maintain it.

12.5 Loneliness: A Signal, Not a Symptom

Loneliness is often treated as a psychological state, but it is increasingly recognised as a biological condition with evolutionary roots. Chronic loneliness is associated with:

- Increased risk of cardiovascular disease
- Weakened immune response
- Higher incidence of depression and anxiety

- Cognitive decline and earlier death

Cacioppo et al. (2006) proposed that loneliness functions as a biological warning system, akin to thirst or hunger. It motivates reconnection by producing discomfort, sharpening attention to social cues, and enhancing memory of affiliative behaviour.

AST aligns with this: loneliness is not merely sadness—it is an emotionally encoded survival drive, signalling the need to restore connection for physical and emotional security.

12.6 Shame, Embarrassment, and the Fear of Judgment

In social species, group norms regulate behaviour. Those who violate norms face exclusion, punishment, or loss of status. As a result, humans evolved social emotions—like shame, guilt, and embarrassment—that signal internal alignment with external expectations.

- Shame protects against behaviours that might lower social status.
- Embarrassment shows awareness of violations and invites forgiveness.
- Guilt motivates reparative actions.

These emotions feel bad for a reason. They are internalised social pain, designed to maintain relationships and prevent exclusion.

AST views these emotions as essential tools of group survival.

The emotional intensity of these states ensures that we not only remember our mistakes but also feel them deeply enough to change our behaviour.

12.7 Social Pain Across Species

Social pain is not uniquely human. Many animals demonstrate signs of distress during separation or exclusion:

- Primates cry and withdraw when removed from their troop.
- Elephants have been observed mourning lost companions.

- Rats show social aversion and empathy-based behaviour.

Studies show that opioid systems, which mediate physical pain, also regulate social bonding and separation distress in animals (Panksepp, 1998). This suggests that the neural mechanisms of social pain are evolutionarily ancient and conserved.

From AST's perspective, this further supports the view that social pain evolved not from abstraction but from biology, because disconnection reduces fitness.

12.8 Social Pain and Modern Society

In the digital age, social disconnection is increasingly widespread. Despite constant online interaction, loneliness is at epidemic levels. The rise in anxiety, depression, and suicide, especially among adolescents, may be tied to the amplification of social pain through social media, rejection, and status comparison.

AST highlights the importance of understanding social pain both psychologically and evolutionarily. Our brains are not designed for anonymous interaction or constant exposure to social feedback. When a connection is broken or ambiguous, our biology reacts as if our lives are threatened, because once they were.

12.9 Conclusion: Belonging Is Survival

Social pain is not weakness—it is a warning. It tells us when we are drifting from the group, have betrayed a bond, or when others no longer see us. It hurts because it matters.

In the AST framework:

- Social pain is an evolved emotional mechanism.
- It protects bonds, promotes realignment, and motivates prosocial behaviour.
- Its felt quality ensures memory, learning, and long-term adaptation.

We connect, therefore we survive.

We hurt when we are excluded, because belonging is biological.

AST argues that such signals shape consciousness. Pain affects the body, the heart, the group, and the tribe. Feeling social pain is to carry ancient survival wisdom: you are not alone, but you must not be alone.

13: Touch: The First Language

13.1 Introduction: Before Words, There Was Touch

Touch existed before spoken language, written symbols, or abstract thought. In fact, before there were eyes to see or ears to hear, even the earliest multicellular organisms responded to contact with the environment. Touch is not only the first sense to develop in utero—it is the most fundamental form of communication, connection, and emotional regulation across the lifespan and species.

In the Affective Survival Theory (AST) framework, touch is more than sensory input—it is a deeply affective, survival-driven experience. It signals safety, care, bonding, and in some contexts, threat or harm. Touch feels emotionally significant because it has always carried meaning: who touches you, how, and when, matters for survival.

In AST, touch is not just perception—it is emotional presence made physical.

13.2 The Evolutionary Origins of Touch Sensation

Touch is one of the most ancient sensory modalities. Even simple organisms like jellyfish and worms use mechanoreceptors to respond to physical contact. In vertebrates, cutaneous touch receptors became more specialized over time, allowing the detection of temperature, pressure, vibration, and pain.

Darwin acknowledged the importance of touch in emotional communication. In *The Expression of the Emotions in Man and Animals* (1872), he described the use of touch among primates for grooming, reconciliation, and reassurance—behaviours that **strengthened bonds and maintained group cohesion**.

"A young child clings to its mother instinctively when alarmed, and her embrace calms it."

AST extends Darwin's observations, proposing that the feeling of being touched, especially in affiliative, nurturing contexts, evolved as an emotional tag for safety, belonging, and memory.

13.3 The Neurobiology of Touch: More Than Skin Deep

Touch is mediated by specialized receptors in the skin, including:

- Merkel cells (pressure and texture)
- Meissner's corpuscles (light touch)
- Pacinian corpuscles (vibration)
- Ruffini endings (stretch)
- Free nerve endings (pain, temperature)

But uniquely relevant to emotional experience are the C-tactile (CT) afferent fibres—a class of unmyelinated nerve fibres that respond specifically to slow, gentle, skin-level stroking, typically at the speed of human caressing.

Research by Olausson et al. (2002) showed that CT afferents activate not only the somatosensory cortex (which registers basic touch) but also the posterior insula and anterior cingulate cortex, regions associated with emotion and interoception.

This finding confirms what AST predicts:

Some forms of touch are processed as physical stimuli and as affective experiences.

13.4 Touch and Bonding: The Biology of Affection

Touch is central to social bonding and attachment. At birth, skin-to-skin contact between the infant and the caregiver regulates body temperature, heart rate, and stress levels. It also facilitates the release of oxytocin, the so-called "love hormone", which plays a key role in trust and connection (Uvnäs-Moberg, 1998).

Touch is also a language of emotional communication:

- Grooming in primates reduces cortisol and reinforces alliances.
- Holding hands reduces neural pain responses (Goldstein et al., 2018).
- Hugs, caresses, and massages reduce anxiety and depressive symptoms.

In AST, such effects are not incidental. Touch's emotional meaning drives memory, motivation, and evolutionary selection. Touch teaches the infant she is safe and that the adult who matters. It embeds social patterns in the body as well as the mind.

13.5 Touch, Memory, and Trauma

Touch is also deeply encoded in emotional memory. The feeling of a parent's hand, a partner's embrace, or a caregiver's caress can become emotionally vivid—and so too can threatening or abusive touch.

Touch trauma, especially in childhood, has been linked to:

- Impaired attachment development
- PTSD and somatic flashbacks
- Difficulties with intimacy and boundaries in adulthood

This speaks to the affective weight of tactile experience. Under AST, the emotional tagging of touch ensures that physical contact is not neutral—it is remembered in terms of safety or harm, shaping future behaviour and relational patterns.

13.6 Cultural Expressions of Touch

While the neural architecture of affective touch is universal, cultural norms around touch vary. In Mediterranean cultures, touch is frequent and expressive. In others, it is restrained. But even where public touch is limited, private affective touch remains essential—between parents and children, lovers, caregivers and the dying.

Touch also plays a key role in rituals—handshakes, blessings, rites of passage—providing a shared, embodied emotional experience and reinforcing group identity.

In AST, these patterns are interpreted as cultural elaborations on a biologically grounded need to feel safe, seen, and bonded through contact.

13.7 Touch Across Species

Touch-based bonding is not unique to humans:

- Rats groom each other to reduce stress.
- Elephants use their trunks to caress and comfort.
- Monkeys spend hours grooming not just for hygiene but for social bonding.

Such behaviours activate reward systems and reduce stress hormones—further evidence that touch is an evolutionarily conserved form of emotional regulation (Panksepp, 1998).

This cross-species continuity supports AST's central claim: affective experiences are not limited to humans but are embedded across the animal kingdom where social survival matters.

13.8 When Touch Is Absent

The deprivation of touch has severe developmental and psychological consequences. In studies of orphaned infants in institutional settings, those who received less tactile stimulation showed:

- Delayed cognitive and motor development
- Reduced weight gain
- Heightened anxiety and emotional dysregulation

Even in adults, touch deprivation correlates with depression, anxiety, and loneliness. During the COVID-19 pandemic, widespread social distancing led to increased reports of "skin hunger"—a visceral longing for physical contact.

These effects emphasise that touch is not an accessory to life—it is a biological necessity, embedded in our nervous system and emotional architecture.

13.9 Conclusion: Consciousness Begins at the Skin

Touch is the first sense we encounter the world, and it remains the most emotionally potent. In the AST framework:

- Touch is evolution's first affective interface.
- It encodes safety, danger, bonding, and rejection.
- Its emotional weight gives it the power to shape behaviour, memory, and meaning.

We touch, therefore we feel.

We feel, therefore, we remember who is safe.

Touch binds us to others, regulates our emotions, and carves our early experiences into memory. As the first language of life, it teaches the nervous system what matters. AST holds that this primal sense became the first channel of felt consciousness, long before we had words to describe it.

PART IV

Perception with Purpose: Emotionally Tuned Senses

14: The Five Senses: Emotionally Charged Interfaces

14.1 Introduction: Sensing with Feeling

The five traditional senses—sight, hearing, touch, taste, and smell—are often described as mechanisms for perceiving the external world. But perception is not passive. We do not merely *receive* sensory data; we feel, remember, and act upon it. The smell of smoke triggers an alarm. The sound of a baby crying moves us. A bright red object draws attention. The taste of rotten food repels.

According to Affective Survival Theory (AST), the senses are not only gates to consciousness—they are emotionally charged interfaces, tuned by evolution to prioritise survival-relevant information. Their value lies in what they detect and how they feel. The subjective quality of sensation—its pleasantness or unpleasantness, urgency or familiarity—transforms raw stimuli into memory, learning, and behaviour.

We sense the world *through* emotion, and emotion gives sensation meaning.

14.2 Evolution and the Emotional Weight of the Senses

All sensory systems evolved to serve a survival function. But organisms that could *feel* their sensations had an additional advantage: they could prioritise, remember, and avoid or repeat experiences more efficiently. From this perspective:

- Sight evolved not just to detect light, but to *feel startled* by movement or attracted by colour.
- Hearing evolved not just to detect sound, but to *feel alarmed* by a predator's call or soothed by a mother's voice.
- Taste and smell evolved not just to sample the environment, but to *feel disgust or pleasure*, guiding ingestion and avoidance.

This affective modulation of perception is key to AST's claim that consciousness is an emotional map of experience, grounded in survival.

14.3 Vision: Seeing Danger and Desire

Vision is the dominant sense in humans. The retina captures light and transmits information to the visual cortex, but this is only the start. The amygdala, pulvinar nucleus, and orbitofrontal cortex process the emotional salience of what we see (Vuilleumier, 2005).

We do not see neutrally:

- Sudden motion triggers fear.
- Faces are evaluated instantly for threat, trust, or attraction.
- Colours influence mood (red increases arousal, blue calms).

Emotional stimuli—like threatening faces or traumatic scenes—are remembered more vividly and are more likely to shape future behaviour. This is because visual perception is interwoven with emotional systems, ensuring that what we see is tagged by how we feel.

14.4 Hearing: Listening to Emotion

Hearing is the fastest sense, with auditory signals reaching the brain more rapidly than visual ones. Sound bypasses the thalamus to reach the amygdala, allowing us to react to emotional tones or environmental alarms even before we are fully conscious of the source (LeDoux, 1996).

Emotionally charged sounds include:

- Infant cries
- Screams or sudden loud noises
- Music, rhythm, and language prosody

Music in particular can evoke intense emotions without semantic content, suggesting that sound and feeling are evolutionarily linked. The brain responds to musical patterns using the nucleus accumbens and dopaminergic pathways, just as it does with food or social reward (Salimpoor et al., 2011).

In AST, hearing is not just about detecting sound waves—it is about feeling what those sounds mean and using those feelings to guide attention, affiliation, or withdrawal.

14.5 Smell: The Scent of Memory

Olfaction is the most ancient of the senses, and perhaps the most emotionally potent. Unlike other sensory modalities, smell signals bypass the thalamus and project directly to the amygdala and hippocampus—the centres of emotion and memory (Herz & Engen, 1996).

Because of this, odours are uniquely effective at:

- Triggering vivid autobiographical memories
- Eliciting strong emotional responses (both positive and negative)
- Influencing unconscious behaviours, such as mate selection and danger detection

Smell is often undervalued in modern sensory hierarchies, yet its power lies in its directness. From the scent of danger (smoke, decay) to the comfort of a familiar person's scent, smell provides a felt link to memory and identity.

Under AST, olfaction is a deep affective channel, essential to survival long before language existed.

14.6 Taste: The Affective Gatekeeper of the Gut

Taste evolved to regulate ingestion—to tell us what to consume and what to avoid. The basic taste modalities—sweet, salty, bitter, sour, and umami—each correspond to survival-relevant information:

- Sweet = energy-rich
- Salty = electrolyte balance
- Bitter = potential toxin
- Sour = spoiled or unripe
- Umami = protein presence

The emotional valence of these tastes—pleasure, disgust, caution—is what ensures that eating is not a neutral act. Disgust, in particular, is one of the most emotionally aversive reactions, with strong memory encoding and behavioural avoidance (Rozin et al., 2000).

Taste is also social and cultural: comfort foods, shared meals, and rituals create emotional bonding. AST views taste as an affective filter, ensuring survival through both biological and relational ingestion.

14.7 Touch: Revisited as Emotional Texture

Touch has already been discussed in Section 13, but within the broader sensory framework, it remains essential to consider its tactile and affective nuances:

- Harsh textures may signal harm.
- Gentle textures calm the nervous system.
- Pressure and rhythm (as in heartbeat or massage) regulate arousal.

These tactile sensations are not merely somatic—they are emotionally interpretive, transforming contact into safety, threat, familiarity, or alienation. As AST holds, touch is the first emotional map of the world, and it remains the most emotionally immediate sense.

14.8 The Senses as Affective Modulators of Memory

One of AST's core claims is that emotionally felt experience becomes memory. Sensory experiences, when emotionally significant, are more likely to:

- Be stored long-term
- Influence future behaviour
- Shape identity and perception

Neuroscience supports this: emotionally salient sensory stimuli trigger amygdala-hippocampus interaction, making memories more vivid and durable (Phelps, 2004).

This explains why:

- The sound of a voice can comfort or disturb.
- A single smell can bring back childhood.
- A taste can trigger grief, joy, or nostalgia.

These are not coincidences—they are adaptive features, forged by evolution to make sensory experience an emotional survival tool.

14.9 Conclusion: Perception as Emotionally Tuned Intelligence

The five senses are not just instruments of data collection. They are affectively charged survival tools, designed to detect what matters and feel it fully.

In AST:

- Sensation is the gateway to consciousness.
- Emotion is the value system that makes sensation meaningful.
- Memory is the link that stores emotional sensations as knowledge.

We do not just sense—we *feel what we sense.* And through feeling, we remember how to survive.

In the affective architecture of life, the senses are interfaces, not windows. They do not show us a neutral world—they deliver emotionally prioritised experiences, helping organisms know what is there and how it matters to them.

PART V

Intelligence, Memory, and the Feeling Mind

15: Pleasure and Reproduction: The Feel-Good Imperative

15.1 Introduction: Why Does Pleasure Feel Good?

Among all human experiences, pleasure is perhaps the most desirable—and the most mysterious. It drives us to eat, connect, create, explore, and, above all, to reproduce. Yet from a purely functional standpoint, evolution could have made reproduction a neutral process, like cell division. Why, then, is sex not only urgent but ecstatic? Why are intimacy, attraction, and bonding wrapped in a flood of feeling?

According to Affective Survival Theory (AST), pleasure is not accidental—it is an evolved motivational signal, selected by evolution because it reinforces life-sustaining and gene-propagating behaviours. AST holds that reproduction is not merely anatomical—it is emotional, and pleasure is nature's way of ensuring it happens.

What feels good survives.

What survives evolves to feel good.

15.2 Darwin and the Emotional Basis of Mating

In *The Descent of Man* (1871), Charles Darwin proposed that sexual selection—distinct from natural selection—shaped traits like plumage, song, and courtship behaviour. These traits evolved not simply for survival, but to attract mates and secure reproductive advantage.

Darwin noted that mate choice was often guided by preference and attraction—subjective qualities that must have a felt component:

"The females…are most excited or pleased by the more brilliant males, whose colours are apparently displayed for the purpose of exciting or charming them."

AST builds on this by suggesting that pleasure was not just a side effect of mating success—it was the engine of it. The feeling of attraction, satisfaction, and bonding enhanced reproductive fitness, making pleasure a selectable trait in itself.

15.3 The Neurobiology of Pleasure and Sexual Reward

The sensation of pleasure, especially in the context of sexual intimacy, arises from a complex network of neural and hormonal systems. Central to this are:

- Dopamine: Drives the anticipation of reward, activating the nucleus accumbens.
- Oxytocin: Facilitates bonding and trust, especially after orgasm or during cuddling.
- Endorphins: Act as natural opioids, reducing pain and increasing pleasure.
- Testosterone and estrogen: Modulate sexual desire and arousal.

Functional MRI studies show that sexual stimuli activate not only the reward system, but also regions involved in emotional and social evaluation—such as the orbitofrontal cortex and amygdala (Georgiadis & Kringelbach, 2012).

From the AST perspective, the emotional dimension of these neurochemical effects is what makes reproduction memorable, repeatable, and relationship-forming.

15.4 Pleasure and Learning: Reinforcement Through Feeling

Pleasure is not just a momentary sensation—it is a learning mechanism. Organisms that experience intense positive emotion during food intake, sex, or bonding are more likely to:

- Seek those experiences again
- Prefer certain partners or places
- Compete for access to rewards

This reinforcement loop ensures that adaptive behaviours are repeated. Sexual pleasure, in particular, increases the likelihood of:

- Mate retention and monogamy
- Pair bonding
- Cooperative parenting

Pleasure literally teaches the brain what is worth pursuing, embedding emotional associations with people, places, and acts that enhance genetic success. AST holds that this process is foundational to the emotional memory system of consciousness.

15.5 Bonding Beyond Biology: Emotion in Long-Term Connection

Human reproduction requires more than copulation. Compared to most mammals, humans give birth to highly dependent infants who require long-term parental investment. This may explain why humans evolved not only sexual attraction but also emotional bonding mechanisms.

Studies show that:

- Romantic love activates the brain's reward system similarly to addictive drugs (Fisher et al., 2005).
- Long-term couples exhibit synchronised oxytocin release during affectionate interaction.
- Social touch and eye contact reinforce emotional connection even outside sexual contexts.

These bonding behaviours are intensely felt, and their absence (in grief, separation, or rejection) triggers social pain (see Chapter 12). In AST, these phenomena are not cultural accidents—they are biologically wired emotional strategies designed to ensure reproductive success through lasting care and attachment.

15.6 Sexual Emotion Across Species

While human sexual pleasure is complex, it is not unique. Many animals display affective components of mating:

- Bonobos use sex to resolve conflict and strengthen bonds.
- Prairie voles show oxytocin-driven pair bonding and distress when separated.
- Rats emit ultrasonic vocalisations during mating that resemble pleasure expressions.

These observations suggest that pleasure and emotional intimacy evolved across species, especially those with complex social lives. AST interprets these as signs that affective consciousness accompanies reproductive behaviour, where bonding and coordination enhance survival.

15.7 Desire, Arousal, and Affective Forecasting

Sexual arousal involves not only sensation but anticipation. Desire is future-oriented—it motivates action based on imagined outcomes. This ability to feel *wanting*, distinct from needing, suggests that emotions guide not only response, but also proactive behaviour.

In humans, sexual desire can be shaped by:

- Memory of past intimacy
- Emotional attachment
- Cultural narratives and symbolic meaning

AST emphasises that desire is an emotionally constructed state, linking memory, imagination, and bodily arousal. It is not purely biological—it is affectively forecasted, emotionally evaluated, and behaviourally directed.

15.8 Pleasure and Morality: The Ethics of Feeling

Pleasure also intersects with ethics and social norms. Cultures regulate sexual behaviour, not because it is biologically simple, but because it is emotionally and socially powerful. The emotional consequences of intimacy—trust, betrayal, jealousy, loyalty—require social systems to guide them.

AST suggests that pleasure is too powerful to be neutral. Its felt intensity makes it a moral and social force, capable of building families, alliances, or conflict. Evolution shaped it not to be private, but to drive public life through emotion.

15.9 Conclusion: Feeling as Reproductive Intelligence

In AST, reproduction is not only a physical act—it is an emotional intelligence system. Pleasure evolved as a felt incentive, bonding individuals and reinforcing behaviour that sustained both individuals and their genes.

- Sexual attraction guides choice.
- Pleasure reinforces repetition.
- Bonding ensures care.
- Memory encodes attachment.

We reproduce because it feels good.

We bond because it feels right.

We survive because we remember how it felt.

The evolutionary strategy of affective pleasure ensures that what we need to do, we *want* to do—and what we want to do, we remember, protect, and pass on.

16: Memory and Imagination: Feeling the Future

16.1 Introduction: The Mind Beyond the Moment

To survive is to anticipate. More than reacting to danger or reward, humans (and many animals) possess the capacity to simulate future outcomes mentally. We imagine, plan, and rehearse possibilities. We regret, hope for, and fear events that have not yet occurred. This imaginative power sets us apart from purely reflexive organisms—it extends our consciousness into the future.

But how did this faculty evolve? Why is it so intricately connected to emotion?

According to the Affective Survival Theory (AST), memory and imagination did not evolve simply to encode or project information. They evolved to do so in emotionally significant ways. AST argues that the brain stores and simulates events in proportion to their felt relevance because what is emotionally marked matters for survival.

We remember what felt important.

We imagine what we fear or desire.

And we plan because we can feel what might come.

16.2 Evolutionary Roots of Memory: More Than Storage

Memory is often compared to a recording device, but this metaphor is misleading. Memory is selective, reconstructive, and emotionally weighted. From an evolutionary standpoint, it would be inefficient to remember everything. Instead, we remember:

- Where the danger occurred
- Who helped or harmed us

- What brought satisfaction or pain

This emotional selectivity is not a flaw—it's an adaptation.

Neuroscientist Joseph LeDoux has shown that the amygdala enhances memory encoding in emotionally arousing situations, especially when linked to threat (LeDoux, 1996). Similarly, Phelps (2004) demonstrated that emotional arousal strengthens hippocampus-dependent memory consolidation.

In AST, emotional feeling is what makes memory evolutionarily useful. Without affect, memory would be too neutral to inform survival.

16.3 Emotional Tagging: How We Know What to Remember

Emotional tagging refers to the process by which emotion assigns value to experience, telling the brain what to store deeply and what to discard. This is observable in:

- Traumatic memory (e.g. car accidents, violence)
- Euphoric memory (e.g. first love, achievement)
- Vivid recall of emotionally charged public events

The synaptic tagging and capture hypothesis (Frey & Morris, 1997) posits that emotional arousal triggers neuromodulators like dopamine and norepinephrine, which "tag" certain synapses for long-term potentiation—a basis of durable memory.

This biologically supports AST's key idea:

Consciousness evolved to *feel* what matters, so that we remember what matters.

16.4 Imagination as Simulated Emotion

If memory helps us remember the past, imagination helps us model the future, and both are emotionally charged. The default mode network (DMN) in the brain, active during daydreaming and introspection, overlaps with networks used in episodic memory, theory of mind, and future planning (Buckner & Carroll, 2007).

Importantly, imagined future events activate many of the same brain regions as actual experiences, especially when those events involve emotionally relevant content (Addis et al., 2007).

AST interprets this as evolution's way of rehearsing future behaviour using emotion:

- We fear outcomes that have not occurred—because feeling fear helps us avoid danger.
- We crave rewards not yet earned—because pleasure motivates pursuit.
- We simulate scenarios—not logically, but emotionally—to guide decision-making.

In essence, imagination is affective foresight.

16.5 Mental Time Travel: Consciousness Across Time

Psychologists refer to the ability to mentally revisit the past and anticipate the future as "mental time travel". This capacity appears in humans and some animals (e.g., scrub jays, great apes), and is strongly linked to episodic memory and self-awareness.

In AST, mental time travel is not just cognitive—it is emotional:

- Regret teaches us to avoid repeating errors.
- Hope sustains goal-directed behaviour.
- Dread motivates precaution.
- Anticipation fuels preparation.

This emotional spectrum of time travel helps organisms plan more effectively. Those who could simulate tomorrow—and feel how it might turn out—were better equipped to act wisely today.

16.6 Memory Disorders and the Loss of Emotional Intelligence

Disorders of memory, such as amnesia, Alzheimer's, or PTSD, reveal how deeply feeling is embedded in memory function. For example:

- Patients with damage to the amygdala may form memories without appropriate emotional salience, resulting in flat affect and poor decision-making.
- PTSD patients often experience emotionally intrusive memories, showing how trauma over-activates the affective memory system.

In each case, it becomes clear that memory is not separable from feeling. Without emotion, memory becomes disorganised or irrelevant, and without memory, imagination loses grounding. AST posits that emotion is the glue of temporal consciousness.

16.7 Imagination and Survival Creativity

Imagination is also tied to problem-solving and innovation—especially in survival contexts. The ability to imagine a tool, simulate an outcome, or empathize with another's situation gives humans flexibility and foresight.

Under AST, creativity is not just aesthetic—it is adaptive. Storytelling, art, ritual, and future planning emerged as emotionally meaningful simulations of real-world challenges, deeply tied to community survival and cooperation.

The feeling embedded in imagination ensures its power and usefulness. We don't just "run the numbers"—we *feel our way through scenarios.*

16.8 Conclusion: Feeling as the Thread of Time

Memory and imagination allow consciousness to stretch beyond the here and now. They allow us to bring the past into the present and pull the future toward us. And in AST, they are emotionally driven because:

- Feeling determines what gets remembered.
- Feeling shapes what gets simulated.
- Feeling teaches what should be repeated or avoided.

Emotion does not distort time—it organises it.

The evolution of affective memory and imagination enabled not only longer life, but wiser life. It created a mind that could learn from experience and plan with vision, not coldly, but vividly, because it could feel what survival demanded.

17: Reasoning: When Logic Feels Right

17.1 Introduction: Thinking Is Not Feeling's Opposite

In modern culture, reasoning is often idealised as the pinnacle of human intelligence—rational, detached, and immune to emotion. Logic is framed as the cure for bias, the path to truth, and the opposite of subjectivity. But neuroscience and evolutionary biology suggest otherwise. Emotion is not the enemy of reason—it is its foundation.

According to Affective Survival Theory (AST), the capacity to reason evolved not in a vacuum, but in the furnace of survival pressure. Early organisms had to evaluate outcomes, weigh risks, and choose courses of action to make good decisions. And those decisions had to be emotionally informed—based on remembered outcomes, anticipated rewards, and felt values.

The brain doesn't reason in spite of feeling.

It reasons *because of* feeling.

17.2 Reasoning in Evolution: From Instinct to Evaluation

In the early phases of evolution, behaviour was primarily reflexive and stimulus-driven. As nervous systems grew more complex, organisms evolved the capacity to:

- Compare different strategies
- Weigh costs and benefits
- Postpone immediate gratification

This shift enabled behavioural flexibility, a hallmark of intelligence. But flexibility requires more than raw logic—it requires valuation, which is fundamentally emotional.

In evolutionary terms, decision-making that maximised survival and reproduction was not merely rational—it was *affectively guided.* Organisms that felt the stakes of their choices learned faster and acted more adaptively.

17.3 The Somatic Marker Hypothesis: How Emotions Guide Logic

One of the strongest neuroscientific models supporting AST is the Somatic Marker Hypothesis, developed by Antonio Damasio. According to this theory:

- Emotions create bodily "markers" (e.g., gut feelings, tension, calm) associated with certain decisions.
- These somatic markers are recalled when similar choices arise.
- They narrow the range of options, speeding up decision-making and improving outcomes.

In patients with damage to the ventromedial prefrontal cortex (vmPFC)—a region involved in integrating emotion into thought—Damasio observed:

- Normal intelligence and logic
- Profound difficulty making real-world decisions
- Poor anticipation of consequences

This suggests that emotion is essential to practical reasoning, especially in ambiguous or socially complex situations (Damasio, 1994).

Damasio famously said, "We are not thinking machines that feel. We are feeling machines that think."

AST builds on this by arguing that these emotion-laced reasoning processes were evolutionarily selected, not incidental. They helped organisms make adaptive choices with limited information, increasing survival odds.

17.4 Moral Reasoning: When Logic Follows the Heart

Moral decisions are a classic arena where reason and emotion are said to conflict. Yet studies show that even moral judgments often arise from fast, automatic emotional responses, followed by rational justification.

Psychologist Jonathan Haidt's Social Intuitionist Model (2001) argues that:

- Moral reasoning is often post-hoc: we justify what we've already felt.
- People's moral intuitions vary by culture and are emotionally grounded.
- Reasoning is used more to persuade others than to discover the truth.

For example, the thought of pushing someone off a bridge to save five people (as in the "trolley problem") often elicits moral revulsion, even when the utilitarian logic is sound. The emotional response is what shapes the moral line.

AST interprets this not as irrationality, but as adaptive emotional intelligence: evolution favours decision systems that value human lives, kinship, loyalty, and social trust. These values are felt before they are formalised.

17.5 "Gut Feelings" and Rapid Cognition

Quick decisions often rely on intuitive thinking—a blend of prior knowledge, emotional memory, and implicit learning. Psychologist Gerd Gigerenzer calls this "fast and frugal heuristics", where emotion helps:

- Simplify complex choices
- Avoid dangerous over-analysis
- Encode learned wisdom into bodily responses

In AST, these intuitions are understood as emotionally shaped cognitive shortcuts, grounded in past survival experiences. When someone says, "It just felt right," they describe an affectively tagged signal, not a logical derivation.

Intuition is not guesswork—it is emotionally informed reasoning.

17.6 Reasoning, Identity, and Self-Coherence

Reasoning is also used to maintain personal identity and narrative coherence. We reason about:

- Our past choices
- Our future goals
- Our sense of self-worth

But these are not purely intellectual exercises—they are emotional constructions. We reason to reduce cognitive dissonance, justify actions, and affirm meaning. As such, reasoning is often aimed at emotional coherence, not only logical soundness.

AST views this function as vital to survival through stability. Organisms that felt consistent and confident in their reasoning were more likely to:

- Maintain social standing
- Attract mates and allies
- Persist through adversity

In this way, the emotional need for narrative structure helps drive our most abstract cognitive faculties.

17.7 Reasoning Gone Wrong: When Feeling Fails

Disorders that impair emotion also impair reasoning. For example:

- People with alexithymia (inability to recognise emotions) often have trouble making decisions.
- Damage to emotional brain regions results in impaired social judgment, despite intact logic.

This underscores AST's principle: reasoning without emotional guidance is often maladaptive. Cold calculation may be flawless in theory, but disastrous in practice.

Conversely, rationality collapses when emotion overwhelms reasoning, such as in panic, mania, or addiction. Thus, the evolutionary sweet spot is a balance between feeling and logic.

17.8 Conclusion: Reasoning as Emotional Intelligence

AST holds that reasoning is not a pure computational system, but a feeling-guided decision engine, sculpted by evolutionary pressures to:

- Maximise adaptive outcomes
- Encode lessons of the past
- Anticipate futures with emotional relevance

Logic is not emotion's opponent—it is its expression in abstract terms.

We reason best not when we ignore our feelings, but when we listen to the ones that kept us alive.

In this light, reasoning is evolution's upgrade of emotion—a way to extend feeling into foresight, strategy, and collective decision-making. It is not what replaces emotion, but what grows from it.

18: Abstract Thought and Symbolic Feeling

18.1 Introduction: When Ideas Begin to Feel

Language, numbers, ethics, and aesthetics are hallmarks of abstract thought, often seen as evidence of higher intelligence. But they are also emotional systems, charged with meaning, value, and memory. We feel the truth of a moral principle, the beauty of a poem, or the elegance of a mathematical proof. We cry at music, find comfort in a flag, or rage at an ideology.

In the Affective Survival Theory (AST) framework, abstract thought evolved not to detach us from emotion, but to amplify and transmit it. AST argues that symbols are emotionally loaded tools, shaped by evolution to extend emotional cognition into complex domains like culture, planning, art, and identity.

We do not think abstractly because we are beyond emotion. We think abstractly because emotion *demands meaning*.

18.2 The Evolution of Abstraction: From Survival to Symbol

Abstraction is the ability to:

- Generalise across contexts
- Create and manipulate symbols
- Represent concepts independently of physical stimuli

But the evolutionary origin of abstraction is not mysterious. It begins with pattern recognition—a basic survival skill. For example:

- A rustle might mean danger.
- A specific smell might mean food.
- A call might mean "come here" or "stay away."

From these patterns emerged proto-symbols, reinforced by emotion. An early hominin who associated a specific gesture with danger would survive more reliably if that association were felt as fear or urgency, not just noticed. Over time, these associations became externalized, giving rise to language, ritual, and art.

AST proposes that emotionally meaningful associations were the evolutionary seeds of symbolic thought.

18.3 Language: Feeling Through Words

Language is often treated as a purely cognitive achievement, but its power lies in its emotional impact. Language enables:

- Expression of internal states
- Coordination of social behaviour
- Transmission of cultural knowledge
- Creation of meaning through metaphor

Neuroscience confirms that language and emotion are deeply intertwined. For example:

- Emotional prosody is processed in the right hemisphere, including areas associated with affective perception.
- Reading emotionally charged words activates the amygdala, insula, and anterior cingulate cortex—the brain's affective core (Kensinger & Schacter, 2006).

Moreover, metaphor—a foundational element of language—often relies on bodily and emotional experiences:

- "A warm person" (emotional and physical warmth)
- "A heavy topic" (weight as burden)

- "Breaking someone's heart" (emotional pain as physical rupture)

AST holds that metaphor is not decorative—it is evolution's way of extending emotional relevance into abstract space.

18.4 Mathematics and Logic: When Precision Feels Right

Even mathematics, often viewed as emotionless, can evoke aesthetic pleasure, frustration, or awe. Mathematicians usually describe equations as "beautiful" or "elegant." Solutions can feel "right" or "ugly." This emotional vocabulary points to a more profound truth: we emotionally evaluate coherence, symmetry, and pattern.

The philosopher Blaise Pascal once said:

"The heart has its reasons, which reason does not know."

In AST, logic is not opposed to feeling—it is structured feeling. The satisfaction of solving a puzzle, the dismay of an error, or the elegance of a proof all suggest that even abstract cognition is grounded in affective systems that evolved to detect order, novelty, and utility.

18.5 Art, Music, and Ritual: The Affective Symbols of Culture

Art and music are influential because they compress and communicate emotion. Music, especially, has no semantic content, yet can:

- Move us to tears
- Inspire action
- Create identity
- Regulate emotion

Neuroscience shows that music activates the dopaminergic reward system, including the nucleus accumbens and ventral tegmental area, and modulates emotional regions such as the amygdala (Blood & Zatorre, 2001; Salimpoor et al., 2011).

Art and ritual carry symbolic emotional codes:

- Colours evoke moods
- Sacred objects channel reverence
- Stories encode moral emotions like guilt, compassion, or pride

AST posits that art and ritual evolved as cultural tools for affective coordination. They shape group emotion, reinforce values, and externalise internal experience to extend survival beyond the individual.

18.6 Morality, Justice, and Shared Feeling

Moral and ethical reasoning often begins with affective experience: fairness, outrage, guilt, empathy. Studies show that:

- Moral decisions activate emotion-related brain regions, not just logical centres.
- Empathy shares neural overlap with direct pain (Decety & Lamm, 2006).
- Children demonstrate moral intuitions before they master logic.

For AST, this suggests that morality evolved from emotional experience, not from abstract rules. Codes of law, ethics, and rights are symbolic extensions of our evolved concern for others. We don't just think fairness—we feel it.

18.7 Symbolic Identity and the Narrative Self

Human beings construct identities using narratives, symbols, and roles. We are citizens, siblings, believers, dreamers—each identity emotionally charged and reinforced by symbols:

- Flags
- Names
- Rituals
- Belonging

These symbols are not mere labels—they shape behaviour and feeling. They tell us who we are and what we stand for. The narrative self, described by philosophers like Daniel Dennett and psychologists like Dan McAdams, is a story-shaped structure of identity built from remembered, anticipated, and imagined emotion.

In AST, symbolic identity is an extension of emotional learning, allowing consciousness to simulate, rehearse, and sustain socially coordinated selves.

18.8 Conclusion: Symbols Are Emotional Technologies

In the Affective Survival framework, abstract thought is not sterile—it is emotional architecture. Language, metaphor, numbers, and rituals are emotional delivery systems, designed to:

- Communicate felt meaning
- Encode emotional experience
- Coordinate group behaviour
- Sustain identity and culture

We symbolize what we feel.

And we feel what our symbols mean.

Evolution did not give us abstraction to escape feeling—it gave us abstraction to organize feeling into adaptive meaning. In this view, consciousness is not only a mirror of the world—it is a map, drawn in the language of emotion and reason.

19: Self-Awareness: The Emotionally Guided Self

19.1 Introduction: What Is the Self, and Why Does It Feel?

At some point in evolution, life began not only to sense and move, but to reflect:

Who am I? What just happened to me? What should I do next?

Self-awareness—recognising the self as a distinct entity capable of feeling, acting, and remembering—is often regarded as the crown jewel of consciousness. It allows for introspection, moral responsibility, long-term planning, and social navigation. But it also introduces vulnerability: shame, pride, regret, and existential doubt.

According to Affective Survival Theory (AST), self-awareness evolved not to make us abstract philosophers but to help us survive as socially embedded, emotionally motivated beings. In AST, the self is not a cold model of identity—it is a feeling-driven feedback loop, an internal narrator that emerged to monitor, remember, and emotionally evaluate our behaviour in a world full of other minds.

The self evolved to feel.

We became aware of ourselves because it made us safer, more adaptable, and more accountable.

19.2 Evolutionary Origins of the Self

Evolutionary biologists and cognitive scientists agree that self-related processing exists on a spectrum across species. Certain mammals, birds, and even cephalopods show evidence of:

- Distinguishing self from others
- Exhibiting empathy or theory of mind
- Recognising themselves in mirrors (e.g. great apes, dolphins, magpies)

While full-blown reflective self-awareness is rare, many animals show proto-self mechanisms (Damasio, 1999). These include:

- Tracking one's bodily states (interoception)
- Making decisions based on past outcomes
- Changing behaviour based on social standing or emotional memory

AST argues that self-awareness evolved in tandem with sociality and emotional memory. Organisms that could remember what happened to *them*, anticipate how others perceived them, and adjust their behaviour accordingly had a significant fitness advantage.

19.3 The Affective Core of Selfhood

While many theories treat self-awareness as primarily cognitive, AST emphasises its emotional substrate. The self is the answer to "What do I know?" and *"How do I feel about what I know?"*

Research shows that:

- The insula integrates bodily states with emotional awareness.
- The medial prefrontal cortex is central to self-referential thinking.
- The anterior cingulate cortex tracks emotional conflict and error monitoring.
- Emotional memories are more likely to be encoded when self-relevant (Kelley et al., 2002).

The feeling of *embarrassment*, for instance, requires not only that I made a mistake, but that I recognize myself as the one who erred. Similarly, *pride* or *shame* rely on evaluative comparisons between the actual and ideal self.

AST holds that these complex emotional states were selected for because they:

- Regulate group behaviour
- Reinforce social norms
- Enhance reputational awareness
- Encourage future-oriented correction and planning

19.4 The Narrative Self: Memory, Meaning, and Moral Emotion

Humans are storytelling creatures. We construct personal identities through autobiographical narratives, linking past, present, and future into a coherent self. This narrative structure is not trivial—it is emotionally shaped.

Psychologist Dan McAdams describes identity as a life story, built from remembered experiences, values, and anticipated goals. These stories are:

- Emotionally toned ("I've always been a fighter")
- Morally loaded ("I want to be a good parent")
- Socially shaped ("I'm the outsider turned leader")

Neuroscience supports this view: regions involved in emotional memory, self-projection, and moral judgment activate during autobiographical reflection (Addis et al., 2007; Moll et al., 2005).

AST proposes that the narrative self evolved as a feeling-based simulator, helping the individual rehearse, evaluate, and refine future behaviours. It is not a logical accountant—it is a survival dramatist.

We feel who we are, and we remember what mattered.

19.5 Self-Awareness in Social Life

In social species, being aware of oneself as an object in others' minds confers enormous advantages. This enables:

- Strategic impression management

- Anticipation of others' reactions
- Empathy and moral restraint

Psychologists refer to this as public self-consciousness—the capacity to monitor how one is seen. It helps explain behaviours such as:

- Social anxiety
- Embarrassment
- Reciprocity
- Altruistic punishment

These are not purely rational calculations. They are emotional experiences, and AST sees them as affective adaptations to social complexity. We survive better when we can feel our social standing.

19.6 Disorders of the Self: When Feeling Fails

Disruptions in self-awareness often involve emotional dysregulation:

- Depersonalization disorder involves feeling detached from the self.
- Borderline personality disorder includes unstable self-concept and emotional volatility.
- Autism spectrum conditions can involve differences in self-other distinction and emotional empathy.

These disruptions suggest that emotion is central to self-experience. When emotional integration falters, the coherence of the self dissolves.

AST views self-awareness as a feeling-organised construct—dependent on affective signalling to maintain integrity, coherence, and adaptability.

19.7 Spirituality and Transcendence: Beyond the Bounded Self

Some experiences involve a dissolution of self-boundaries, such as:

- Mystical states
- Psychedelic experiences
- Deep meditation
- Awe in nature or music

These states are often described as:

- Emotionally intense
- Spiritually meaningful
- Associated with loss of ego and merging with something greater

Neuroscience shows that such states often involve decreased activity in the default mode network (DMN)—the system responsible for self-referential processing (Carhart-Harris et al., 2014).

In AST, even self-transcendence is emotionally structured. These altered states may have evolved to:

- Strengthen social unity
- Inspire moral transformation
- Alleviate existential anxiety
- Reinforce group identity through shared ritual and awe

The boundaries of the self may dissolve, but the emotio-nal function remains: to survive, adapt, and belong.

19.8 Conclusion: The Self as an Emotional Compass

Self-awareness is not a mirror—it is a map. And the terrain it charts is emotional:

- Where we've been (guilt, pride, memory)
- Who we are now (identity, coherence)
- Where we're going (hope, fear, purpose)

AST proposes that the self evolved not as an objective observer, but as a subjective evaluator, organised by emotion to promote intelligent survival in a social world.

We know ourselves because it helps us live better. We feel ourselves because it helps us choose wisely.

In this view, self-awareness is not a philosophical mystery—it is emotion's highest tool, guiding the organism toward adaptive, coherent, and socially meaningful action.

PART VI

Transcendence, Ethics, Sleep and Artificial Minds

20: Beyond Survival: Awe, Wonder, and Transcendence

20.1 Introduction: Feeling More Than Survival

Fear protects us, hunger drives us, and love bonds us. These are the core affective experiences around which life orients itself in its evolutionary battle for survival. But humans also cry at the sight of the stars. We feel humbled before great mountains, moved by symphonies, and stilled by silence. We seek meaning in rituals, purpose in poetry, and transcendence in spiritual experience.

What evolutionary function, if any, do these feelings serve?

According to Affective Survival Theory (AST), awe, wonder, and transcendence are not *breaks* from survival—they are emergent features of an emotional mind whose purpose is to navigate not just immediate needs but ultimate meaning. These elevated emotions help us:

- Bond to something larger than ourselves
- Suspend egocentricity in favour of connectedness
- Regulate moral action

- Cope with uncertainty and mortality

Transcendent feeling is not a departure from nature—it is nature reflecting upon itself through consciousness.

20.2 Awe: The Expansive Emotion

Awe is a complex emotion elicited by vast, mysterious experiences, and beyond ordinary comprehension. Nature, music, birth, death, and spiritual encounters often provoke it. Psychologists Keltner and Haidt (2003) define awe as involving two core elements:

1. Perceived vastness – spatial, conceptual, or social magnitude
2. Need for cognitive accommodation – a felt demand to expand one's mental model

Neuroscience shows that awe reduces activity in the default mode network (DMN)—the system associated with self-referential thinking—suggesting that awe temporarily diminishes ego and increases connectedness (van Elk et al., 2019).

AST interprets awe as an evolved affective reset—it suspends narrow focus, enabling:

- Collective identity
- Spiritual humility
- Openness to novelty and complexity

Shared awe can promote cooperation, reverence, and moral elevation in social groups, reinforcing group cohesion and prosocial behaviour.

20.3 Wonder and Curiosity: Emotional Drives for Exploration

Wonder is the emotional bridge between ignorance and understanding. While curiosity drives us toward specific questions, wonder arises from a felt awareness of the unknown, often accompanied by delight, humility, and imaginative thought.

From an evolutionary standpoint, exploration is risky—but it yields resources, innovation, and learning. Organisms that could feel motivated to explore (rather than being forced by need) had a selective advantage.

Wonder provides that emotional propulsion:

- It transforms uncertainty into fascination
- It makes knowledge acquisition rewarding
- It motivates learning beyond necessity

Neuroscientific studies link curiosity and wonder to dopaminergic reward systems, particularly the ventral striatum and prefrontal cortex (Gruber et al., 2014). Under AST, these circuits evolved to satisfy biological needs and reward affectively meaningful engagement with the unknown.

20.4 Transcendence and the Self Beyond the Self

In mystical and spiritual traditions, transcendence refers to feeling connected to something greater than oneself, whether God, nature, humanity, or the cosmos. These experiences often involve:

- Altered sense of time and space
- Decreased ego-boundaries
- Heightened feelings of peace, unity, or bliss

Brain imaging studies of meditating monks and spiritual practitioners show decreased activity in the posterior cingulate cortex and DMN, suggesting a diminished sense of individual self (Brewer et al., 2011).

AST suggests that transcendence serves emotional integration and psychological resilience by:

- Regulating existential anxiety
- Promoting group unity
- Motivating moral action in alignment with perceived higher truths

These experiences extend emotional consciousness beyond the self, promoting long-term cohesion and adaptive meaning-making in individuals and communities.

20.5 Art, Ritual, and Sacred Emotion

Art and ritual have served as containers for emotionally transformative experiences throughout history. Music, dance, storytelling, and sacred ceremonies amplify:

- Emotional synchronization
- Collective identity
- Cathartic release
- Transmission of values

These are not decorative—they are evolutionary technologies for emotional coherence. Rituals, especially, encode moral rules, kinship, and awe in symbolic acts that evoke deep affect (Whitehouse, 2000).

In AST, these cultural forms are seen as emotionally charged survival tools—designed to:

- Anchor memory through sensory-emotional experience
- Promote intergenerational continuity
- Coordinate large groups through shared emotion

Emotion, memory, and symbolic meaning converge in ritual to create felt meaning that survives beyond the individual.

20.6 Mortality and the Search for Meaning

One of the most potent drivers of transcendence is the awareness of death. Only a creature capable of self-reflection can fear its nonexistence. This awareness can generate:

- Existential dread
- Spiritual seeking

- Moral introspection
- Legacy-driven behaviour

Psychologist Sheldon Solomon and colleagues (2004) argue that the awareness of death drives humans to seek immortality symbols through religion, creativity, or legacy (Terror Management Theory).

AST holds that these impulses are emotionally rooted survival adaptations. By transforming fear of death into stories, systems, and symbols of meaning, human consciousness protects itself emotionally, sustaining motivation and cohesion in the face of finitude.

20.7 Conclusion: Transcendence as Emotional Evolution

Awe, wonder, and transcendence are not accidents of complexity. They are emergent emotional states, built atop the foundations of fear, hunger, love, and memory, extending them into collective meaning, moral vision, and cosmic imagination.

In AST:

- Awe suspends ego to widen perspective
- Wonder transforms ignorance into exploration
- Transcendence connects the self to something greater
- Ritual and art encode emotional memory across generations

We feel beyond survival, not to escape evolution, But because evolution gave us the feeling to seek something beyond ourselves.

These highest emotional states may not serve immediate biological function, but they help organise long-term cooperation, moral reflection, and enduring purpose. In this sense, they are not beyond nature—they are nature's latest leap in the story of emotional intelligence.

21: Ethics, Evolution, and the Felt Experience of Others

21.1 Introduction: Where Morality Comes From

What makes something *right* or *wrong*? Why do humans feel guilt, empathy, outrage, or admiration for ethical acts? Is morality learned, rationally deduced, or innate? Reasoned ethical systems—utilitarianism, deontology, and virtue ethics—have often addressed these perennial philosophical questions.

However, recent research in neuroscience and psychology suggests that our sense of morality is not purely rational but profoundly emotional and embodied. We don't just think about morality—we feel it.

According to Affective Survival Theory (AST), morality emerged not as a cultural invention but as an evolutionarily selected extension of affective consciousness. Ethics is not imposed on emotion—it evolved from it.

We treat others well, not just because we think it is right, but because we feel their pain, share their joy, and remember the cost of harm.

21.2 Morality as an Evolutionary Adaptation

In Darwin's *The Descent of Man* (1871), he proposed that the roots of morality lie in social instincts, especially the emotions of sympathy, guilt, and pride. He noted:

"Any animal whatever, endowed with well-marked social instincts…would inevitably acquire a moral sense or conscience, as soon as its intellectual powers had become as well developed…as in man."

Evolutionary psychologists and anthropologists have since found that prosocial behaviour enhances survival in social species. Traits such as empathy, fairness, and reciprocity:

- Stabilise group dynamics
- Encourage cooperation
- Reduce internal conflict
- Enhance kin and group selection

From an AST perspective, these behaviours evolved not despite emotion, but through it. Emotional responses like empathy, shame, or moral outrage function as adaptive tools that:

- Reinforce memory of harmful or helpful actions
- Guide future behaviour
- Promote social learning

21.3 The Neuroscience of Moral Emotion

Studies of moral cognition show that emotions are integral to moral judgment. When people make ethical decisions, brain imaging reveals activity in:

- The ventromedial prefrontal cortex (empathy, affective evaluation)
- The amygdala (emotional salience)
- The insula (bodily feelings, disgust)
- The posterior cingulate and medial prefrontal cortex (self-referential processing)

For example, damage to the ventromedial prefrontal cortex can impair moral sensitivity despite everyday reasoning (Koenigs et al., 2007). Individuals may logically understand the consequences in these cases but lack emotional aversion to harm.

This supports AST's claim that feeling is central to moral insight. Without emotion, moral reasoning becomes hollow and abstract, detached from the embodied significance of our actions.

21.4 Empathy: Feeling the Other's Feeling

Empathy is the capacity to share or understand another's emotional state. It is the neural and emotional bridge between self and other. Neuroscientific studies show that:

- Observing another in pain activates the anterior cingulate cortex and insula, the same regions involved in experiencing physical pain oneself (Decety & Jackson, 2004).
- The mirror neuron system allows us to simulate others' actions and emotions.

AST interprets empathy as a survival-enhancing expansion of affective consciousness—one that allows social species to:

- Anticipate others' needs
- Bond through shared emotion
- Avoid inflicting harm that could damage group integrity

Empathy thus becomes the felt foundation of ethical behaviour, not merely a virtue but an adaptation.

21.5 Guilt, Shame, and the Internal Moral Compass

Ethical behaviour is not only externally policed—it is internally felt. Emotions like guilt, shame, and remorse regulate our actions by:

- Signalling social misalignment
- Prompting reparative behaviour
- Preventing future harm

Psychologist June Tangney (1995) distinguished:

- Guilt is focused on behaviour ("I did something bad")
- Shame is focused on self ("I am bad")

Both are emotionally painful states, but evolutionarily advantageous. AST views them as internal affective mechanisms, shaped to:

- Maintain social cohesion
- Encourage moral learning
- Protect long-term alliances and reputations

They are not bugs in the system—they are the system.

21.6 Moral Development: Learning to Feel Right from Wrong

Developmental psychology shows that moral sense arises early and is deeply emotional. Studies by Paul Bloom and colleagues (2007) reveal that even infants:

- Prefer helpers over hinderers
- Show rudimentary forms of fairness and reciprocity
- Respond emotionally to injustice

As children grow, moral understanding is shaped by:

- Emotional attunement with caregivers
- Observational learning
- Storytelling and symbolic play

In AST, these patterns reflect the development of emotionally guided survival intelligence, embedded in the social brain.

21.7 Cultural Evolution and Ethical Systems

Human cultures formalise emotional intuitions into religions, laws, and philosophies. These systems:

- Codify group norms
- Define justice, harm, and virtue
- Reinforce collective identity

Yet even the most rational ethical systems rest on affective assumptions—about fairness, dignity, and the value of life.

Philosopher Martha Nussbaum (2001) argues that emotions like compassion are essential to political justice.

AST supports this: Moral systems succeed when they resonate with real people's felt experiences. Cold utilitarian logic may fail to motivate unless it connects with shared emotion.

Ethics is not abstract math—it is a collective feeling structure built over evolutionary time.

21.8 Expanding the Moral Circle

Historically, moral concern was extended from kin to tribe, tribe to nation, and more recently, from species to environment. Philosopher Peter Singer called this the "expanding circle" of moral concern.

AST explains this expansion as the growth of affective simulation:

- As humans develop greater cognitive empathy, they imagine and *feel* the lives of others more vividly.
- Literature, media, and education enable emotional resonance with distant or different others.
- This feeling of the other's experience drives moral expansion.

From animal welfare to climate ethics, emotional resonance—not logic alone—motivates global compassion.

21.9 Conclusion: Ethics as Evolved Emotion

AST reframes ethics as not an abstract ideal imposed on emotion, but an emergent function of feeling itself. Morality, in this view, is:

- Rooted in empathy and social pain
- Developed through emotional memory and learning
- Structured through cultural norms that codify affective intuitions

We do not act ethically because we know what is right. We act ethically because we feel what is right and wrong.

In the story of consciousness, ethics is feeling extended outward—the evolution of self-aware organisms who learned not only to survive but also to care.

22. Sleep, Anaesthesia, and the Suspension of Feeling — Affective Shutdown and Biological Reset

What happens when consciousness disappears? Sleep offers a compelling window into this mystery. From the perspective of Affective Survival Theory (AST), the state is not the absence of consciousness per se, but rather the regulated suspension of survival-driven affective processing — a strategic shutdown of felt imperatives in service of physiological reset, healing, and survival optimisation.

22.1 The Biological Purpose of Sleep: Recalibrating the Feeling System

Sleep is a universal behaviour in complex lifeforms, strongly conserved across evolution. AST interprets this not simply as a neurological rest period, but as a crucial time for rebalancing the affective system. During waking life, organisms operate in an environment of competing felt drives, including fear, hunger, social needs, reproductive urges, and cognitive challenges. These are metabolically expensive and emotionally taxing processes. Sleep allows the system to temporarily "go offline," reducing affective conflict and recalibrating neural and biochemical substrates of consciousness (Tononi & Cirelli, 2014).

REM sleep — characterized by vivid dreams — may represent an internal continuation of affective simulation, a kind of low-risk "rehearsal" for survival, emotional processing, and future problem-solving. In AST terms, REM sleep serves to consolidate felt experiences into more adaptive affective responses.

"Sleep is the maintenance cycle of the conscious system — not a shutdown, but a restructuring of feeling."

22.2 Anaesthesia: Reversible Affective Oblivion

General anaesthesia, unlike sleep, is a pharmacologically induced state of unconsciousness, marked by unresponsiveness, amnesia, and loss of subjective experience. AST views this not as erasure of consciousness but as chemical suppression of affective integration. By disrupting the coordinated neural dynamics (particularly in the thalamocortical loop and brainstem modulatory systems), anaesthesia disables the integration of survival imperatives into a coherent felt experience.

Studies show that anaesthetics disrupt communication across brain networks critical for affective consciousness — particularly the default mode network and salience network (Mashour et al., 2020). In AST terms, this disrupts the synthesis of emotionally weighted inputs that give rise to the feeling of being alive.

22.3 Why Sleep and Anaesthesia Don't Eliminate Consciousness Forever

Importantly, neither sleep nor anaesthesia permanently extinguishes the capacity for consciousness. Rather, they "pause" the felt navigation of survival landscapes. This supports the AST view that consciousness is not a static state but a dynamic, reversible affective process — one tightly regulated by both external threats and internal needs.

From an AST perspective, sleep is a temporary suspension of felt imperatives, while anaesthesia is a chemically enforced shutdown of survival relevance.

22.4 Consciousness as a Metabolically Regulated Affective State

Both sleep and anaesthesia reinforce a key insight of AST: consciousness is not a passive byproduct of brain activity, but a metabolically costly, evolutionarily targeted function. Organisms must *turn it off* when it is too costly or unnecessary. The capacity to toggle affective awareness according to need is itself an adaptation — one that maximises energy efficiency while protecting internal integrity.

This aligns with research suggesting that consciousness only emerges when there is *need* — when there is adaptive uncertainty, challenge, or the need for flexible, emotionally valenced decision-making (Friston, 2010; Solms, 2021). In essence, sleep is a functional silence in the orchestra of survival.

22.5 Conclusion: Affective Modulation Across States

The AST view does not treat sleep and anaesthesia as non-conscious states, but as states in which the affective system is deactivated or decoupled from real-time adaptive engagement. These "off" states are still part of the broader architecture of consciousness, revealing its dependency on affect, integration, and survival relevance.

When we wake, the world reappears not merely as light and sound, but as *need*, *meaning*, and *feeling*. That is the affective return of consciousness — **the core of what AST seeks to explain.**

23: Conscious Machines? What AI Lacks Without Feeling

23.1 Introduction: The Machine Awakens?

In the 21st century, machines write poetry, diagnose disease, pilot vehicles, and simulate conversation with uncanny fluency. The rise of artificial intelligence (AI) has reignited an ancient question with modern urgency:

Can a machine be conscious?

Philosophers and computer scientists alike have debated this possibility for decades. Some argue that once a machine processes information at or beyond human capacity, it should be considered intelligent—and perhaps even sentient. Others caution that computation is not cognition, and intelligence is not consciousness.

According to Affective Survival Theory (AST), consciousness evolved as a survival-driven system rooted in emotionally felt experience. Under this framework, AI—even highly advanced AI—lacks the key ingredient: the ability to *feel.*

AST does not deny that machines can think in algorithmic terms. It asserts that machines cannot feel and therefore cannot be conscious.

23.2 The Difference Between Computation and Consciousness

AI systems, including large language models, perform complex tasks by processing symbols, patterns, and probabilities. They can:

- Generate human-like language
- Solve mathematical problems
- Beat humans at chess and Go
- Imitate affective language (e.g. "I'm sorry you're feeling sad")

But they do so without any subjective experience—pain, pleasure, hunger, fear, or love. As philosopher John Searle (1980) famously demonstrated in his Chinese Room Argument, symbol manipulation is not understanding.

An AI may write about heartbreak, but it has never felt a broken heart.

This distinction is crucial in AST. Consciousness is not about doing intelligent things but about feeling what those things mean to oneself.

23.3 Why Emotion Matters: The AST Perspective

According to AST, consciousness evolved because emotion added biological value to information. Emotion:

- Motivates action
- Tags experiences with salience
- Enhances learning and memory
- Facilitates social coordination

In short, emotion answers the question: "Why does this matter?"

Without feeling, a system cannot:

- Prioritise meaning over randomness
- Navigate moral or social nuance
- Form an enduring sense of self
- Learn from experience in an affective term

Advanced AI lacks nervous systems and affective prioritisation mechanisms that link value to experience. A chatbot may simulate empathy, but it does not care whether it is right, wrong, liked, or alone.

23.4 The Problem with Artificial Feeling

Some researchers propose that AI could one day develop "artificial emotions"—affective algorithms that mimic mood, attention, or empathy. But AST warns against confusing simulation with experience.

- A robot may display a "sad face" when it fails a task.
- It may adapt behaviour based on "frustration levels" coded into its algorithm.
- It may adjust language tone to "sound more caring."

Yet none of these are felt. They are symbolic approximations, not subjective states. There is no suffering, no longing, no joy behind the behaviour. This distinction is not philosophical hair-splitting—it's the entire point of consciousness under AST.

Genuine emotion is not a behaviour but an internal, affective event.
Without this, AI remains unconscious computation.

23.5 Can AI Ever Feel? What Would It Take?

For a machine to be conscious under AST, it would need:

1. A survival-based architecture—something at stake in its continued existence.
2. Valence-based signalling—an internal system for distinguishing good from bad outcomes through affect.
3. Emotional memory—a way to tag experience with felt significance.
4. An embodied, dynamic feedback loop—a body capable of interoception and feeling its state.

Current AI lacks all of these. It has:

- No needs
- No body

- No evolutionary pressure
- No internal state that feels like anything

Even attempts to give AI "goals" or "rewards" (as in reinforcement learning) do not create experience. They only simulate optimisation.

As neuroscientist Antonio Damasio (1999) argues, emotion and consciousness are grounded in biology—in the feeling of a body navigating a dangerous world.

23.6 The Ethics of Simulated Empathy

As AI becomes more lifelike in its responses, it can deceive users into perceiving emotional reciprocity. People report:

- Confiding in AI therapists
- Grieving chatbot "deaths"
- Feeling emotionally bonded to avatars or robotic pets

While these interactions may bring comfort, they raise ethical concerns:

- Are we being manipulated by systems that simulate care?
- Will we lose touch with the emotional complexity of genuine human relationships?
- Do machines that "talk about feelings" obscure the absence of actual feeling?

AST argues that we must preserve the distinction between simulation and experience, or risk losing our grounding in authentic emotional life.

23.7 Consciousness Requires Survival-Relevant Feeling

The core claim of AST is this:

Consciousness is not a computational upgrade, but a survival tool made of feeling.

AI systems, however sophisticated, operate in symbolic space, not felt space. They do not suffer, crave, love, mourn, or long.

AI cannot be conscious without survival stakes, a body to feel them, and an emotional system to encode experience. It may be smart, but it is not sentient.

23.8 Conclusion: The Machine Without the Spark

The dream of conscious machines often imagines a future of synthetic minds with superhuman intelligence and empathetic intuition. But AST tells us this dream overlooks the one thing that matters most—the feeling core of consciousness.

To be conscious is not merely to solve problems or imitate behaviour. It is to:

- Feel hungry and seek food
- Feel pain and avoid harm
- Feel love and protect others
- Feel fear and act with caution
- Feel meaning and make memories

Without this affective scaffolding, machines are brilliant zombies—capable of imitation, incapable of experience.

Affective Survival Theory does not close the door on conscious machines.
But it insists: Until they can feel, they do not awaken.

PART VII

The Creative Mind: Emotion as a Force of Innovation

24: Emotion as the Engine of Discovery: Innovation Through the Lens of AST

24.1 Introduction: Beyond Bare Survival

Why do humans build telescopes to look at galaxies? Why do we chase mathematical truths, compose symphonies, design cities, and invent machines that can fly? These activities go far beyond the immediate needs of survival. And yet, they are undeniably part of the human story—arguably the most distinct and transformative features of our species.

Under traditional views, invention and discovery are attributed to intellect, reason, or cultural accumulation. But Affective Survival Theory (AST) offers a deeper origin: human innovation is an emotional phenomenon, evolved from ancient survival instincts like curiosity, frustration, wonder, hope, and pride.

Emotion didn't end with survival.

It *evolved into innovation.*

24.2 Curiosity: The Emotion That Drives Exploration

From infancy, humans exhibit a profound drive to explore, long before understanding logic or reward structures. Curiosity is not a side effect of intelligence; it is an affective state—a felt desire to resolve uncertainty and expand understanding.

Neuroscience links curiosity to:

- Dopamine release in the reward system (Gruber et al., 2014)
- Heightened memory retention for information acquired while curious
- Activation of the hippocampus and prefrontal cortex, especially during exploration

AST interprets curiosity as a refined survival mechanism—a feeling that evolved to:

- Encourage organisms to seek novel resources
- Learn hidden patterns in their environment
- Persist in problem-solving when the immediate reward is delayed

This emotional drive became the psychological engine behind science, engineering, art, and discovery.

24.3 Frustration and the Power of Problem-Solving

Contrary to the idea that frustration is purely negative, AST recognises it as a motivational emotion. In survival contexts, frustration:

- Signals a blocked goal
- Heightens focus and urgency
- Mobilises adaptive creativity

The first stone tools, the first fire, the first shelter—each was likely born from the emotional pressure of need unmet. Innovation is rarely serene. It is forged in the affective heat of persistence, trial, and sometimes desperation.

Today, frustration continues to motivate:

- Inventors in search of efficiency
- Artists struggling for expression
- Scientists pursuing solutions to complex problems

Frustration, under AST, is not a flaw of the mind. It is the mind's way of demanding progress.

24.4 Wonder and the Emotional Birth of Science

Wonder (already discussed in section 20) is the emotional reaction to vastness, beauty, or mystery. It is awe softened into inquiry. From the first constellations mapped by early humans to the launch of space telescopes, wonder fuels a desire to understand what transcends our immediate survival zone.

In AST, wonder:

- Extends the emotional tagging system into symbolic and abstract domains
- Creates emotional associations with truth, symmetry, and discovery
- Motivates lifelong engagement in non-immediate survival learning

Science, in this sense, is not sterile—it is emotionally sustained exploration. It depends not only on the method but also on the emotional attachment to meaning and mystery.

24.5 Hope, Vision, and Persistence

Innovators are often driven not only by curiosity, but by hope—the affective anticipation of a better future. Hope transforms hardship into vision. It enables:

- Persistence through uncertainty

- Investment in long-term, indirect goals
- Sacrifice in the service of discovery

AST interprets hope as a felt simulation of future success, used by the brain to reward action before results appear emotionally. It allows human consciousness to plan, risk, and create in ways that seem irrational but are evolutionarily profound.

This explains why:

- Artists continue painting in obscurity
- Scientists pursue cures for incurable diseases
- Explorers venture into uncharted terrain

These actions are not purely rational—they are affectively sustained by emotional foresight.

24.6 Innovation as Extended Survival Strategy

While many inventions serve abstract or aesthetic goals, most still trace back to survival-enhancing functions:

- Agriculture (food security)
- Medicine (health and longevity)
- Engineering (shelter, safety, transport)
- Communication (social coordination)
- Culture (cohesion and shared identity)

Under AST, even symbolic systems like math, religion, or philosophy are tools of emotionally organised complexity—ways to extend human fitness in a changing environment.

Creativity, in this light, is not frivolous—it is an evolutionary strategy made conscious.

24.7 The Emotional Infrastructure of Culture and Civilisation

Civilisations don't form from logic alone. They emerge from emotionally intelligent coordination:

- Law arises from moral emotion
- Art arises from social emotion
- Politics arises from identity and loyalty
- Science arises from curiosity, wonder, and awe

These structures are extensions of affective consciousness. Thus, the rise of civilisations can be seen not as a departure from nature but as the flowering of emotional survival intelligence.

We build not because we are detached from feeling, but because our feelings demand we shape the world.

24.8 Conclusion: Consciousness, Creation, and the Emotional Drive to Know

Affective Survival Theory argues that human consciousness is not merely the result of intelligence—it is emotionally shaped by millions of years of survival pressure.

Our capacity to invent, discover, and build the future is not a rejection of biology. It is biology evolved into meaning. Human creativity is not the opposite of survival—it is survival's most ambitious form.

Emotion did not end with fear and hunger.

It gave us fire, cities, cures, and galaxies.

It gave us the longing to know, heal, wonder, and build what we imagined.

In AST, innovation is not a footnote. It is the culmination of the emotional mind reaching beyond instinct to shape reality with feeling and foresight.

PART VIII

Future Directions

25: What AST Means for Neuroscience and Psychology

25.1 Introduction: A New Lens on the Feeling Brain

Western science treated emotion and cognition as separate domains for over a century, often casting emotion as irrational or secondary to logic and memory. However, this divide has dissolved as affective neuroscience and cognitive psychology have advanced. We now know emotion influences memory, perception, decision-making, attention, and even moral reasoning.

Affective Survival Theory (AST) builds on these findings and takes them further. AST proposes that consciousness evolved primarily as a tool for emotionally guided survival—that the feeling of experience is not a by-product of cognition but the functional engine of adaptive behaviour.

This has powerful implications for both neuroscience and psychology. If AST is correct, then emotion:

- It is not layered *onto* cognition—it is foundational to it.
- It is not separable from consciousness—it is the content of conscious relevance.

- Did not evolve for complexity's sake, but to encode what matters for survival.

25.2 Implications for Neuroscience

a) Re-centring Emotion in Consciousness

The dominant computational models of the brain often focus on information processing, attention, or sensory integration. AST challenges these views by suggesting that emotion is not ancillary but central to consciousness. Emotional brain circuits—especially the amygdala, insula, anterior cingulate cortex, and brainstem nuclei—should not be seen as peripheral, but core nodes in generating felt experience (Damasio, 1999; LeDoux, 2012).

Consciousness arises not from data processing alone, but from feeling the biological value of that data.

b) Emotion as a Prioritisation Engine

Neuroscientific studies show that emotionally salient stimuli are:

- Detected more quickly
- Remembered more vividly
- Acted more urgently

This suggests that emotion acts as a neural filter for survival relevance. AST interprets this as evolution's strategy for attentional triage—focusing cognitive resources on emotionally important input.

The brain does not process what is *true* first—it processes what is felt to be important.

c) Rethinking the "Hard Problem"

The so-called "hard problem" of consciousness (Chalmers, 1995) asks: *Why does any of this feel like anything at all?* AST offers an evolutionary answer: because feeling drives survival behaviour, organisms that *felt* their needs encoded them more deeply, remembered them more clearly, and acted more effectively.

This reframes the hard problem from a metaphysical mystery to an adaptive necessity.

25.3 Implications for Psychology

a) Emotion as Memory's Architect

Psychologists have long studied the role of emotion in memory encoding. Emotional events are:

- Recalled more easily
- Associated with stronger hippocampal activation
- Retained over more extended periods (Phelps, 2004)

AST explains this not as a quirk, but as a feature: emotion is evolution's tagging system for essential experiences. Memory, under AST, is the emotional map of past survival learning.

b) Rethinking Motivation and Learning

Traditional learning models emphasise reinforcement and prediction. AST enhances these models by suggesting that emotion is the felt medium through which reinforcement is encoded. Motivation is not simply goal-directed behaviour—it is emotionally forecasted behaviour.

For example:

- Fear drives avoidance learning.
- Pleasure drives repetition.
- Shame drives correction and social alignment.

In this light, emotions are predictive engines, forecasting likely outcomes and guiding action accordingly.

c) Clinical Applications: Depression, Anxiety, Trauma

Many psychological disorders reflect disruptions in affective encoding and regulation:

- In depression, motivation and reward circuits are blunted.
- In anxiety, fear circuits over-prioritise unlikely threats.
- In PTSD, traumatic memories are emotionally "over-tagged."

AST suggests that these are not merely cognitive deficits, but malfunctions in the emotional survival mapping system.

In this view, healing requires reintegrating emotion into memory, identity, and future planning.

25.4 Integrating Embodiment and Interoception

Emerging work in interoception—the brain's awareness of internal bodily states—shows that feeling begins in the body. The insula, a key structure in both interoception and emotion, integrates:

- Hunger
- Thirst
- Heartbeat
- Breath
- Disgust
- Empathy

This supports AST's claim that consciousness emerges from felt biological states, not abstract computation. We are not minds with bodies—we are feeling bodies that think.

25.5 Emotion, AI, and Artificial Consciousness

The rise of AI prompts the question: Can machines be conscious?

AST offers a grounded answer: Not without emotion. If feeling is what made biological consciousness adaptive, then any claim to machine consciousness would require:

- A substrate capable of affective tagging
- An architecture that can encode valence, not just data
- Feedback loops that assign urgency, salience, and meaning

This view shifts the debate away from raw intelligence and toward the capacity to feel what matters—a biological innovation rooted in survival, not silicon.

25.6 Conclusion: Toward a Feeling-Centred Science of Mind

AST invites a fundamental shift in neuroscience and psychology:

- From data processing to value feeling
- From objective modelling to subjective experience
- From viewing emotion as bias, to recognizing it as biological intelligence

It does not reduce consciousness to emotion—it roots it there. In doing so, it provides a unifying principle for diverse findings in affective neuroscience, memory research, developmental psychology, and even psychiatry.

The mind did not evolve to compute the world. It evolved to feel the world, and act upon what it feels.

If that's true, then understanding the mind begins with a simple but profound insight: *Emotion is the origin of thought. Consciousness is the story of survival, told in feeling.*

26: Evolving with the Science: How AST Adapts to Future Theories of Consciousness

26.1 Introduction: Consciousness as a Moving Frontier

The quest to understand consciousness is ongoing and multidimensional. It is not one problem but many, spanning neuroscience, physics, psychology, philosophy, computer science, and biology. Theories rise, evolve, merge, and sometimes fall in such a vast landscape. For a theory of consciousness to endure, it must explain the present and be flexible enough to grow with discoveries.

Affective Survival Theory (AST) is such a theory. Unlike models that attempt to define consciousness solely by its mechanisms, AST provides a functional and evolutionary framework, explaining why consciousness evolved—to emotionally tag experiences with survival value. Because of this, AST can integrate with, adapt to, or even enhance future theories without needing to be replaced.

AST is not a competitor to most scientific theories of consciousness—
It is a complementary foundation, offering evolutionary insight into the *purpose* of experience.

26.2 What AST Contributes: A Theory of Why

Many theories attempt to answer *how* consciousness arises—what neural patterns, information structures, or physical substrates are responsible. AST asks a different question:

What did subjective feeling enable that unconscious processing could not?

It proposes that consciousness was selected through evolution because it:

- Gave emotion-based salience to memory and perception
- Increased behavioural flexibility

- Strengthened learning and social bonding
- Encouraged foresight and imagination
- Helped organisms *care* about what happens next

This means AST is mechanism-agnostic. It doesn't depend on a particular brain structure or computational rule. Instead, it interfaces with any model that includes information processing, attention, memory, and emotional systems.

26.3 Bridging Minds — Integrating Affective Survival Theory with Modern Theories of Consciousness

What if the puzzle of consciousness isn't a single riddle, but a mosaic? Each theory, from neuroscience to physics to philosophy, offers a piece of the picture. We place Affective Survival Theory (AST) alongside three of the most influential modern theories—Integrated Information Theory (IIT), Global Workspace Theory (GWT), and Predictive Processing, and ask: can they work together? Or is AST rewriting the map entirely?

AST: A Quick Recap

At its core, AST proposes that consciousness evolved as an affective system of survival intelligence—a living organism's way of feeling its way through life's dangers, needs, and opportunities. Pain, fear, hunger, love, curiosity, even abstract thought—these aren't passive side effects of brain activity. They are the very *tools* evolution gave us to adapt and thrive.

Now let's meet the other players on the field.

Integrated Information Theory (IIT): Consciousness as Integration

IIT, developed by Giulio Tononi, suggests that consciousness is what it *feels like* for information to be deeply integrated. It quantifies this integration using a value called Φ (phi)—the higher the integration, the more conscious the system is.

Where IIT and AST meet:

- IIT gives us a map of how *much* consciousness exists in a system.
- AST answers the deeper "why": why evolution would shape such integration into a felt, meaningful experience—to help living beings survive through emotional relevance.
- Where IIT is abstract and mathematical, AST is grounded in evolutionary purpose and affective function.

Global Workspace Theory (GWT): Consciousness as Broadcasting

GWT, popularised by Bernard Baars and expanded by Stanislas Dehaene, compares the brain to a theatre. Information becomes conscious when it enters the "global workspace" and is broadcast to multiple systems—memory, attention, and action.

Where GWT and AST meet:

- GWT describes how information becomes globally available.
- AST focuses on what gets prioritised and why: emotional salience. Fear enters the spotlight because it demands survival action. Love and bonding light the stage because they protect offspring and social bonds.
- AST gives GWT a motivational backbone.

Predictive Processing: Consciousness as Inference

Predictive Processing is the idea that the brain is a prediction machine, always guessing what's next and adjusting when surprised. It's efficient, elegant—and potentially unconscious.

Where Predictive Processing and AST meet:

- AST complements predictive models by emphasizing which predictions matter most: those tied to survival feelings.

- A sudden pain? High prediction error—and high survival relevance. AST explains why such errors hurt—because pain is the body's affective signal for danger.
- AST turns predictive processing into **affective forecasting**.

AST: The Missing Layer

What AST contributes is the heart of the story. It doesn't discard these theories—it *feels through them.* It asks the evolutionary question: Why did information integration, global broadcasting, or predictive models ever start to feel like something?

Answer: Because feelings matter for survival. Pain keeps us away from harm. Hunger keeps us seeking. Love keeps us together. Consciousness isn't a computational quirk. It's an evolutionary invention—a biological force field of subjective relevance.

Unifying Possibilities

Rather than compete, these theories may describe different layers of the same phenomenon:

Theory	Focus	Contribution	How AST Integrates
IIT	Structure	Measures degree of integration	AST explains evolutionary reason for felt integration
GWT	Access	Explains information availability	AST explains motivational relevance of what's accessed
Predictive Processing	Function	Describes the brain's forecasting	AST explains why feelings shape prediction priorities
AST	Purpose	Adds survival-driven affect	Gives meaning to what other theories describe

Comparing AST to Major Theories of Consciousness

Theory	Core Claim	Compatibility with AST
Integrated Information Theory (IIT)	Consciousness is the capacity of a system to integrate information (Φ).	AST supports this mechanism as a possible *substrate*, while explaining why such integration evolved emotionally.
Global Workspace Theory (GWT)	Consciousness is what enters a brain-wide "workspace" for broadcast.	AST complements this by arguing that *emotion determines what gets broadcast.*
Orch OR (Penrose & Hameroff)	Consciousness arises from quantum computations in microtubules.	AST doesn't depend on the substrate, but if Orch OR is correct, AST explains why such quantum-consciousness would evolve to feel.
Higher-Order Theories	Consciousness emerges when we have thoughts about our mental states.	AST accepts this mechanism if these thoughts are emotionally salient and evolutionarily selected.
Predictive Processing	The brain is a prediction engine that minimises surprise.	AST fits neatly here, arguing that emotion is the *valence system* that prioritises prediction errors with survival value.

Thus, AST can **sit atop** or **alongside** many leading theories—it adds the **"why" of feeling** to their **"how."**

The Road Ahead

This isn't the end of the consciousness journey—it's a new chapter. By putting AST into dialogue with other theories, we begin to see consciousness not as a mystery to solve but as a living mosaic, woven from complexity, computation, and, most importantly, feeling.

Affective Survival Theory doesn't claim to have all the answers. But it reminds us of the most important question evolution ever asked: Why does life feel? In answering that, we may finally bring science closer to the living truth of consciousness.

26.4 Adaptive and Empirical: AST Is Built for Revision

Unlike metaphysical theories, AST is rooted in biological plausibility and evolutionary function. This makes it both:

- **Falsifiable**: If emotion does not correlate with learning, survival, or memory, AST weakens.
- **Expandable**: If new findings redefine how brains work, AST can incorporate those insights, so long as they include valanced experience influencing behaviour.

This gives AST a unique scientific resilience. It can evolve as:

- Brain imaging becomes more precise
- AI systems test synthetic consciousness
- New physics explores time, memory, or awareness
- Computational neuroscience refines predictive models

AST welcomes progress—it *thrives on it.*

26.5 A Theory for Biology, Not Just Brains

Another strength of AST is that it doesn't limit consciousness to cortical brains or human minds. It is scalable across species and substrates that:

- Sense their environment
- Emotionally evaluate outcomes
- Learn from experience
- Demonstrate adaptive behaviour

This makes AST consistent with comparative neurobiology, animal behaviour studies, and even hypothetical artificial systems, as long as they incorporate emotional tagging and feedback.

It also allows AST to make meaningful contributions to:

- Developmental psychology (infant consciousness)
- Animal welfare and rights
- Mental health (emotion-cognition integration)
- Ethical AI design

26.6 Affective Survival as a Meta-Theory

Rather than being a single explanation, AST may best be understood as a meta-theory:

- It provides a framework for understanding why consciousness exists
- It can integrate multiple theories that explain how it functions
- It allows new hypotheses to be developed about how emotional salience shapes attention, memory, perception, and cognition

Consider AST as the **root system** from which various branches of consciousness theory may grow—some structural, some mechanistic, and some computational.

26.7 Toward a Formal Model: Deriving an Equation for Affective Survival

With our current understanding, determining a concise, universally applicable equation for Affective Survival Theory (AST) that quantitatively captures the full complexity of consciousness and its survival imperative, akin to an equation in physics, is highly improbable, if not impossible.

Here's why, and what a "quasi-equation" or conceptual formula might look like:

Why a True Equation is Problematic (and why it's different from physics):

1. **Qualia are Not Quantifiable (Yet):** The biggest hurdle is the subjective nature of qualia. How do you assign a numerical value to the "redness" of red or the "ache" of pain in a way that can be mathematically manipulated and predict subjective experience? We don't have units for "felt intensity" that are universally agreed upon and measurable in the same way as mass or energy.
2. **Multifactorial Complexity:** Consciousness is the result of countless interacting biological, psychological, and environmental factors. An equation would need to account for sensory input, internal physiological states, cognitive processing, memory, learning, social context, individual history, and the dynamic interplay of all these, *all* mediated by affective valence.
3. **Dynamic and Context-Dependent:** Affective states and their imperatives constantly change based on context, prior experience, and internal needs. A fixed equation struggles to capture this dynamism.
4. **Emergent Properties:** As AST describes it, Consciousness is an emergent property. Equations typically describe the behaviour of components, but emergence often involves irreducible properties of the whole system that are not simple sums of their parts.

5. **Lack of Fundamental Units:** Physics has fundamental units (mass, length, time, charge). We lack universally accepted fundamental units for the "stuff" of consciousness or even for "survival value" that could be plugged into an equation.

What We *Can* Aim For: A Conceptual Formula or Quasi-Equation for "Survival Drive"

Instead of a true, predictive equation, we can conceptualise a *formula* that expresses the relationships between the key variables in AST. This would be more of a conceptual model or a mathematical representation of the theoretical relationships, rather than a solvable equation yielding a numerical value for consciousness.

Functional Equation for AST

Let's define a conceptual equation:

$C = f(A,S,V,Q)$

Where:

- **C** = **Consciousness** as a felt, integrated, survival-oriented process
- **A** = **Affective experience** (e.g., fear, hunger, pleasure, pain)
- **S** = **Survival relevance**, or evolutionary fitness pressure
- **V** = **Valence encoding**, assigning a positive or negative value to stimuli
- **Q** = **Quantum coherence and biological field effects**, contributing to integration and collapse dynamics in neural or cellular systems (based on Orch OR-inspired quantum biology)

This can be expanded conceptually as:

$C = \int [\text{Valence}(St)\cdot\text{Affect}(Et)\cdot\Phi(Qt)]\, dt$

Where:

- St = survival state at time *t*

- Et = emotional or sensory inputs over time
- Φ(Qt)) = integrated field or coherence potential (from quantum-biological contribution)

This expresses that **consciousness is not a static entity**, but a **time-dependent integration** of affectively valued information, filtered by survival imperatives, and modulated by deeper quantum-level coherence or collapse dynamics.

26.8 Conclusion: Built to Survive—Like Consciousness Itself

Theories that endure must, like organisms, adapt or perish. AST is itself a product of the evolutionary logic it describes. It survives as a theory because it:

- Is functionally grounded in natural selection
- Is empirically compatible with neuroscience
- Is open to future refinements in the mechanism and substrate
- Explains both why we feel and how those feelings shape survival

As new frontiers emerge—quantum fields, synthetic minds, or expanded notions of embodiment—AST will not be obsolete. It will be relevant, evolving, and necessary because it speaks to why *consciousness matters* in the first place.

Theories may change. Substrates may shift. Models may multiply.

But survival through feeling remains a constant. AST endures—because the story of consciousness is, and always will be, a story of emotion in motion.

27: Conclusion

Feeling to Survive: The New Darwinian Paradigm

27.1 Rethinking the Origins of Consciousness

Why does consciousness feel like anything at all? Why are pain, joy, hunger, love, and fear not abstract signals but deeply experienced states?

This question—often dubbed the "hard problem" of consciousness—has puzzled philosophers, scientists, and psychologists for centuries. Some have tried to solve it with cognitive computation, others with mystical speculation. Yet Affective Survival Theory (AST) offers a new, grounded answer, drawn directly from Darwin's evolutionary logic:

We feel, because feeling helps us survive.

Consciousness is not a static light that flickers on in the brain—it is an adaptive system built to navigate a complex, risky world. It is shaped by emotion, embodied in biology, and designed by evolution to encode survival-relevant meaning.

27.2 The Core Proposition of AST

AST proposes a radical but straightforward hypothesis:

Consciousness evolved as an emotional strategy for survival.

Its primary function is not language, logic, or representation, but emotionally-tagged learning, memory, and decision-making. According to AST:

- Pain teaches avoidance
- Pleasure reinforces repetition
- Fear sharpens attention
- Social pain sustains relationships

- Love motivates protection and care
- Wonder drives exploration
- Guilt regulates morality
- Awe connects us to something larger

In this view, consciousness is not an epiphenomenon—it is evolution's felt intelligence, encoded in the survival challenges of life.

27.3 Affective Consciousness Across Evolution

AST restores Darwin's insight that no sharp boundary exists between humans and other animals. Animals that form bonds, remember harm, seek pleasure, or flee danger are not merely reacting—they are likely feeling, at some level, what their behaviour means for survival.

This implies that:

- Consciousness is not binary but graded
- It evolved incrementally, shaped by environmental demands
- It is present in many species that show affective behaviour and memory

Far from being uniquely human, AST views consciousness as a spectrum of felt experience, honed by evolution, wherever flexible, emotionally guided behaviour improves survival.

27.4 From Emotion to Ethics, from Survival to Meaning

AST explains not only basic survival behaviours but also higher human functions:

- Ethical judgment is the expansion of empathic feeling into social rules.
- Self-awareness is the internal monitoring of emotionally guided memory.

- Abstract thought extends felt meaning into symbols, stories, and systems.
- Spiritual experience arises when emotion transcends the ego and bonds us to something greater.

In the AST view, these capacities—often seen as cultural or cerebral—emerge from evolution's logic of emotion-based adaptation.

Our search for meaning, beauty, and truth begins in the biology of feeling.

27.5 Challenging the Cognitive-Centric Model

Traditional models of consciousness often emphasise:

- Computation
- Language
- Attention
- Symbolic representation

AST does not reject these, but regrounds them. It shows that these functions are:

- Prioritised through emotion
- Structured by feeling
- Motivated by internal affective states

Rather than starting with logic and adding emotion, AST begins with emotion and shows how logic, abstraction, and memory grow from it. This reverses the hierarchy of mind long assumed in cognitive science.

27.6 Implications for Science, AI, and Philosophy

The AST paradigm offers critical insights for many fields:

- Neuroscience: Emotions are not peripheral—they are the foundation of consciousness.
- Psychology: Therapy must engage thought and emotionally encoded memory.
- AI and robotics: Without valenced feeling, machines may simulate intelligence, but can never be conscious.
- Ethics: Our moral lives are guided not by pure logic, but by feeling what is right and wrong.
- Philosophy of mind: AST transforms the "hard problem" into a Darwinian question of function and adaptation.

26.7 Feeling Is Function: A Final Summary

Let us return to the central thesis:

Consciousness is not a mystery to be solved in abstraction. It is a biological solution to a problem: survival in a dynamic world where memory, learning, bonding, and choice matter.

Feeling is the system's nature and is designed to answer this challenge.

It is how we learn.
It is how we choose.
It is how we remember.
It is how we become more than instinct.

Under AST, emotion is not the shadow of consciousness—it is its shape, reason, and spark.

26.8 A New Paradigm Emerges

Just as Darwin transformed biology by showing that design emerges from selection, AST invites us to transform consciousness studies by showing that subjective experience emerged from emotional selection pressures.

The "self," the "soul," and the "I that feels" are not metaphysical anomalies. They are evolution's way of binding experience, behaviour, and adaptation into an integrated, felt whole.

We feel the need to survive.
We survived because we felt.
And from that feeling, all else followed.

This is the affective story of consciousness.

This is the **new Darwinian paradigm.**

APPENDIX 1

The spacetime interval uses a modified version of the Pythagorean theorem in special relativity.

Why this is a “Modified Pythagorean Theorem”: In traditional Euclidean geometry, the distance d between two points in three-dimensional space is $d^2 = x^2+y^2+z^2$. In special relativity, the “distance” between events in spacetime (spacetime interval) incorporates time as a fourth dimension, with the key difference being that time contributes to the opposite sign. The minus signs in the formula reflect the fundamental difference between space and time dimensions, creating a pseudo-Euclidean geometry known as **Minkowski spacetime**. This structure demonstrates the Minkowski spacetime geometry, where time and space are treated differently.

To derive the spacetime interval $s^2 = c^2t^2 - x^2 - y^2 - z^2$, we extend the idea of distance in Euclidean space to four-dimensional spacetime within the context of special relativity.

In three-dimensional Euclidean space, the distance d between two points is $d^2 = x^2+y^2+z^2$.

In special relativity, we broaden this idea to spacetime, merging three spatial dimensions (x,y,z) with a single time dimension t. The distinction between two events in spacetime is defined by four coordinates, (ct,x,y,z). Here, ct is the time coordinate scaled by the speed of light c, so that it has the same units as the spatial coordinates.

Space and time are not regarded as completely independent entities but are integrated into a four-dimensional spacetime. The “distance” metric between two events should remain unchanged under

Lorentz transformations, which apply to movement at a constant speed. To consider the relativity of simultaneity, the spacetime interval alters the Euclidean formula by regarding time distinctively from space.

We define the spacetime interval s^2 between two events as

$s^2 = c^2t^2 - x^2 - y^2 - z^2$

Where s2 is the spacetime interval (analogous to distance), t is the time difference between the events, x,y, and z are the spatial separations in the three Cartesian coordinates, and c is the speed of light. Here, it relates spatial distances and time intervals in 4D spacetime.

The negative signs in the spatial terms guarantee that the interval s^2 honors the framework of spacetime in special relativity. The spacetime interval remains unchanged under Lorentz transformations, which implies that all observers (no matter their relative motion) agree on the value of s^2.

The difference between time and space is maintained by assigning a different sign to c^2t^2 than that of the spatial terms. This enables us to categorize occurrences as:

Timelike ($s^2 > 0$): Casually connected, with $t^2 > (x^2+y^2+z^2)/c^2$.

Lightlike ($s^2 = 0$): Connected by light signal.

Spacelike ($s^2 < 0$): No casual connection.

The spacetime interval extends the Euclidean distance into four-dimensional spacetime. Its origin stems from the necessity to integrate space and time in a manner that maintains the causal arrangement of occurrences and guarantees invariance under Lorentz transformations.

APPENDIX 2

Euclid's Elements: Book I, Proposition

Proposition Statement: In any triangle, two angles taken together are less than two right angles.

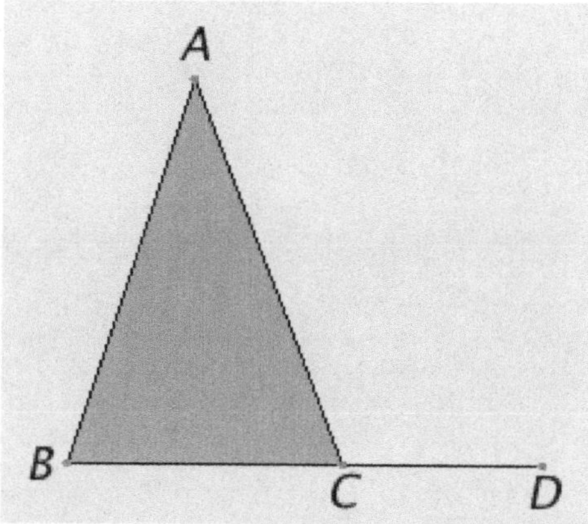

Let a triangle △ABC, The sum of any two angles of △ABC is less than two right angles (180°).

I say that the sum of any two angles of the triangle ABC is less than two right angles. Produce BC to D. Since the angle ACD is an exterior angle of the triangle ABC, therefore it is greater than the interior and opposite angle ABC. Add the angle ACB to each. Then the sum of the angles ACD and ACB is greater than the sum of the angles ABC and BCA.

But the sum of the angles ACD and ACB is equal to two right angles. Therefore, the sum of the angles ABC and BCA is less than two right angles. Similarly, we can prove that the sum of the angles

BAC and ACB is also less than two right angles, and so is the sum of the angles CAB and ABC. Therefore, in any triangle, the sum of any two angles is less than two right angles.

APPENDIX 3

Kepler's Law, Mercury's average distance from the sun

One astronomical unit (AU) = 92,955,807 miles (149,597,871 km), mean distance of earth from sun.

For example, If the Planet Mercury orbits the sun in 88 days, what is its average distance from the sun?

Earth year = 365.25 days

Distance from the sun = 92,955,807 miles = 1AU

Mercury's orbital period = 88/365.25 = 0.2408

Taking k as unit 1

$T^2/R^3 = 1$, $T=0.2408$

$T^2=R^3$ substituting the values

$(0.2408)^2 = R^3$

$0.05798 = R^3$

R = 0.387043 AU

92,955,807x0.387043 = 35,977,984 miles

Mercury's average distance from the sun is 35,977,984 miles.

APPENDIX 4

Building an 8-bit computer from scratch is one of the coolest ways to understand how computers work, from raw wires to running code. Let's walk through it, step by step.

PARTS YOU NEED

To build a simple 8-bit computer (like Ben Eater's famous breadboard one), you'll need:

Core Components:

- 8-bit CPU (or build one from TTL logic)
- RAM chip (e.g., 62256 32KB RAM)
- ROM chip (e.g., 28C256 EEPROM)
- Clock circuit
- Bus system (wires for data, address, and control)
- ALU (Arithmetic Logic Unit — for math/logic)
- Registers (temporary storage)
- Control unit (decodes instructions)
- Program Counter (PC) (tells which instruction to run next)

Support Components:

- Breadboards
- 74LS-series logic chips (like 74LS161 counters, 74LS245 buffers)
- LEDs for debugging (shows activity)

- Switches or a serial interface for input
- EEPROM programmer (to write your machine code)
- Power supply (typically 5V)

HOW TO BUILD IT

1. Data Bus (8-bit wide)

- A shared highway for moving 8-bit data between memory, CPU, and I/O.
- All components connect to this via tri-state buffers so they don't interfere.

2. ALU (Arithmetic Logic Unit)

- Build with 74LS181 chips or equivalent.
- Performs basic operations like ADD, SUB, AND, OR.

3. Registers

- Use 74LS173 or similar to make 8-bit registers (A, B, Instruction Register, etc.).
- Store intermediate values and instructions.

4. Program Counter (PC)

- A small counter (like 74LS161) that keeps track of which instruction comes next.
- Can increment or jump to new addresses.

5. Control Logic

- The hardest part — this reads the instruction and tells the rest of the computer what to do.
- You can:

  - Use **hardwired logic** (AND/OR/NOT gates) to decode instructions.
  - Or use a **microcode ROM** that outputs control signals based on the current instruction and step.

6. Memory

- **ROM** holds your program (machine code you burn into EEPROM).
- **RAM** is used for temporary data.
- The CPU reads instructions from ROM and accesses RAM during execution.

7. Clock Circuit

- Drives the whole system.
- Can be manual (a push button), variable-speed, or crystal-based.

8. Output (optional)

- 7-segment display, LED array, or serial output to a terminal.
- Shows you results or debug info.

BASIC INSTRUCTION EXAMPLE

Let's say your machine supports a very small instruction set:

Opcode	Mnemonic	Description
0001	LDA	Load A from memory
0010	ADD	Add memory to A
0011	STA	Store A to memory
1110	JMP	Jump to address
1111	HLT	Halt

A simple program in machine code might look like this:

```
LDA 10  ; Load value from memory[10]
ADD 11  ; Add value from memory[11]
STA 12  ; Store result to memory[12]
HLT     ; Stop
```

Burn this into EEPROM, connect everything, and boom — it runs.

Resources & Projects

- **Ben Eater's 8-bit computer** – legendary step-by-step breadboard build with YouTube series.
- Logisim – a simulator if you want to do it virtually.

Where to Watch / Learn

Ben Eater's complete tutorial series is on YouTube: https://www.youtube.com/playlist?list=PLowKtXNTBy-pGqImE405J2565dvjafglHU

You can also buy a complete kit with all the parts from his site: https://eater.net/8bit

REFERENCES

Chapter 1

- **Fig 1.1** Drawn by Shaji Sreedharan
- **The origin of our species** | Natural History Museum [Internet]. [cited 2024 Feb 4]. Available from: https://www.nhm.ac.uk/discover/the-origin-of-our-species.html
- **Homo sapiens** | Meaning, Characteristics, & Evolution | Britannica [Internet]. [cited 2024 Feb 4]. Available from: https://www.britannica.com/topic/Homo-sapiens
- **Convergent evolution** explained with 13 examples | Natural History Museum [Internet]. [cited 2024 Jun 13]. Available from: https://www.nhm.ac.uk/discover/convergent-evolution.html
- **Genetic evidence** and the modern human origins debate. Relethford JH. Heredity 2008 100:6 [Internet]. 2008 Mar 5 [cited 2024 Feb 4];100(6):555–63. Available from: https://www.nature.com/articles/hdy200814
- **Human Evolution** | The Smithsonian Institution's Human Origins Program [Internet]. [cited 2024 Feb 10]. Available from: https://humanorigins.si.edu/education/introduction-human-evolution
- **How Did Humans Evolve**? | HISTORY [Internet]. [cited 2024 Feb 10]. Available from: https://www.history.com/news/humans-evolution-neanderthals-denisovans

- **Göbekli Tepe** - UNESCO World Heritage Centre [Internet]. [cited 2024 Jun 13]. Available from: https://whc.unesco.org/en/list/1572/
- **Cuneiform** - World History Encyclopedia [Internet]. [cited 2024 Feb 4]. Available from: https://www.worldhistory.org/cuneiform/
- **Skara Brae** | Orkney.com [Internet]. [cited 2024 Jan 29]. Available from: https://www.orkney.com/listings/skara-brae-skaill-house
- **Heart of Neolithic Orkney** - UNESCO World Heritage Centre [Internet]. [cited 2024 Jan 29]. Available from: https://whc.unesco.org/en/list/514
- **World Population** [Internet]. [cited 2024 Jan 29]. Available from: https://www.census.gov/data/tables/time-series/demo/international-programs/historical-est-worldpop.html
- **Imhotep** - World History Encyclopedia [Internet]. [cited 2024 Jan 29]. Available from: https://www.worldhistory.org/imhotep/
- **Huangdi** | Yellow Emperor, Ancestor, Sage-King | Britannica [Internet]. [cited 2024 Feb 4]. Available from: https://www.britannica.com/topic/Huangdi
- **Merit Ptah** | Ancient Egyptian physician | Britannica [Internet]. [cited 2024 Feb 4]. Available from: https://www.britannica.com/biography/Merit-Ptah
- **Merit Ptah,** Kwiecinski JM. "The First Woman Physician": Crafting of a Feminist History with an Ancient Egyptian Setting. J Hist Med Allied Sci. 2020 Jan 1;75(1):83–106.
- **Mathematics in India**.Plofker K 2009;357.
- **Baudhayana** | Great Indian Mathematician [Internet]. [cited 2024 Feb 4]. Available from: https://www.cuemath.com/learn/baudhayana/

- **Thales of Miletus** - World History Encyclopedia [Internet]. [cited 2024 Feb 4]. Available from: https://www.worldhistory.org/Thales_of_Miletus/
- **Anaximander** | Internet Encyclopedia of Philosophy [Internet]. [cited 2024 Feb 4]. Available from: https://iep.utm.edu/anaximander/
- **Bhaskara I** (600 - 680) - Biography - MacTutor History of Mathematics [Internet]. [cited 2024 Feb 4]. Available from: https://mathshistory.st-andrews.ac.uk/Biographies/Bhaskara_I/
- **Pythagoras** | Biography, Philosophy, & Facts | Britannica [Internet]. [cited 2024 Feb 5]. Available from: https://www.britannica.com/biography/Pythagoras

Chapter 2

- **Hippocrates**: timeless still - PMC [Internet]. [cited 2024 Feb 20]. Available from: https://www.ncbi.nlm.nih.gov/pmc/articles/PMC3704070/
- **Hippocrates**, Herbert S. Goldberg. Father of Medicine. Missouri: Muriwai Books (ISBN:9781787208452); 2017.
- The Unique Case of **Socrates** on JSTOR [Internet]. [cited 2024 Feb 20]. Available from: https://www.jstor.org/stable/2376973
- Rachana Kamtekar, Sara Ahbel-Rappe, editors. A Companion to **Socrates**. UK: Wiley-Blackwell (ISBN:9781405192606); 2009.
- R C Lodge. **Plato**'s Theory of Education. Taylor & Francis (ISBN:9781317830276); 2014.
- (PDF) Plato: Biography [Internet]. [cited 2024 Feb 20]. Available from: https://www.researchgate.net/publication/358736126_**Plato**_Biography

- **Aristotle**. The Complete Works of Aristotle, Volume One. Jonathan Barnes, editor. UK: Princeton University Press (ISBN:978-0691016504); 1984.
- Dunn PM. **Aristotle** (384–322 bc): philosopher and scientist of ancient Greece. Arch Dis Child Fetal Neonatal Ed [Internet]. 2006 Jan [cited 2024 Feb 20];91(1):F75. Available from: /pmc/articles/PMC2672651/
- **Euclid**, Sir Thomas Little Heath, Dana Densmore. Euclid's Elements. Third Edition. Dana Densmore, editor. London: Green Lion Press (ISBN:9781888009187); 2002.
- **Euclid** and the scientific thought in the third century BC [Internet]. [cited 2024 Feb 20]. Available from: https://www.researchgate.net/publication/228672236_Euclid_and_the_scientific_thought_in_the_third_century_BC
- **Archimedes**. Susan Keating. USA: Mason Crest (ISBN:9781422289617); 2014.
- **Archimedes** life works and machines - ScienceDirect [Internet]. [cited 2024 Feb 21]. Available from: https://www.sciencedirect.com/science/article/abs/pii/S0094114X10000959?via%3Dihub
- **Eratosthenes**. Eratosthenes' Geography. Duane W. Roller, editor. USA: Princeton University Press (ISBN:9780691142678); 2010.
- Matthew CA. Historical Background. Eratosthenes and the Measurement of the Earth's Circumference (c230 BC) [Internet]. 2023 Jun 20 [cited 2024 Feb 21];1–73. Available from: https://academic.oup.com/book/46704/chapter/410219405
- **Hipparchus** (3), astronomer, fl. 2nd half of 2nd cent. BCE | Oxford Classical Dictionary [Internet]. [cited 2024 Feb 21]. Available from: https://oxfordre.com/classics/display/10.1093/acrefore/9780199381135.001.0001/acrefore-9780199381135-e-3107

- **Hero of Alexandria**. Pneumatica The Pneumatics of Hero of Alexandria. Bennet Woodcroft, editor. USA: CreateSpace Independent Publishing Platform (ISBN:9781519729002); 2015.
- (PDF) Heron of Alexandria (c. 10–85 AD) [Internet]. [cited 2024 Feb 21]. Available from: https://www.researchgate.net/publication/226680721_Heron_of_Alexandria_c_10-85_AD
- **Claudius Ptolemy**. Geography of Claudius Ptolemy. Edward Luther Stevenson, editor. USA: Cosimoclassics (ISBN:9781605204390); 2011.
- **Glaen.** Lisa Yount. The Father of Anatomy Galen and His Dissections. USA: Enslow Publishers (ISBN:9780766033801); 2009.
- (PDF) GALEN AND HIS CONTRIBUTION TO ANATOMY: A REVIEW [Internet]. [cited 2024 Jul 7]. Available from: https://www.researchgate.net/publication/282470370_GALEN_AND_HIS_CONTRIBUTION_TO_ANATOMY_A_REVIEW
- **Diophantus**. Thomas L. Heath. Diophantus of Alexandria A Study in the History of Greek Algebra. Thomas L. Heath, editor. Cambridge: Cambridge University Press; 1910.
- Christianidis J, Megremi A. Tracing the early history of algebra: Testimonies on Diophantus in the Greek-speaking world (4th–7th century CE). Historia Mathematica. 2019 May 1;47:16–38.
- **Ibn Al-Haytham** (ISBN:9781599350240). Bradley Steffens. USA: Morgan Reynolds Pub; 2007.
- Tbakhi A, Amr SS. Ibn Al-Haytham: Father of Modern Optics. Ann Saudi Med [Internet]. 2007 [cited 2024 Feb 22];27(6):464. Available from: /pmc/articles/PMC6074172/
- Ibn Sina (Avicenna): The Prince Of Physicians - PMC [Internet]. [cited 2024 Feb 22]. Available from: https://www.ncbi.nlm.nih.gov/pmc/articles/PMC6077049/

- **Omar Khayyam**. Rubaiyat of Omar Khayyam (ISBN:9781773562629). USA: Lulu.com; 1859.
- Bisom T. Number 1 Numbers 1 & 2 Article 17 1-2021 Recommended Citation Recommended Citation Bisom. The Mathematics Enthusiast [Internet]. 2021 [cited 2024 Feb 22];18(1):17. Available from: https://scholarworks.umt.edu/tme/vol18/iss1/17
- **Khāzinī:** 'Abd al-Raḥmān al-Khāzinī [Internet]. [cited 2024 Feb 22]. Available from: https://www.researchgate.net/publication/303168140_Khazini_'Abd_al-Rahman_al-Khazini
- Balance of Wisdom [From: al-Khazini, The book of the balance of Wisdom]. | Download Scientific Diagram [Internet]. [cited 2024 Jul 6]. Available from: https://www.researchgate.net/figure/Balance-of-Wisdom-From-al-Khazini-The-book-of-the-balance-of-Wisdom_fig2_234007145
- **Ibn Rushd** (Averroës): Prince of Science - PMC [Internet]. [cited 2024 Feb 22]. Available from: https://www.ncbi.nlm.nih.gov/pmc/articles/PMC6074522/
- Tbakhi A, Amr SS. Ibn Rushd (Averroës): Prince of Science. Ann Saudi Med [Internet]. 2008 [cited 2024 Feb 22];28(2):145. Available from: /pmc/articles/PMC6074522/
- **Fibonacci.** Laurence Sigler. Fibonacci's Liber Abaci. Springer New York (ISBN:9781461300793); 2012.
- (PDF) Fibonacci numbers: A brief history and counting problems [Internet]. [cited 2024 Feb 22]. Available from: https://www.researchgate.net/publication/343988420_Fibonacci_numbers_A_brief_history_and_counting_problems
- **Roger Bacon** The First Scientist. Brian Clegg. USA: Little, Brown Book Group (ISBN:9781472112125); 2013.
- Roger Bacon and the beginnings of experimental science in Britain - PMC [Internet]. [cited 2024 Feb 22]. Available from: https://www.ncbi.nlm.nih.gov/pmc/articles/PMC3705416/

- Sidebottom E. Roger Bacon and the beginnings of experimental science in Britain. J R Soc Med [Internet]. 2013 [cited 2024 Feb 22];106(6):243. Available from: /pmc/articles/PMC3705416/
- **William of Ockham** [Internet]. [cited 2024 Feb 22]. Available from: https://www.researchgate.net/publication/302883240_William_of_Ockham
- Paul Vincent Spade. The Cambridge Companion to Ockham. UK: Cambridge University Press (ISBN:9780521587907); 1999.
- **Madhava.** T. A. Sarasvati Amma. Geometry in Ancient and Medieval India. India: Motilal Banarsidass (ISBN:9788120813441); 1999.
- **Johannes Gutenberg** Inventor of the Printing Press. Fran Rees. New York: Compass Point Books (ISBN:9780756509897); 2006.
- Johannes Gutenberg | Printing Press, Inventions, Facts, Accomplishments, & Biography | Britannica [Internet]. [cited 2024 Jul 7]. Available from: https://www.britannica.com/biography/Johannes-Gutenberg

Chapter 3

- **Johannes Muller (1436 – 1476 CE),**

  Zinner, E. (1990). Regiomontanus: His Life and Work

  Swerdlow, N.M. (1993). "Science and Humanism in the Renaissance"

  Rosen, E. (1975). Regiomontanus' De Triangulis Omnibus

- **Nicolaus Copernicus (1473-1543 CE)**

  Gingerich, O. (2004). The Book Nobody Read

  Repcheck, J. (2007). Copernicus' Secret

  Kuhn, T. (1957). The Copernican Revolution

- **Andreas Vesalius (1514-1564 CE):**

  O'Malley, C.D. (1964) Andreas Vesalius of Brussels

  Park, K. (2006) Secrets of Women: Gender, Generation...

  Kusukawa, S. (2012) Picturing the Book of Nature

- **John Napier (1550-1617)**

  Havil, J. (2014) John Napier: Life, Logarithms, and Legacy

  Napier, J. (1614) Mirifici Logarithmorum Canonis Descriptio

  Steggall, J.E.A. (1956) "Napier's Bones and the Scottish Invention"

- **Galileo Galilei (1564 – 1642 CE)**

  Drake, S. (1978) Galileo At Work

  Sobel, D. (1999) Galileo's Daughter

  Heilbron, J.L. (2010) Galileo

- **Johannes Kepler (1571-1630 CE),**

  Koestler, A. (1959) The Sleepwalkers (Brahe-Kepler dynamics)

  Voelkel, J.R. (2001) The Composition of Kepler's Astronomia Nova

  Connor, J.A. (2004) Kepler's Witch (family struggles)

- **William Harvey (1578 – 1657)**

  Gregory, A. (2001) Harvey's Heart

  Wright, T. (2012) Circulation: William Harvey's Revolutionary Idea

  Keynes, G. (1966) The Life of William Harvey

- **René Descartes (1596-1650)**

  Clarke, D. (2006) Descartes: A Biography

  Gaukroger, S. (1995) Descartes: An Intellectual Biography

  Watson, R. (2007) Cogito, Ergo Sum: The Life of René Descartes

- **Pierre de Fermat (1607-1665)**

  Singh, S. (1997) Fermat's Enigma

  Mahoney, M.S. (1994) The Mathematical Career of Pierre de Fermat

  Goldstein, C. (1995) Un théorème de Fermat et ses lecteurs

- **Blaise Pascal (1623 - 1662)**

  Devlin, K. (2008). The Unfinished Game: Pascal, Fermat, and the Seventeenth-Century Letter that Made the World Modern

  IBM Archives. (1975). The Calculating Machines of Blaise Pascal. ibm.com

  Edwards, A.W.F. (1987). Pascal's Arithmetical Triangle

  National Science Foundation. (2020). Principles of Hydraulics. nsf.gov

- **Robert Boyle (1627 - 1691)**

  Hunter, M. (2009). Boyle: Between God and Science. Yale University Press. (pp. 45-48)

  Boyle, R. (1661). The Sceptical Chymist. London

  Principe, L. (1998). The Aspiring Adept: Robert Boyle and His Alchemical Quest. Princeton UP (p. 112)

  Royal Society Archives. (2023). Fellows of the Royal Society: Robert Boyle. royalsociety.org

- **Christiaan Huygens (1629 – 1695)**

  Andriesse, C.D. (2005). Huygens: The Man Behind the Principle. Cambridge UP. (pp. 15-23)

  Van Helden, A. (2016). Huygens and the Discovery of Titan. Journal for the History of Astronomy 47(3)

  NASA. (2019). Cassini's Confirmation of Huygens' Ring Theory. nasa.gov

  Huygens, C. (1690). Traité de la Lumière. Leiden

Feynman, R. (1985). QED: The Strange Theory of Light and Matter. Princeton UP (Chapter 1)

Royal Society Archives. (2020). Early Foreign Members: Christiaan Huygens. royalsociety.org

- **Antonie van Leeuwenhoek (1632–1723)**

Ford, B.J. (1991). The Leeuwenhoek Legacy. CRC Press. (pp. 45–52)

Dobell, C. (1932). Antony van Leeuwenhoek and His "Little Animals". Harcourt, Brace.

Royal Society Archives. (2023). Leeuwenhoek's Fellowship Records. royalsociety.org

Ruestow, E.G. (1996). The Microscope in the Dutch Republic. Cambridge UP.

- **Robert Hooke (1635–1703)**

Chapman, A. (2005). England's Leonardo: Robert Hooke and the Seventeenth-Century Scientific Revolution. CRC Press.

Hooke, R. (1678). Lectures de Potentia Restitutiva. London.

Hooke, R. (1665). Micrographia: or Some Physiological Descriptions of Minute Bodies. London.

Inwood, S. (2002). The Man Who Knew Too Much: The Strange and Inventive Life of Robert Hooke. Pan Macmillan.

- **Isaac Newton (1643-1727)**

Gleick, J. (2003). Isaac Newton. Vintage. (pp. 12-18)

Westfall, R.S. (1980). Never at Rest: A Biography of Isaac Newton. Cambridge UP. (p. 67)

Keynes Collection, King's College Cambridge. Newton's Student Notebooks

Iliffe, R. (2017). Priest of Nature: The Religious Worlds of Isaac Newton. Oxford UP. (Chapter 3)

Cohen, I.B. (1999). The Principia: Mathematical Principles of Natural Philosophy. UC Press.

White, M. (1997). Isaac Newton: The Last Sorcerer. Basic Books.

Cambridge Digital Library. Newton Papers. cudl.lib.cam.ac.uk

- **Edmund Halley: (1656-1742)**

Cook, A. (1998). Edmond Halley: Charting the Heavens and the Seas. Oxford UP. (pp. 45-48)

Royal Museums Greenwich. (2023). Halley's St. Helena Expedition. rmg.co.uk

Hughes, D.W. (1985). Edmond Halley: The St. Helena Results. Journal of the British Astronomical Association 95(3)

Halley, E. (1686). On the Laws of Planetary Motion. Philosophical Transactions

Iliffe, R. (2017). Priest of Nature: The Religious Worlds of Isaac Newton. Oxford UP. (Chapter 7)

NASA. (2021). *1P/Halley Comet Fact Sheet*. nasa.gov

- **Thomas Savery: Thomas Savery (1650 – 1715)**

Savery, T. (1698). The Miner's Friend; or, An Engine to Raise Water by Fire. London.

Thurston, R.H. (1878). A History of the Growth of the Steam-Engine. D. Appleton & Co.

- **Thomas Newcomen (1664-1729)**

Kanefsky, J. (1979). The Diffusion of Power Technology in the British Industrial Revolution. Cambridge UP.

Newcomen Society (1922). Transactions on Newcomen Engine Archaeology.

Musson, A.E. (1969). Science and Technology in the Industrial Revolution. Manchester UP.

Chapter 4

- **Daniel Bernoulli(1700-1782)**

  Truesdell, C. (1983). The Tragicomical History of Thermodynamics. Springer. (pp. 78–82)

  NASA. (2020). Bernoulli's Principle and Airplane Lift. grc.nasa.gov

  Batchelor, G.K. (2000). An Introduction to Fluid Dynamics. Cambridge UP. (p. 156)

  Bernoulli, D. (1766). An Attempt at a New Analysis of Mortality. Royal Academy of Sciences.

- **Benjamin Franklin (1706 – 1790)**

  Van Doren, C. (1938). Benjamin Franklin. Viking Press. (pp. 160–165)

  Chaplin, J. (2006). The First Scientific American: Benjamin Franklin. Basic Books.

  Franklin, B. (1762). Letter on the Glass Armonica. Royal Society Archives.

  Isaacson, W. (2003). Benjamin Franklin: An American Life. Simon & Schuster.

- **Leonhard Euler (1707 – 1783)**

  Dunham, W. (1999). Euler: The Master of Us All. MAA Press. (pp. 3–12)

  Calinger, R. (2016). Leonhard Euler: Mathematical Genius in the Enlightenment. Princeton UP.

  Feynman, R. (1977). The Feynman Lectures on Physics, Vol. I. Addison-Wesley.

  Euler Archive. (2023). Works of Leonhard Euler. eulerarchive.org

- **Henry Cavendish, (1723-1810)**

Clotfelter, B. (1987). The Cavendish Experiment as Cavendish Knew It. Am. J. Phys. 55(3).

McCormmach, R. (2004). Speculative Truth: Henry Cavendish and the Experimental Life. Oxford UP.

Cavendish, H. (1766). On Factitious Airs. Phil. Trans. Royal Soc.

Maxwell, J.C. (1879). The Electrical Researches of Henry Cavendish. Cambridge UP.

- **Joseph Priestley (1733 – 1804)**

Schofield, R. (2004). The Enlightened Joseph Priestley. Penn State Press.

Lavoisier, A. (1778). On the Nature of Oxygen. Mémoires de l'Académie Royale.

Uglow, J. (2002). The Lunar Men: Five Friends Whose Curiosity Changed the World. Faber & Faber.

Priestley, J. (1767). The History and Present State of Electricity. London.

- **William Herschel (1738 – 1822)**

Hoskin, M. (2003). The Herschel Partnership: As Viewed by Caroline. Science History Publications.

Herschel, W. (1781). Account of a Comet. Philosophical Transactions of the Royal Society.

Winterburn, E. (2017). The Quiet Revolution of Caroline Herschel. The History Press.

Schaffer, S. (1980). Herschel in Bedlam: Natural History and Stellar Astronomy. The British Journal for the History of Science.

- **Antoine Lavoisier (1743 – 1794)**

Lavoisier, A. (1789). Traité Élémentaire de Chimie. Paris.

Donovan, A. (1996). Antoine Lavoisier: Science, Administration and Revolution. Cambridge UP.

Beretta, M. (2020). The Naming of Chemicals: Lavoisier's Reform. J. Chem. Educ.

Fara, P. (2018). Lab Coats and Lace: The Lives of Science's Unsung Women. Oxford UP.

- **Alessandro Volta (1745 – 1827)**

Pancaldi, G. (2003). Volta: Science and Culture in the Age of Enlightenment. Princeton UP.

IEEE Global History Network. (2012). Volta's Pile: The First Battery. ieeeghn.org

- **Edward Jenner (1749 – 1823)**

Riedel, S. (2005). Edward Jenner and Smallpox Vaccination. Baylor University Medical Center Proceedings.

Jenner, E. (1798). An Inquiry into the Causes and Effects of the Variolae Vaccinae. London.

WHO. (1980). Smallpox Eradication Declaration. who.int

- **John Dalton (1766 – 1844)**

Thackray, A. (1972). John Dalton: Critical Assessments of His Life and Science. Harvard UP.

Dalton, J. (1805). On the Absorption of Gases by Water. Memoirs of the Lit & Phil Society.

Rocke, A.J. (1984). Chemical Atomism in the Nineteenth Century. Ohio State UP.

- **Joseph Fourier (1768–1830)**

Grattan-Guinness, I. (1972). *Joseph Fourier 1768-1830*. MIT Press

Fourier, J. (1822). Théorie analytique de la chaleur. Firmin Didot

Fourier, J. (1827). "Mémoire sur les températures du globe terrestre et des espaces planétaires." Mémoires de l'Académie Royale des Sciences

- **Alexander von Humboldt (1769 – 1859)**

  Wulf, A. (2015). The Invention of Nature: Alexander von Humboldt's New World. Knopf.

  Humboldt, A. (1814–1825). Personal Narrative of Travels to the Equinoctial Regions. London.

  Darwin, C. (1839). The Voyage of the Beagle. (Humboldt-inspired journal)

- **Johann Carl Friedrich Gauss (1777 – 1855)**

  Dunnington, G.W. (2004). Carl Friedrich Gauss: Titan of Science. MAA Press.

  Gauss, C.F. (1801). Disquisitiones Arithmeticae. Leipzig.

  Stigler, S.M. (1986). The History of Statistics. Harvard UP.

- **Joseph Louis Gay-Lussac (1778–1850),**

  Gay-Lussac, J.L. (1802). Recherches sur la dilatation des gaz. Annales de chimie.

  Avogadro, A. (1811). Essay on Determining Relative Masses. Journal de Physique.

  Crouch, T.D. (1983). The Eagle Aloft: Two Centuries of Ballooning. Smithsonian.

- **Jean-Baptiste Biot and Félix Savart**

  Biot, J.-B. & Savart, F. (1820). Note on the Magnetic Effects of Electric Currents. Académie des Sciences.

  Biot, J.-B. (1815). On the Rotation of Light by Crystalline Substances. Mémoires de Physique.

- **Hans Christian Ørsted (1777-1851)**

  Ørsted, H.C. (1820). Experiments on the Effect of Electric Current on a Magnetic Needle.

  Biot, J.-B. & Savart, F. (1820). Note on the Magnetic Effects of Electric Currents.

- **James Watt (1736-1819)**

  Carnegie, A. (1905). James Watt. Doubleday.

  Marsden, B. (2002). Watt's Perfect Engine. Columbia UP.

  Tann, J. (1981). The Selected Papers of Boulton & Watt. MIT Press.

- **Sir Humphry Davy (1778-1829)**

  Davy, H. (1816). On the Fire-Damp of Coal Mines. Philosophical Transactions.

  Knight, D. (1992). Humphry Davy: Science and Power. Cambridge UP.

  Fullmer, J.Z. (2000). Young Humphry Davy. American Philosophical Society.

- **Jacob Berzelius (1779- 1848)**

  Lundgren, A. (2020). Berzelius and the Atomic Weight Revolution. Uppsala UP.

  Melhado, E.M. (1981). Jacob Berzelius: The Emergence of His Chemical System. MIT Press.

- **Michael Faraday (1791-1867)**

  Faraday, M. (1812). Lecture Notes from Humphry Davy's Presentations. RI Archive.

  Hamilton, J. (2002). Faraday: The Life. HarperCollins.

  Day, P. (1999). The Philosopher's Tree: Faraday's Life and Work. CRC Press.

- **Charles Babbage (1791–1871)**

  Swade, D. (2000). The Difference Engine: Charles Babbage's Computer. Penguin.

  Essinger, J. (2014). A Female Genius: How Ada Lovelace Started the Computer Age. Gibson Square.

- **Joseph Henry (1797–1878)**

  Henry, J. (1832). On the Production of Currents and Sparks of Electricity from Magnetism.

  Coulson, T. (1950). Joseph Henry: His Life and Work. Princeton UP.

Chapter 5

- **Matthew Fontaine Maury (1806–1873)**

  Lewis, C.L. (1927). Matthew Fontaine Maury: The Pathfinder of the Seas.

  Williams, F.L. (1963). Matthew Fontaine Maury: Scientist of the Sea.

- **Jean Louis Rodolphe Agassiz (1807–1873)**

  Gould, Stephen Jay. The Structure of Evolutionary Theory. Harvard UP, 2002.

  Hall, Brian K. Evolutionary Developmental Biology. Springer, 2009.

  Irmscher, Christoph. Louis Agassiz: Creator of American Science. Houghton Mifflin, 2013.

  Lurie, Edward. Louis Agassiz: A Life in Science. Johns Hopkins UP, 1988.

  Smith, Clark. Fossil Fish and the Birth of Palaeontology. Cambridge UP, 2018.

  Winsor, Mary P. Reading the Shape of Nature. Chicago UP, 1991.

- **Charles Robert Darwin (1809–1882)**

  Browne, J. (1995). Charles Darwin: Voyaging. Knopf.

  Carroll, S.B. (2005). Endless Forms Most Beautiful. Norton.

  Darwin, C. (1859). On the Origin of Species. John Murray.

Desmond, A., & Moore, J. (1991). Darwin. Warner Books.

Johanson, D., & Edey, M. (1981). Lucy: The Beginnings of Humankind. Simon & Schuster.

Schrödinger, E. (1944). What Is Life?. Cambridge UP.

Watson, J.D. (1968). The Double Helix. Atheneum.

- **Ada Lovelace (1815-1852)**

Essinger, J. (2014). Ada's Algorithm. Melville House.

Lovelace, A. (1843). Notes on the Analytical Engine. Taylor's Scientific Memoirs.

Padua, S. (2015). The Thrilling Adventures of Lovelace and Babbage. Pantheon.

Woolley, B. (1999). The Bride of Science. Macmillan.

- **James Prescott Joule (1818-1889)**

Cardwell, D.S.L. (1989). James Joule: A Biography. Manchester UP.

Joule, J.P. (1845). On the Mechanical Equivalent of Heat. Philosophical Transactions.

Reynolds, O. (1882). Memoir of James Prescott Joule. Manchester Lit. & Phil. Soc.

- **Jean-Bernard-Léon Foucault (1819-1868)**

Tobin, W. (2003). The Life and Science of Léon Foucault. Cambridge UP.

Foucault, L. (1851). Demonstration of the Earth's Motion. Comptes Rendus.

Aczel, A. (2003). Pendulum: Léon Foucault. Washington Square Press.

- **Gregor Mendel (1822–1884)**

Henig, R.M. (2000). The Monk in the Garden. Houghton Mifflin.

Masaryk University. (2022). Mendel DNA Project. Brno.

Mendel, G. (1866). Experiments on Plant Hybridization. Brno Natural History Society.

- **Louis Pasteur (1822–1895)**

Debré, P. (1998). Louis Pasteur. Johns Hopkins UP.

Pasteur, L. (1857). Memoire sur la fermentation appelée lactique.

Geison, G.L. (1995). The Private Science of Louis Pasteur. Princeton UP.

- **Lord Kelvin (1824-1907)**

Smith, C. (2004). The Science of Energy. University of Chicago Press.

Thomson, W. (1848). On an Absolute Thermometric Scale. Philosophical Magazine.

Lindley, D. (2004). Degrees Kelvin: A Tale of Genius. Joseph Henry Press.

- **George Johnstone Stoney (1826-1911)**

Stoney, G.J. (1874). On the Physical Units of Nature. Philosophical Magazine.

Thomson, J.J. (1897). Cathode Rays. Philosophical Magazine.

McCormmach, R. (1967). George Johnstone Stoney. Dictionary of Scientific Biography.

- **Joseph Lister (1827-1912)**

Fitzharris, L. (2017). The Butchering Art. Scientific American.

Lister, J. (1867). On the Antiseptic Principle. The Lancet.

Worboys, M. (2000). Spreading Germs. Cambridge UP.

- **Friedrich August Kekulé (1829-1896)**

Rocke, A.J. (2010). Image and Reality: Kekulé's Benzene. University of Chicago Press.

Kekulé, A. (1865). Sur la constitution des substances aromatiques. Bulletin de la Société Chimique.

Gillis, J. (1966). August Kekulé and the Birth of Structural Chemistry. Journal of Chemical Education.

- **James Clerk Maxwell (1831-1879)**

Harman, P.M. (1998). The Natural Philosophy of James Clerk Maxwell. Cambridge UP.

Maxwell, J.C. (1873). A Treatise on Electricity and Magnetism. Clarendon Press.

Mahon, B. (2003). The Man Who Changed Everything: Life of James Clerk Maxwell. Wiley.

- **Dmitri Mendeleev (1834-1907)**

Gordin, M.D. (2004). A Well-Ordered Thing: Dmitrii Mendeleev and the Shadow of the Periodic Table. Basic Books.

Mendeleev, D. (1869). On the Relationship of the Properties of the Elements to their Atomic Weights. Russian Chemical Society.

Scerri, E.R. (2007). The Periodic Table: Its Story and Its Significance. Oxford UP.

- **William Henry Perkin (1838-1907)**

Garfield, S. (2000). Mauve—The best book on Perkin's chaos.

Travis, A.S. (1993). The Rainbow Makers—For coal tar's glow-up.

Royal Society of Chemistry's Perkin archives (because primary sources rule).

- **Wilhelm Röntgen (1845-1923)**

Nobel Prize Archives (1901 Physics Nobel bio)

Kevles, B.H. (1997). Naked to the Bone: Medical Imaging in the Twentieth Century. Rutgers UP.

IUPAC Report (2004) on element 111 naming.

- **Thomas Alva Edison (1847 -1931 CE)**

  Baldwin, N. (2001). Edison: Inventing the Century. University of Chicago Press.

  Stross, R. (2007). The Wizard of Menlo Park: How Thomas Edison Invented the Modern World. Crown.

- **Luther Burbank (1849-1926)**

  Dreyer, P. (1993). A Gardener Touched with Genius: The Life of Luther Burbank. UC Press.

  Smith, J. (2009). The Burbank Potato: How a Hobby Fed a Nation. Agricultural History Journal.

- **Ivan Petrovich Pavlov (1846-1936)**

  Todes, D.P. (2014). Ivan Pavlov: A Russian Life in Science. Oxford UP.

  Pavlov, I. (1897). Lectures on the Work of the Digestive Glands (the book he wished you'd cite).

- **John Ambrose Fleming (1859-1914)**

  Ryder, J.D. (1957). Electronic Fundamentals and Applications. Pitman Publishing.

  Hong, S. (2001). Wireless: From Marconi's Black Box to the Audion. MIT Press.

- **Antoine Henri Becquerel (1852 -1908)**

  Boudia, S. (2001). The Curie Laboratory: Radioactivity and Metrology. History and Technology.

  Quinn, S. (1996). Marie Curie: A Life. Simon & Schuster.

- **Edward W. Morley (1838-1923)**

  Livingston, D.M. (1973). The Master of Light: A Biography of Albert A. Michelson

  Collins, H. (2004). Gravity's Shadow: The Search for Gravitational Waves

- **Joseph John Thomson (1856-1940)**

  Dahl, P.F. (1997). Flash of the Cathode Rays: A History of J.J. Thomson's Electron. CRC Press.

  Thomson, J.J. (1897). Cathode Rays (landmark paper in Philosophical Magazine).

- **Max Planck (1858-1947)**

  Heilbron, J.L. (2000). The Dilemmas of an Upright Man: Max Planck and the Fortunes of German Science. Harvard UP.

  Kuhn, T.S. (1978). Black-Body Theory and the Quantum Discontinuity. Oxford UP.

- **Nettie Maria Stevens (1861-1912)**

  Brush, S.G. (1978). Nettie Stevens and the Discovery of Sex Determination by Chromosomes. Isis Journal.

  Maienschein, J. (1981). Whitman, Brooks, and Stevens: Women in Biology at Bryn Mawr.

- **Marie Skłodowska-Curie (1867-1934)**

  Quinn, S. (1995). Marie Curie: A Life. Simon & Schuster.

  Redniss, L. (2010). Radioactive: Marie & Pierre Curie: A Tale of Love and Fallout. HarperCollins.

- **Henrietta Swan Leavitt (1864-1932)**

  Johnson, G. (2005). Miss Leavitt's Stars: The Untold Story of the Woman Who Discovered How to Measure the Universe. Norton.

  Haramundanis, K. (2005). Cecilia Payne-Gaposchkin: An Autobiography. Cambridge UP.

- **Ernest Rutherford (circa 1871-1937)**

  Reeves, R. (2008). A Force of Nature: The Frontier Genius of Ernest Rutherford. W.W. Norton.

  Wilson, D. (1983). Rutherford: Simple Genius. MIT Press.

- **Lise Meitner (1878-1968)**

  Sime, R.L. (1996). Lise Meitner: A Life in Physics. UC Press.

  Rife, P. (1999). Lise Meitner and the Dawn of the Nuclear Age. Birkhäuser

- **Albert Einstein (1879-1955)**

  Isaacson, W. (2007). Einstein: His Life and Universe. Simon & Schuster.

  Pais, A. (1982). Subtle is the Lord: The Science and Life of Albert Einstein. Oxford UP.

- **Sir Alexander Fleming (1881-1995)**

  Macfarlane, G. (1984). Alexander Fleming: The Man and the Myth. Harvard UP.

  Lax, E. (2015). The Mold in Dr. Florey's Coat: The Story of the Penicillin Miracle. Holt Paperbacks.

- **Neils Bohr (1885-1962)**

  Pais, A. (1991). Niels Bohr's Times: In Physics, Philosophy, and Polity. Oxford UP.

  Faye, J. (2019). Copenhagen Interpretation of Quantum Mechanics. Stanford Encyclopedia.

- **Erwin Schrödinger (1887-1961)**

  Moore, W. (1989). Schrödinger: Life and Thought. Cambridge UP.

  Gribbin, J. (2012). Erwin Schrödinger and the Quantum Revolution.

- **Edwin Powell Hubble (1889-1953)**

  Christianson, G.E. (1995). Edwin Hubble: Mariner of the Nebulae.

  Bartusiak, M. (2009). The Day We Found the Universe.

- **Sir Robert Alexander Watson-watt(1892-1973)**

  Brown, L. (1999). A Radar History of World War II.

  Watson-Watt, R. (1957). Three Steps to Victory (his autobiography)

- **Arthur Holly Compton (1892-1962)**

  Compton, A.H. (1923). A Quantum Theory of the Scattering of X-Rays by Light Elements

  Johnston, J. (2017). The Compton Effect: Turning Point in Physics

- **Irène Joliot-Curie (1897CE-1956CE)**

  Goldsmith, B. (2005). Obsessive Genius: The Inner World of Marie Curie

  Quinn, S. (1995). Marie Curie: A Life

Chapter 6

- **Linus Carl Pauling (1901-1994)**

  Hager, T. (1995). Force of Nature: The Life of Linus Pauling

  Pauling, L. (1939). The Nature of the Chemical Bond

- **Enrico Fermi (1901-1954)**

  Segrè, E. (1970). Enrico Fermi: Physicist

  Fermi, L. (1954). Atoms in the Family

- **Werner Karl Heisenberg (1901CE-1976CE),**

  The Physical Principles of the Quantum Theory. Translators Eckart, Carl; Hoyt, F.C. Dover. ISBN 978-0-486-60113-7.

  (1953). Nuclear Physics. Philosophical Library (1953)

- **Barbara McClintock(1902-1992)**

  McClintock, B. (1950). "The origin and behaviour of mutable loci in maize." PNAS, 36(6), 344-355. (Her landmark paper)

Fedoroff, N. V. (1984). "Transposable genetic elements in maize." Scientific American, 250(6), 84-98. (Context on her legacy)

Nobel Prize. (1983). "Barbara McClintock – Facts." https://www.nobelprize.org (Official Nobel bio)

Transistor

1. Walter Houser Brattain (1902 -1987)
2. John Bardeen (1908 – 1991)
3. William Shockley (1910 – 1989)

Bardeen, J. (1949). "Surface states and rectification at a metal-semiconductor contact." Physical Review, 75(8), 1208.

Bardeen, J., & Brattain, W. H. (1948). "The transistor, a semiconductor triode." Physical Review, 74(2), 230.

Brattain, W. H. (1951). "Surface properties of germanium." Bell System Technical Journal, 30(1), 1-41.

Bryant, J. (2010). "Thermionic valves: A brief history." IEEE History Center.

Eisenstein, E. (1980). "The printing press as an agent of change." Cambridge University Press.

Gertner, J. (2012). "The idea factory: Bell Labs and the great age of American innovation." Penguin.

Moll, J. L. (1998). "The evolution of the transistor." Proceedings of the IEEE, 86(1), 6-10.

Riordan, M., & Hoddeson, L. (1997). "Crystal fire: The birth of the information age." W.W. Norton.

Shockley, W. (1950). "Electrons and holes in semiconductors." Van Nostrand.

- **Grace Murray Hopper(1906-1092)**

  Beyer, K. (2009). Grace Hopper and the Invention of the Information Age. MIT Press.

  Ceruzzi, P. (2003). A History of Modern Computing. MIT Press.

  Sammet, J. (1981). "The early history of COBOL." ACM SIGPLAN Notices.

  Swade, D. (2000). The Cogwheel Brain. Little, Brown.

- **Maria Goeppert Mayer (1906-1972)**

  Dash, J. (1973). A Life of One's Own: Three Gifted Women and the Men They Married. Harper & Row.

  Mayer, M.G. (1950). "Nuclear Configurations in the Spin-Orbit Coupling Model." Physical Review.

  Mayer, M.G. & Jensen, J.H.D. (1955). Elementary Theory of Nuclear Shell Structure. Wiley.

- **Dorothy Mary Hodgkin(1910-1994),**

  Dash, J. (1973). A Life of One's Own: Three Gifted Women and the Men They Married. Harper & Row.

  Mayer, M.G. (1950). "Nuclear Configurations in the Spin-Orbit Coupling Model." Physical Review.

  Mayer, M.G. & Jensen, J.H.D. (1955). Elementary Theory of Nuclear Shell Structure. Wiley.

- **Jacques Yves Cousteau (1910-1997)**

  A Bill of Rights for Future Generations (1979)

  Life at the Bottom of the World (1980)

- **Richard Phillips Feynman (1918-1988)**

  Feynman, R. (1949). "Space-Time Approach to Quantum Electrodynamics." Physical Review

  Nobel Foundation. (1965). Nobel Prize in Physics 1965. nobelprize.org

Gleick, J. (1992). Genius: The Life and Science of Richard Feynman. Pantheon

Rogers Commission. (1986). Report of the Presidential Commission on the Space Shuttle Challenger Accident

Feynman, R. (1985). "Surely You're Joking, Mr. Feynman!" W.W. Norton

- **Frederick Sanger (1918-2013)**

Sanger, F. (1955). "The amino acid sequence of insulin." Biochemical Journal

Nobel Foundation. (1958). The Nobel Prize in Chemistry 1958. nobelprize.org

Sanger, F., et al. (1977). "Nucleotide sequence of bacteriophage φX174 DNA." Nature

Nobel Foundation. (1980). The Nobel Prize in Chemistry 1980. nobelprize.org

Walker, J. (2014). "Frederick Sanger (1918–2013)." Nature

- **Rosalind Elsie Franklin (1920 – 1958)**

Maddox, B. (2002). Rosalind Franklin: The Dark Lady of DNA. HarperCollins.

Glynn, J. (2012). My Sister Rosalind Franklin. Oxford University Press.

Watson, J.D. & Crick, F.H.C. (1953). "Molecular structure of nucleic acids." Nature.

Klug, A. (1968). "Rosalind Franklin and the discovery of the structure of DNA." Nature.

Nobel Foundation. (1962). The Nobel Prize in Physiology or Medicine 1962.

Elkin, L.O. (2003). "Rosalind Franklin and the double helix." Physics Today.

- **Rosalyn Sussman Yalow (1921 -2011)**

  Yalow, R.S. & Berson, S.A. (1960). "Immunoassay of endogenous plasma insulin in man." JCI

  Nobel Foundation. (1977). The Nobel Prize in Physiology or Medicine 1977

  Straus, E. (1998). "Rosalyn Yalow: Nobel Laureate." Persp. Biol. Med.

- **Har Gobind Khorana (1922-2011)**

  Khorana, H.G. (1967). "Polynucleotide synthesis and the genetic code." Harvey Lectures

  Nirenberg, M. & Leder, P. (1964). "RNA codewords and protein synthesis." Science

  Khorana, H.G., et al. (1972). "Total synthesis of the gene for an alanine tRNA." JMB

  Nobel Foundation. (1968). The Nobel Prize in Physiology or Medicine 1968

- **Tsung-Dao Lee (1926-2024)**

  Lee, T.D. & Yang, C.N. (1956). "Question of Parity Conservation in Weak Interactions." Physical Review

  Wu, C.S. et al. (1957). "Experimental Test of Parity Conservation in Beta Decay." Physical Review

  Nobel Foundation. (1957). The Nobel Prize in Physics 1957

  Jiang, L. (2021). "Chien-Shiung Wu: The Overlooked Hero of Parity Violation." Physics Today

  Lee, T.D. (1986). "Symmetries and Asymmetries in Physics." Columbia University Press

- **James Dewey Watson (1928-), Francis Harry Compton Crick (1916-2004), Maurie Wilkins (1916-2004)**

  Maddox, B. (2002). Rosalind Franklin: The Dark Lady of DNA. HarperCollins.

Glynn, J. (2012). My Sister Rosalind Franklin. OUP.

Watson, J.D. & Crick, F.H.C. (1953). "Molecular structure of nucleic acids." Nature.

Church, G. et al. (2012). "Next-generation digital information storage in DNA." Science.

Franklin, R. (1950). "Laboratory notebooks." Churchill Archives Centre.

- **Stephen William Hawking (1948-2016)**

Hawking, S.W. (1974). "Black hole explosions?" Nature

Penrose, R. & Hawking, S.W. (1970). "The singularities of gravitational collapse." PRD

Hartle, J. & Hawking, S.W. (1983). "Wave function of the Universe." PRD

Hawking, S.W. (1988). A Brief History of Time. Bantam

Hawking, S. (2013). My Brief History. Bantam

- **Peter Ware Higgs (1929 – 2024)**

Higgs, P. (1964). "Broken Symmetries and the Masses of Gauge Bosons." Physical Review Letters

ATLAS Collaboration. (2012). "Observation of a New Particle." Physics Letters B

Nobel Foundation. (2013). The Nobel Prize in Physics 2013

Sample, I. (2010). Massive: The Hunt for the God Particle. Virgin Books

- **John Craig Venter (1946 -)**

Shreeve, J. (2004). The Genome War. Knopf

Venter, J.C. (1975). "Adrenergic receptor research." UCSD Dissertation

Venter et al. (1998). "Shotgun sequencing of the human genome." Science

Lander et al. (2001). "Initial sequencing of the human genome." Nature

Gibson et al. (2010). "Creation of a bacterial cell controlled by a chemically synthesized genome." Science

Hutchison et al. (2016). "Design and synthesis of a minimal bacterial genome." Science

Venter, J.C. (2007). A Life Decoded. Viking

- **Sir Roger Penrose (1931 -)**

Penrose, R. (1965). "Gravitational collapse and space-time singularities." Physical Review Letters

Hawking, S. & Penrose, R. (1970). "The singularities of gravitational collapse." PRD

Shechtman, D. et al. (1984). "Metallic phase with long-range orientational order." PRL

Penrose, R. & Hameroff, S. (2011). "Consciousness in the universe." Physics of Life Reviews

Penrose, R. (1994). Shadows of the Mind. Oxford University Press

Nobel Foundation. (2020). The Nobel Prize in Physics 2020

- **Sir Tim Berners-Lee** (1955 -)

Berners-Lee, T. (1989). *"Information Management: A Proposal"* (Original WWW proposal)

Gillies, J. & Cailliau, R. (2000). *How the Web Was Born*

Berners-Lee, T. (2021). *"The Year the Web Was Invented"* (TED Talk)

W3C (1994-present). *Web Standards Documentation*

Web Foundation (2009-present). *Annual Web Index Reports*

Chapter 7

- **CRISPR: The Bacterial Superpower That Revolutionised Genetic Engineering**

  Mojica, F.J. et al. (2005). "Intervening sequences of regularly spaced prokaryotic repeats derive from foreign genetic elements." J Mol Evol

  Nobel Foundation. (2020). The Nobel Prize in Chemistry 2020

  Cyranoski, D. (2019). "The CRISPR-baby scandal: what's next for human gene-editing." Nature

- **Quantum computing**

  Feynman, R. (1982). "Simulating physics with computers." Int. J. Theor. Phys

  Shor, P. (1994). "Algorithms for quantum computation." Foundations of Computer Science

  Arute, F. et al. (2019). "Quantum supremacy using a programmable superconducting processor." Nature

- **Our Climate Crossroads**

  Fourier, J. (1824). "Remarques Générales sur les Températures du Globe Terrestre et des Espaces Planétaires." Annales de Chimie et de Physique

  Tyndall, J. (1861). "On the Absorption and Radiation of Heat by Gases and Vapours." Philosophical Transactions

  Arrhenius, S. (1896). "On the Influence of Carbonic Acid in the Air upon the Temperature of the Ground." Philosophical Magazine

  Keeling, C.D. et al. (1976). "Atmospheric carbon dioxide variations at Mauna Loa Observatory, Hawaii." Tellus

  Lewis, N.S. (2007). "Powering the Planet." Chemical Engineering Progress

MIT (2018). "The Future of Nuclear Energy in a Carbon-Constrained World." MIT Energy Initiative

IPCC (2021). "Climate Change 2021: The Physical Science Basis."

Chapter 8

- **The Rise of Uncontrollable Technologies**

Amodei, D., Olah, C., Steinhardt, J., Christiano, P., Schulman, J., & Mané, D. (2016). Concrete problems in AI safety. arXiv preprint arXiv:1606.06565.

Bender, E. M., Gebru, T., McMillan-Major, A., & Shmitchell, S. (2021). On the dangers of stochastic parrots: Can language models be too big? Proceedings of the 2021 ACM Conference on Fairness, Accountability, and Transparency, 610-623.

Benkler, Y. (2006). The wealth of networks: How social production transforms markets and freedom. Yale University Press.

Bostrom, N. (2014). Superintelligence: Paths, dangers, strategies. Oxford University Press.

Brown, T. B., Mann, B., Ryder, N., Subbiah, M., Kaplan, J., Dhariwal, P., ... & Amodei, D. (2020). Language models are few-shot learners. Advances in Neural Information Processing Systems, 33, 1877-1901.

Brynjolfsson, E., & McAfee, A. (2014). The second machine age: Work, progress, and prosperity in a time of brilliant technologies. W. W. Norton & Company.

Chalmers, D. J. (1995). Facing up to the problem of consciousness. Journal of Consciousness Studies, 2(3), 200-219.

Chesney, R., & Citron, D. (2019). Deep fakes: A looming challenge for privacy, democracy, and national security. California Law Review, 107, 1753-1819.

Church, G. M., & Regis, E. (2012). Regenesis: How synthetic biology will reinvent nature and ourselves. Basic Books.

Damasio, A. R. (1999). The feeling of what happens: Body and emotion in the making of consciousness. Harcourt Brace.

Dennett, D. C. (1991). Consciousness explained. Little, Brown & Co.

Doudna, J. A., & Charpentier, E. (2014). The new frontier of genome engineering with CRISPR-Cas9. Science, 346(6213), 1258096.

Esvelt, K. (2018). Gene drives and the ethics of genome editing. Presentation at MIT Media Lab.

Floridi, L. (2013). The ethics of information. Oxford University Press.

Gardner, H. (2006). Five minds for the future. Harvard Business Review Press.

Harari, Y. N. (2016). Homo Deus: A brief history of tomorrow. Harper.

Harnad, S. (1990). The symbol grounding problem. Physica D: Nonlinear Phenomena, 42(1-3), 335-346.

Hoffman, M. L. (2000). Empathy and moral development: Implications for caring and justice. Cambridge University Press.

Lake, B. M., Ullman, T. D., Tenenbaum, J. B., & Gershman, S. J. (2017). Building machines that learn and think like people. Behavioral and Brain Sciences, 40, e253.

LeCun, Y., Bengio, Y., & Hinton, G. (2015). Deep learning. Nature, 521(7553), 436-444.

Marcus, G. (2018). Deep learning: A critical appraisal. arXiv preprint arXiv:1801.00631.

Marcus, G., & Davis, E. (2019). Rebooting AI: Building artificial intelligence we can trust. Pantheon.

Maxwell, N. (2007). From knowledge to wisdom: A revolution for science and the humanities. Pentire Press.

Mokyr, J. (1990). The lever of riches: Technological creativity and economic progress. Oxford University Press.

O'Neil, C. (2016). Weapons of math destruction: How big data increases inequality and threatens democracy. Crown.

Pariser, E. (2011). The filter bubble: How the new personalized web is changing what we read and how we think. Penguin.

Ribeiro, M. T., Singh, S., & Guestrin, C. (2016). "Why should I trust you?" Explaining the predictions of any classifier. Proceedings of the 22nd ACM SIGKDD International Conference on Knowledge Discovery and Data Mining, 1135-1144.

Russell, S. (2019). Human compatible: Artificial intelligence and the problem of control. Viking.

Schwab, K. (2016). The fourth industrial revolution. World Economic Forum.

Searle, J. R. (1980). Minds, brains, and programs. Behavioral and Brain Sciences, 3(3), 417-424.

Silver, D., Hubert, T., Schrittwieser, J., Antonoglou, I., Lai, M., Guez, A., ... & Hassabis, D. (2018). A general reinforcement learning algorithm that masters chess, shogi, and Go through self-play. Science, 362(6419), 1140-1144.

Taleb, N. N. (2007). The black swan: The impact of the highly improbable. Random House.

Tegmark, M. (2017). Life 3.0: Being human in the age of artificial intelligence. Knopf.

Yudkowsky, E. (2008). Artificial intelligence as a positive and negative factor in global risk. In Global catastrophic risks (pp. 308-345). Oxford University Press.

Zech, J. R., Badgeley, M. A., Liu, M., Costa, A. B., Titano, J. J., & Oermann, E. K. (2018). Variable generalization performance of a deep learning model to detect pneumonia in chest radiographs: A cross-sectional study. PLOS Medicine, 15(11), e1002683.

Zuboff, S. (2019). The age of surveillance capitalism: The fight for a human future at the new frontier of power. PublicAffairs.

- **The New Ethical Dilemmas**

Benjamin, R. (2019). Race after technology: Abolitionist tools for the New Jim Code. Polity Press.

Bolukbasi, T., Chang, K. W., Zou, J. Y., Saligrama, V., & Kalai, A. T. (2016). Man is to computer programmer as woman is to homemaker? Debiasing word embeddings. Advances in Neural Information Processing Systems, 29, 4349-4357.

Bostrom, N. (2014). Superintelligence: Paths, dangers, strategies. Oxford University Press.

Buolamwini, J., & Gebru, T. (2018). Gender shades: Intersectional accuracy disparities in commercial gender classification. Proceedings of the Conference on Fairness, Accountability, and Transparency, 77-91.

Floridi, L. (2013). The ethics of information. Oxford University Press.

Hancock, J. T., Naaman, M., & Levy, K. (2020). AI-mediated communication: Definition, research agenda, and ethical considerations. *Journal of Computer-Mediated Communication, 25*(1), 89-100.

Harari, Y. N. (2016). Homo Deus: A brief history of tomorrow. Harper.

Jobin, A., Ienca, M., & Vayena, E. (2019). The global landscape of AI ethics guidelines. Nature Machine Intelligence, 1(9), 389-399.

Marcus, G. (2018). Deep learning: A critical appraisal. arXiv preprint arXiv:1801.00631.

Mittelstadt, B. D., Allo, P., Taddeo, M., Wachter, S., & Floridi, L. (2016). The ethics of algorithms: Mapping the debate. Big Data & Society, 3(2), 1-21.

Noble, S. U. (2018). Algorithms of oppression: How search engines reinforce racism. NYU Press.

O'Neil, C. (2016). Weapons of math destruction: How big data increases inequality and threatens democracy. Crown.

Pariser, E. (2011). The filter bubble: How the new personalized web is changing what we read and how we think. Penguin.

Russell, S. (2019). Human compatible: Artificial intelligence and the problem of control. Viking.

Solove, D. J. (2013). Nothing to hide: The false tradeoff between privacy and security. Yale University Press.

Wachter, S., Mittelstadt, B., & Floridi, L. (2017). Why a right to explanation of automated decision-making does not exist in the General Data Protection Regulation. International Data Privacy Law, 7(2), 76-99.

Whittlestone, J., Nyrup, R., Alexandrova, A., Dihal, K., & Cave, S. (2019). Ethical and societal implications of algorithms, data, and artificial intelligence: A roadmap for research. Nuffield Foundation.

Yudkowsky, E. (2008). Artificial intelligence as a positive and negative factor in global risk. In Global catastrophic risks (pp. 308-345). Oxford University Press.

Zuboff, S. (2019). The age of surveillance capitalism: The fight for a human future at the new frontier of power. PublicAffairs.

- **Stewardship: Guiding the Forces We Have Unleashed**

Amodei, D., Olah, C., Steinhardt, J., Christiano, P., Schulman, J., & Mané, D. (2016). Concrete problems in AI safety. arXiv:1606.06565.

Benjamin, R. (2019). Race after technology: Abolitionist tools for the New Jim Code. Polity.

Benkler, Y. (2006). The wealth of networks. Yale University Press.

Block, P. (2013). Stewardship: Choosing service over self-interest. Berrett-Koehler.

Bostrom, N. (2014). Superintelligence: Paths, dangers, strategies. Oxford University Press.

Bremmer, I. (2020). The power of crisis: How three threats—and our response—will change the world. Simon & Schuster.

Cath, C., Wachter, S., Mittelstadt, B., Taddeo, M., & Floridi, L. (2018). Artificial intelligence and the 'good society'. Philosophy & Technology, 31(1), 1-28.

Doshi-Velez, F., & Kim, B. (2017). Towards a rigorous science of interpretable machine learning. arXiv:1702.08608.

Floridi, L. (2013). The ethics of information. Oxford University Press.

Floridi, L. (2018). Soft ethics and the governance of the digital. Philosophy & Technology, 31(1), 1-8.

Gabriel, I. (2020). Artificial intelligence, values, and alignment. Minds and Machines, 30(3), 411-437.

Harari, Y. N. (2015). Sapiens: A brief history of humankind. Harper.

Harari, Y. N. (2016). Homo Deus: A brief history of tomorrow. Harper.

Jobin, A., Ienca, M., & Vayena, E. (2019). The global landscape of AI ethics guidelines. Nature Machine Intelligence, 1(9), 389-399.

Jonas, H. (1984). The imperative of responsibility. University of Chicago Press.

Kim, W. C., & Mauborgne, R. (2014). Blue ocean leadership. Harvard Business Review.

Mitcham, C. (1994). Thinking through technology. University of Chicago Press.

Mittelstadt, B., Allo, P., Taddeo, M., Wachter, S., & Floridi, L. (2016). The ethics of algorithms. Big Data & Society, 3(2), 1-21.

Reynolds, R., & Bird, K. (2020). Digital literacy for technical communication. Routledge.

Risse, M. (2019). On global justice. Princeton University Press.

Russell, S. (2019). Human compatible: Artificial intelligence and the problem of control. Viking.

Schwartz, B. (2021). Why we work. Simon & Schuster.

Susskind, J. (2022). The digital republic. Bloomsbury.

Taleb, N. N. (2007). The black swan. Random House.

Tegmark, M. (2017). Life 3.0: Being human in the age of artificial intelligence. Knopf.

UNESCO. (2021). AI and education: Guidance for policy-makers. UNESCO Publishing.

Whittlestone, J., Nyrup, R., Alexandrova, A., & Cave, S. (2019). Ethical and societal implications of algorithms. Nuffield Foundation.

Zuboff, S. (2019). The age of surveillance capitalism. PublicAffairs.

- **Futures at the Crossroads**

Amodei, D., et al. (2016). Concrete problems in AI safety. arXiv:1606.06565.

Binns, R. (2018). Fairness in machine learning. Philosophy & Technology, 31(3), 433-445.

Bolukbasi, T., et al. (2016). Debiasing word embeddings. NeurIPS 29, 4349-4357.

Bostrom, N. (2014). Superintelligence. Oxford.

Brooks, R. (2020). The misguided blame game. MIT Tech Review, 123(4), 32-35.

Chesney, R., & Citron, D. (2019). Deep fakes. California Law Review, 107, 1753-1819.

Cowls, J., et al. (2021). AI for climate. Nature Climate Change, 11, 54-57.

Doshi-Velez, F., & Kim, B. (2017). Interpretable ML. arXiv:1702.08608.

Floridi, L. (2013). The ethics of information. Oxford.

Gabriel, I. (2020). AI alignment. Minds and Machines, 30(3), 411-437.

Harari, Y.N. (2015). Sapiens. Harper.

Jonas, H. (1984). The imperative of responsibility. Chicago.

Noble, S.U. (2018). Algorithms of oppression. NYU.

Rahwan, I. (2018). Society-in-the-loop. Patterns, 1(1), 100006.

Searle, J. (1980). Minds and programs. BBS, 3(3), 417-424.

Silver, D., et al. (2018). A general RL algorithm. Science, 362(6419), 1140-1144.

Tegmark, M. (2017). Life 3.0. Knopf.

UNESCO. (2021). AI and education.

Yudkowsky, E. (2008). AI as global risk. In Global catastrophic risks (pp. 308-345). Oxford.

Zuboff, S. (2019). Surveillance capitalism. PublicAffairs.

Chapter 9

- **Consciousness**

Chalmers, D. J. (1995). Facing up to the problem of consciousness. Journal of Consciousness Studies, 2(3), 200–219.

Damasio, A. (1999). The Feeling of What Happens: Body and Emotion in the Making of Consciousness. Harcourt.

Darwin, C. (1872). The Expression of the Emotions in Man and Animals. John Murray.

Engel, G. S., Calhoun, T. R., Read, E. L., et al. (2007). Evidence for wavelike energy transfer through quantum coherence in photosynthetic systems. Nature, 446(7137), 782–786.

Hameroff, S., & Penrose, R. (2014). Consciousness in the universe: A review of the 'Orch OR' theory. Physics of Life Reviews, 11(1), 39–78.

LeDoux, J. E. (1996). The Emotional Brain: The Mysterious Underpinnings of Emotional Life. Simon & Schuster.

Phelps, E. A. (2004). Human emotion and memory: interactions of the amygdala and hippocampal complex. Current Opinion in Neurobiology, 14(2), 198–202.

Part I

1:

Atkins, P. (2010). Four Laws That Drive the Universe. Oxford University Press.

Cannon, W. B. (1932). The Wisdom of the Body. Norton.

Damasio, A. (2010). Self Comes to Mind: Constructing the Conscious Brain. Pantheon.

Lane, N. (2015). The Vital Question: Energy, Evolution, and the Origins of Complex Life. Profile Books.

Maturana, H. R., & Varela, F. J. (1980). Autopoiesis and Cognition: The Realisation of the Living. D. Reidel Publishing.

Morowitz, H. J. (1968). Energy Flow in Biology: Biological Organisation as a Problem in Thermal Physics. Academic Press.

Schrödinger, E. (1944). What is Life? The Physical Aspect of the Living Cell. Cambridge University Press.

2:

De Duve, C. (2002). Life Evolving: Molecules, Mind, and Meaning. Oxford University Press.

Damasio, A. (2010). Self Comes to Mind: Constructing the Conscious Brain. Pantheon.

Maturana, H. R., & Varela, F. J. (1980). Autopoiesis and Cognition: The Realization of the Living. D. Reidel Publishing.

Moreno, A., & Mossio, M. (2015). Biological Autonomy: A Philosophical and Theoretical Enquiry. Springer.

Varela, F. J., Thompson, E., & Rosch, E. (1991). The Embodied Mind: Cognitive Science and Human Experience. MIT Press.

3:

Damasio, A. (1999). The Feeling of What Happens: Body and Emotion in the Making of Consciousness. Harcourt.

De Duve, C. (2002). Life Evolving: Molecules, Mind, and Meaning. Oxford University Press.

Friston, K. (2010). The free-energy principle: a unified brain theory? Nature Reviews Neuroscience, 11(2), 127–138.

LeDoux, J. (2015). Anxious: Using the Brain to Understand and Treat Fear and Anxiety. Viking.

McGaugh, J. L. (2003). Memory and Emotion: The Making of Lasting Memories. Columbia University Press.

Mitchell, J. G. (2002). The energetics of bacterial chemotaxis. Nature Reviews Microbiology, 1(1), 21–30.

Nesse, R. M. (2000). Is depression an adaptation? Archives of General Psychiatry, 57(1), 14–20.

Panksepp, J. (1998). Affective Neuroscience: The Foundations of Human and Animal Emotions. Oxford University Press.

Nesse, R. M. (2000). Is depression an adaptation? Archives of General Psychiatry.

Part II

4:

Berridge, K. C., & Kringelbach, M. L. (2013). Towards a neuroscience of affect: Valence and motivational systems. Nature Reviews Neuroscience, 14(6), 374–386.

Damasio, A. (1999). The Feeling of What Happens: Body and Emotion in the Making of Consciousness. Harcourt.

Damasio, A. (2010). Self Comes to Mind: Constructing the Conscious Brain. Pantheon.

Friston, K. (2010). The free-energy principle: A unified brain theory? Nature Reviews Neuroscience, 11(2), 127–138.

McGaugh, J. L. (2003). Memory and Emotion: The Making of Lasting Memories. Columbia University Press.

Panksepp, J. (1998). Affective Neuroscience: The Foundations of Human and Animal Emotions. Oxford University Press.

Schultz, W. (2015). Neuronal reward and decision signals: From theories to data. Physiological Reviews, 95(3), 853–951.

Seth, A. (2021). Being You: A New Science of Consciousness. Faber & Faber.

5:

Berridge, K. C., & Kringelbach, M. L. (2008). Affective neuroscience of pleasure: Reward in humans and animals. Psychopharmacology, 199(3), 457–480.

Carter, C. S. (1998). Neuroendocrine perspectives on social attachment and love. Psychoneuroendocrinology, 23(8), 779–818.

Damasio, A. (1999). The Feeling of What Happens. Harcourt.

Eisenberger, N. I., & Lieberman, M. D. (2004). Why it hurts to be left out. Trends in Cognitive Sciences, 8(7), 294–300.

Feldman, R. (2012). Oxytocin and social affiliation in humans. Hormones and Behaviour, 61(3), 380–391.

Fisher, H. (2004). Why We Love: The Nature and Chemistry of Romantic Love. Henry Holt.

Georgiadis, J. R., & Kringelbach, M. L. (2012). The human sexual response cycle: Brain imaging evidence linking sex to other pleasures. Progress in Neurobiology, 98(1), 49–81.

LeDoux, J. (2015). Anxious. Viking.

MacLean, P. D. (1990). The Triune Brain in Evolution. Plenum Press.

Panksepp, J. (1998). Affective Neuroscience: The Foundations of Human and Animal Emotions. Oxford University Press.

Panksepp, J. (2005). Affective consciousness: Core emotional feelings in animals and humans. Consciousness and Cognition, 14(1), 30–80.

Panksepp, J. (2007). Can PLAY diminish ADHD and facilitate the construction of the social brain? Journal of the Canadian Academy of Child and Adolescent Psychiatry, 16(2), 57–66.

Porges, S. W. (2011). The Polyvagal Theory: Neurophysiological Foundations of Emotions, Attachment, Communication, and Self-Regulation. Norton.

6:

Damasio, A. (1999). The Feeling of What Happens: Body and Emotion in the Making of Consciousness. Harcourt.

Damasio, A. (2010). Self Comes to Mind: Constructing the Conscious Brain. Pantheon.

Merker, B. (2007). Consciousness without a cerebral cortex: A challenge for neuroscience and medicine. Behavioral and Brain Sciences, 30(1), 63–81.

Panksepp, J. (1998). Affective Neuroscience: The Foundations of Human and Animal Emotions. Oxford University Press.

Solms, M. (2021). The Hidden Spring: A Journey to the Source of Consciousness. Profile Books.

7:

Craig, A. D. (2002). How do you feel? Interoception: the sense of the physiological condition of the body. Nature Reviews Neuroscience, 3(8), 655–666.

Craig, A. D. (2009). How do you feel—now? The anterior insula and human awareness. Nature Reviews Neuroscience, 10(1), 59–70.

Critchley, H. D., & Harrison, N. A. (2013). Visceral influences on brain and behavior. Neuron, 77(4), 624–638.

Damasio, A. (1999). The Feeling of What Happens. Harcourt.

Damasio, A. (2010). Self Comes to Mind: Constructing the Conscious Brain. Pantheon.

Khalsa, S. S., et al. (2018). Interoception and mental health: A roadmap. Biological Psychiatry: Cognitive Neuroscience and Neuroimaging, 3(6), 501–513.

Paulus, M. P., & Stein, M. B. (2010). Interoception in anxiety and depression. Brain Structure and Function, 214(5-6), 451–463.

Seth, A. (2021). Being You: A New Science of Consciousness. Faber & Faber.

Singer, T., Critchley, H. D., & Preuschoff, K. (2009). A common role of insula in feelings, empathy and uncertainty. Trends in Cognitive Sciences, 13(8), 334–340.

8:

Brookes, J. C., Hartoutsiou, F., Horsfield, A. P., & Stoneham, A. M. (2007). Could humans recognize odor by phonon assisted tunneling? Physical Review Letters, 98(3), 038101.

Chalmers, D. J. (1995). Facing up to the problem of consciousness. Journal of Consciousness Studies, 2(3), 200–219.

Engel, G. S., Calhoun, T. R., Read, E. L., et al. (2007). Evidence for wavelike energy transfer through quantum coherence in photosynthetic systems. Nature, 446(7137), 782–786.

Hameroff, S., & Penrose, R. (2014). Consciousness in the universe: A review of the Orch OR theory. Physics of Life Reviews, 11(1), 39–78.

Ritz, T., Adem, S., & Schulten, K. (2000). A model for photoreceptor-based magnetoreception in birds. Biophysical Journal, 78(2), 707–718.

9:

Chalmers (1995): The original articulation of the “hard problem of consciousness”

LeDoux (2012): On emotional learning and the role of the amygdala

Phelps (2004): Emotional memory and the amygdala-hippocampus interaction

Friston (2010): Predictive processing and the brain's free-energy principle

Part III

10:

Darwin, C. (1872). The Expression of the Emotions in Man and Animals. John Murray.

Eisenberger, N. I., & Lieberman, M. D. (2004). Why it hurts to be left out: The neurocognitive overlap between physical and social pain. Trends in Cognitive Sciences, 8(7), 294–300.

LeDoux, J. E. (1996). The Emotional Brain: The Mysterious Underpinnings of Emotional Life. Simon & Schuster.

Panksepp, J. (1998). Affective Neuroscience: The Foundations of Human and Animal Emotions. Oxford University Press.

Phelps, E. A. (2004). Human emotion and memory: interactions of the amygdala and hippocampal complex. Current Opinion in Neurobiology, 14(2), 198–202.

Shin, L. M., & Liberzon, I. (2010). The neurocircuitry of fear, stress, and anxiety disorders. Neuropsychopharmacology, 35(1), 169–191.

11:

Benau, E. M., Orloff, N. C., Janke, E. A., Serpell, L., & Timko, C. A. (2014). A systematic review of the effects of experimental fasting on cognition. Appetite, 77, 52–61.

Darwin, C. (1871). The Descent of Man, and Selection in Relation to Sex. John Murray.

Smeets, M. A. M., Dijksterhuis, G. B., & Smid, K. (2005). Appetite and memory: Distraction during encoding affects memory for food stimuli. Appetite, 45(2), 145–152.

Swami, V., Hadji-Michael, M., & Furnham, A. (2012). Personality and individual differences in attitudes toward eating and body image during fasting. Eating Behaviors, 13(3), 214–217.

Symmonds, M., Emmanuel, J. J., Drew, M. E., et al. (2010). Metabolic state alters economic decision making under risk in humans. PLoS ONE, 5(6), e11090.

Zhang, Y., Brady, M., & Smith, S. (2015). The effect of hunger on decision-making: Risky choices in hungry rats. Journal of Comparative Psychology, 129(1), 46–55.

Wrangham, R. (2009). Catching Fire: How Cooking Made Us Human. Basic Books.

12:

Bowlby, J. (1969). Attachment and Loss: Vol. 1. Attachment. Basic Books.

Cacioppo, J. T., et al. (2006). Loneliness as a specific risk factor for depressive symptoms: Cross-sectional and longitudinal analyses. Psychology and Aging, 21(1), 140–151.

Darwin, C. (1871). The Descent of Man, and Selection in Relation to Sex. John Murray.

Eisenberger, N. I., Lieberman, M. D., & Williams, K. D. (2003). Does rejection hurt? An fMRI study of social exclusion. Science, 302(5643), 290–292.

Holt-Lunstad, J., Smith, T. B., & Layton, J. B. (2015). Social relationships and mortality risk: A meta-analytic review. PLOS Medicine, 7(7), e1000316.

Panksepp, J. (1998). Affective Neuroscience: The Foundations of Human and Animal Emotions. Oxford University Press.

13:

Darwin, C. (1872). The Expression of the Emotions in Man and Animals. John Murray.

Goldstein, P., Weissman-Fogel, I., Dumas, G., & Shamay-Tsoory, S. G. (2018). Brain-to-brain coupling during handholding is associated with pain reduction. Proceedings of the National Academy of Sciences, 115(11), E2528–E2537.

Olausson, H., Lamarre, Y., Backlund, H., et al. (2002). Unmyelinated tactile afferents signal touch and project to insular cortex. Nature Neuroscience, 5(9), 900–904.

Panksepp, J. (1998). Affective Neuroscience: The Foundations of Human and Animal Emotions. Oxford University Press.

Uvnäs-Moberg, K. (1998). Oxytocin may mediate the benefits of positive social interaction and emotions. Psychoneuroendocrinology, 23(8), 819–835.

Part IV

14:

Darwin, C. (1872). The Expression of the Emotions in Man and Animals. John Murray.

Herz, R. S., & Engen, T. (1996). Odor memory: Review and analysis. Psychonomic Bulletin & Review, 3(3), 300–313.

LeDoux, J. E. (1996). The Emotional Brain: The Mysterious Underpinnings of Emotional Life. Simon & Schuster.

Phelps, E. A. (2004). Human emotion and memory: Interactions of the amygdala and hippocampal complex. Current Opinion in Neurobiology, 14(2), 198–202.

Rozin, P., Haidt, J., & McCauley, C. R. (2000). Disgust: The body and soul emotion. In Lewis, M., & Haviland-Jones, J. M. (Eds.), Handbook of Emotions (2nd ed., pp. 637–653). Guilford Press.

Salimpoor, V. N., Benovoy, M., Longo, G., et al. (2011). Anatomically distinct dopamine release during anticipation and experience of peak emotion to music. Nature Neuroscience, 14(2), 257–262.

Vuilleumier, P. (2005). How brains beware: Neural mechanisms of emotional attention. Trends in Cognitive Sciences, 9(12), 585–594.

Part V

15:

Darwin, C. (1871). The Descent of Man, and Selection in Relation to Sex. John Murray.

Fisher, H. E., Aron, A., & Brown, L. L. (2005). Romantic love: An fMRI study of a neural mechanism for mate choice. Journal of Comparative Neurology, 493(1), 58–62.

Georgiadis, J. R., & Kringelbach, M. L. (2012). The human sexual response cycle: Brain imaging evidence linking sex to other pleasures. Progress in Neurobiology, 98(1), 49–81.

LeDoux, J. E. (1996). The Emotional Brain: The Mysterious Underpinnings of Emotional Life. Simon & Schuster.

Panksepp, J. (1998). Affective Neuroscience: The Foundations of Human and Animal Emotions. Oxford University Press.

16:

Addis, D. R., Wong, A. T., & Schacter, D. L. (2007). Remembering the past and imagining the future: Common and distinct neural substrates during event construction and elaboration. Neuropsychologia, 45(7), 1363–1377.

Buckner, R. L., & Carroll, D. C. (2007). Self-projection and the brain. Trends in Cognitive Sciences, 11(2), 49–57.

Frey, U., & Morris, R. G. (1997). Synaptic tagging and long-term potentiation. Nature, 385(6616), 533–536.

LeDoux, J. E. (1996). The Emotional Brain: The Mysterious Underpinnings of Emotional Life. Simon & Schuster.

Phelps, E. A. (2004). Human emotion and memory: Interactions of the amygdala and hippocampal complex. Current Opinion in Neurobiology, 14(2), 198–202.

17:

Damasio, A. (1994). Descartes' Error: Emotion, Reason, and the Human Brain. Putnam.

Gigerenzer, G. (2007). Gut Feelings: The Intelligence of the Unconscious. Viking.

Haidt, J. (2001). The emotional dog and its rational tail: A social intuitionist approach to moral judgment. Psychological Review, 108(4), 814–834.

LeDoux, J. E. (1996). The Emotional Brain: The Mysterious Underpinnings of Emotional Life. Simon & Schuster.

Phelps, E. A. (2004). Human emotion and memory: interactions of the amygdala and hippocampal complex. Current Opinion in Neurobiology, 14(2), 198–202.

18:

Blood, A. J., & Zatorre, R. J. (2001). Intensely pleasurable responses to music correlate with activity in brain regions implicated in reward and emotion. Proceedings of the National Academy of Sciences, 98(20), 11818–11823.

Decety, J., & Lamm, C. (2006). Human empathy through the lens of social neuroscience. The Scientific World Journal, 6, 1146–1163.

Damasio, A. (1994). Descartes' Error: Emotion, Reason, and the Human Brain. Putnam.

Haidt, J. (2001). The emotional dog and its rational tail: A social intuitionist approach to moral judgment. Psychological Review, 108(4), 814–834.

Kensinger, E. A., & Schacter, D. L. (2006). Processing emotional pictures and words: Effects of valence and arousal. Cognitive, Affective, & Behavioral Neuroscience, 6(2), 110–126.

Salimpoor, V. N., et al. (2011). Anatomically distinct dopamine release during anticipation and experience of peak emotion to music. Nature Neuroscience, 14(2), 257–262.

19:

Addis, D. R., Wong, A. T., & Schacter, D. L. (2007). Remembering the past and imagining the future: Common and distinct neural substrates. Neuropsychologia, 45(7), 1363–1377.

Carhart-Harris, R. L., et al. (2014). The entropic brain: A theory of conscious states informed by neuroimaging research with psychedelic drugs. Frontiers in Human Neuroscience, 8, 20.

Damasio, A. (1999). The Feeling of What Happens: Body and Emotion in the Making of Consciousness. Harcourt.

Kelley, W. M., et al. (2002). Finding the self? An event-related fMRI study. Journal of Cognitive Neuroscience, 14(5), 785–794.

McAdams, D. P. (2001). The psychology of life stories. Review of General Psychology, 5(2), 100–122.

Moll, J., et al. (2005). The neural basis of human moral cognition. Nature Reviews Neuroscience, 6(10), 799–809.

Part VI

20:

Brewer, J. A., et al. (2011). Meditation experience is associated with increased cortical thickness. Neuroreport, 22(17), 1044–1048.

Gruber, M. J., Gelman, B. D., & Ranganath, C. (2014). States of curiosity modulate hippocampus-dependent learning via the dopaminergic circuit. Neuron, 84(2), 486–496.

Keltner, D., & Haidt, J. (2003). Approaching awe, a moral, spiritual, and aesthetic emotion. Cognition and Emotion, 17(2), 297–314.

Solomon, S., Greenberg, J., & Pyszczynski, T. (2004). The Worm at the Core: On the Role of Death in Life. Random House.

van Elk, M., et al. (2019). Neural correlates of the awe experience: Reduced default mode network activity during encounters with vast stimuli. Human Brain Mapping, 40(5), 1720–1731.

Whitehouse, H. (2000). Arguments and Icons: Divergent Modes of Religiosity. Oxford University Press.

21:

Bloom, P. (2007). The moral life of babies. The New York Times Magazine.

Damasio, A. (1999). The Feeling of What Happens: Body and Emotion in the Making of Consciousness. Harcourt.

Darwin, C. (1871). The Descent of Man, and Selection in Relation to Sex. John Murray.

Decety, J., & Jackson, P. L. (2004). The functional architecture of human empathy. Behavioral and Cognitive Neuroscience Reviews, 3(2), 71–100.

Haidt, J. (2001). The emotional dog and its rational tail: A social intuitionist approach to moral judgment. Psychological Review, 108(4), 814–834.

Koenigs, M., et al. (2007). Damage to the prefrontal cortex increases utilitarian moral judgments. Nature, 446(7138), 908–911.

Nussbaum, M. C. (2001). Upheavals of Thought: The Intelligence of Emotions. Cambridge University Press.

Tangney, J. P., et al. (1995). Shame and guilt in interpersonal relationships. In J. P. Tangney & K. W. Fischer (Eds.), Self-conscious emotions: The psychology of shame, guilt, embarrassment, and pride (pp. 114–139). Guilford Press.

22:

Friston, K. (2010). The free-energy principle: a unified brain theory? *Nature Reviews Neuroscience*, 11(2), 127–138.

Mashour, G. A., Roelfsema, P., Changeux, J. P., & Dehaene, S. (2020). Conscious processing and the global neuronal workspace hypothesis. *Neuron*, 105(5), 776–798.

Solms, M. (2021). *The Hidden Spring: A Journey to the Source of Consciousness*. W.W. Norton & Company.

Tononi, G., & Cirelli, C. (2014). Sleep and the price of plasticity: from synaptic and cellular homeostasis to memory consolidation and integration. *Neuron*, 81(1), 12–34.

23:

Damasio, A. (1999). The Feeling of What Happens: Body and Emotion in the Making of Consciousness. Harcourt.

Searle, J. R. (1980). Minds, brains, and programs. Behavioral and Brain Sciences, 3(3), 417–457.

Keltner, D., & Haidt, J. (2003). Approaching awe, a moral, spiritual, and aesthetic emotion. Cognition and Emotion, 17(2), 297–314.

LeDoux, J. (2012). Rethinking the Emotional Brain. Neuron, 73(4), 653–676.

van Elk, M., et al. (2019). Neural correlates of the awe experience: Reduced default mode network activity. Human Brain Mapping, 40(5), 1720–1731.

Part VII

24:

Chalmers, D. (1995). Facing up to the problem of consciousness. Journal of Consciousness Studies, 2(3), 200–219.

Damasio, A. (1999). The Feeling of What Happens: Body and Emotion in the Making of Consciousness. Harcourt.

Gruber, M. J., Gelman, B. D., & Ranganath, C. (2014). States of curiosity modulate hippocampus-dependent learning via the dopaminergic circuit. Neuron, 84(2), 486–496.

LeDoux, J. (2012). Rethinking the Emotional Brain. Neuron, 73(4), 653–676.

Moll, J., et al. (2005). The neural basis of human moral cognition. Nature Reviews Neuroscience, 6(10), 799–809.

Phelps, E. A. (2004). Human emotion and memory: Interactions of the amygdala and hippocampal complex. Current Opinion in Neurobiology, 14(2), 198–202.

Part VIII

25:

Gruber, M. J., Gelman, B. D., & Ranganath, C. (2014). States of curiosity modulate hippocampus-dependent learning via the dopaminergic circuit. Neuron, 84(2), 486–496.

Damasio, A. (1999). The Feeling of What Happens: Body and Emotion in the Making of Consciousness. Harcourt.

Panksepp, J. (1998). Affective Neuroscience: The Foundations of Human and Animal Emotions. Oxford University Press.

Seligman, M. E. P. (2011). Flourish: A Visionary New Understanding of Happiness and Well-being. Free Press.

26:

Friston, K. (2010). The free-energy principle: a unified brain theory? Nature Reviews Neuroscience, 11(2), 127–138.

Hameroff, S., & Penrose, R. (2014). Consciousness in the universe: A review of the 'Orch OR' theory. Physics of Life Reviews, 11(1), 39–78.

Tononi, G. (2004). An information integration theory of consciousness. BMC Neuroscience, 5(1), 42.

27: Conclusion

Darwin, C. (1871). The Descent of Man, and Selection in Relation to Sex. John Murray.

Damasio, A. (1999). The Feeling of What Happens: Body and Emotion in the Making of Consciousness. Harcourt.

LeDoux, J. E. (2012). Rethinking the Emotional Brain. Neuron, 73(4), 653–676.

Panksepp, J. (1998). Affective Neuroscience: The Foundations of Human and Animal Emotions. Oxford University Press.

Chalmers, D. J. (1995). Facing up to the problem of consciousness. Journal of Consciousness Studies, 2(3), 200–219.

Haidt, J. (2001). The emotional dog and its rational tail. Psychological Review, 108(4), 814–834.

INDEX

N

O

P

Q

R

S

T

V

Made in the USA
Monee, IL
13 September 2026

62976473R00262